When the Clock Runs Out

When the Clock Runs Out

20 NFL Greats Share Their Stories
of Hardship and Triumph

Stories by Bill Lyon

Photographs by Cynthia Zordich

TRIUMPH
B O O K S
CHICAGO

Printed in the United States of America

This book is available in quantity at special discounts for your group or
organization. For more information, contact:
Triumph Books
601 South LaSalle Street
Suite 500
Chicago, Illinois 60605
(312) 939-3330
Fax (312) 663-3557

Book and jacket design by Eileen Wagner
Flap photos by Karen McLoughlin

ISBN 1-57243-339-6

TABLE OF CONTENTS

Acknowledgements

To all of those who played the game and made it what it is today, especially the many who responded to my queries and were willing to share their stories, namely: Steve Spurrier, Lance Rentzel, Harry Carson, Harold Carmichael, Merril Hoge, Tim Lewis, Mickey Shuler, Ted Banks, Garo Yepremian, John Rienstra, Mike McCloskey, Troy Benson, Paul Dombrowski, Barry Pettyjohn, Gill Byrd, Marty Lyons, John Spagnola, and Dante Lavelli.

To all the players who took the time to send their photographs, quotes, stories, and poetry, which are scattered throughout the pages of this book, offering content and visuals "you can't make up," as Lance Rentzel put it.

To Cathy and Steve Courson.

To an old war horse who loved the game so much, he couldn't talk about leaving it— John Sandusky.

To my husband, Michael, who would offer only, "I don't want to be in this book"— a single, honest truth that says it all.

To my partner, Bill Lyon. The best part about creating this book has been knowing you, laughing with you, anticipating each story, so eloquently spun and haphazardly received (as you never did learn how to use your fax machine—maybe by the next one?).

To veteran weekend sports photographer Chance Brockway for gracing the pages of our book with his gritty images of yesteryear. Mr. Brockway has photographed more than three-hundred NFL games, eight Super Bowls, and has covered Ohio State football/basketball since 1962. Not to mention his coverage of the NBA, ABA, AL, NL, Indy 500, and Kentucky Derby.

To my printer (counselor, friend) Bob Asman, master of the black and white image (although he'll be the first to admire the grays in between), and to Krista . . . off to the theater.

To everyone at Rudinecs for the overtime and overall enthusiasm. Especially to Cindy and Mikey.

To good friend and agent Jimmy Solano, for his perseverence, loyalty, and genuine interest in everything we do.

To Steve Sabol, Ray Didinger, and Chris Barlow of NFL Films, Inc.

To my office duo, Joanne Componation and Erin Burns.

To Diane Chandler, Brenda Johnston, P. J. Murray, Bill Fralic, and Mark Battaglia for speaking on my behalf and helping add some extraordinary players to the project.

To MaryAnn Zimmer, Ben Lease, and P. J. Murray for their legal advice.

To my parents.

To my publisher Mitch Rogatz, along with Heidi Hill, Anne Schlitt, Peter Balis, and Karyn Viverito of Triumph Books, for believing in *When the Clock Runs Out*, for embracing its differences, and for allowing it to become more than "just another sports book."

To my friends and family, especially Michael Vincent, Alex, and Aidan, whose lives have been one big tailgate party.

Hoist and twirl it, baby!

For Michael.
-CZ

~

For Ethel, always.
For my mother.
For Jim and John and Sandy.
And for my very bestest buddies, Evan and Joshua.
-BL

BLOWING AIR INTO THE BUBBLE

By Cynthia Zordich

I am one of those people who has to analyze everything. My husband says, "Let it go," but I can't. Back in the fall of 1997, a friend of ours was released mid-season. On Sunday, he was a major contributor. On Monday, his coaches were looking for him. On Tuesday, he was cleaning out his locker. This was Andy Harmon's fate.

My sons loved to watch Andy play. My youngest, Alex, wore his jersey to all the home games and tacked all of his clippings to the wall behind his bed. Alex was always Andy Harmon. And he wasn't alone. In fact, just the season before, more number ninety-one jerseys (large and small) had arrived at the Vet (Veteran's Stadium) each Sunday than any other number. And now, except for the many steadfast Harmon followers who continue to wear his jersey proudly in an open gesture of loyalty and disgruntlement, number ninety-one will no longer grace our field.

With so many charity functions and appearances during the season, you take for granted that you're going to see the other players and their families socially. Besides a handful of times, you really don't make "arrangements" to be together. Usually, we all meet for a few drinks in the parking lot after the game to figure out where everybody wants to go. If a player is hurt or doesn't feel like dealing with a crowd, he'll walk straight to his car after a few distant waves and head home with his family. No judgments are made—everyone's been there before.

With Andy and Kristy gone for two weeks now, except for a few visits immediately after his release, we hadn't seen them. So one of the wives actually made plans. It was a casual dinner and Kristy and Andy looked great. Their new son Grant was a favorite topic of conversation. What wasn't an open topic of conversation was certainly felt in the air. A civilized, familiar tension amongst friends. Just what was Andy really going through? In contrast to the media frenzy going on around them and about them, they both seemed relaxed. They were enjoying the time they could spend with the baby, they said, and it was great sleeping in for once. But I couldn't help wondering about the other issues. How does Andy feel when the game is being played without him on Sunday? Can he watch? Is he bitter? Has he cried? These are questions I would have asked if I dared—but I didn't. Why? Initially, I'm sure it was out of respect for their privacy. Besides, that dinner wasn't the time or the place. So I "let it go" until the ride home, when I started running through more questions that I could have asked them both and imagined what their answers might have been. With all these thoughts spinning around in my head, it hit me that I couldn't be the only one with these questions. It was then that I realized what I wanted to do.

Michael has played in the league for eleven seasons now. We have never taken one of those seasons for granted, nor have we ever seriously discussed the notion of one of them being the last. We always figure that we'll cross that bridge when we get to it. This off-season the question being asked of Michael is, "Zordich, you comin' back next year?" His answer has been a consistent, "I plan on it." And yes we are—planning on it, hoping for it. Right now, I'd say we are blowing more and more air into the bubble and getting ready to shut our eyes when it pops. Lots of people have asked me what Michael's going to do when he retires. But lately, I take this question as a personal attack, as if they're suggesting that he is done. When they ask me his age, I imagine them calculating how many years he has left. My guard is constantly up and I know why. I'm running scared. The fact is, Michael would like to play forever. The fact is, nobody does.

Once, when I was thinking about retirement, I said, "You know, Michael, leaving football must leave your system in a state of shock." Think about it—everything your senses are used to and take for granted is lost. Once you leave, you'll never feel impact like that again. You'll never hear the muffled sound of the crowd through your helmet, the rip of the tape, the crashing of the pads. You'll never look into the hostile eyes of an opponent through a face mask or feel the slipperiness of their silk jersey through your hands. If it's not a loss, it certainly is a numbing of the senses. But what does it feel like? While some things are better left unsaid, I bring up these issues in preparation, not only for him, but also for myself. For while he's going through all of these transitions, I'll be there.

I often compare the abruptness of retirement to somebody saying to me, "You are no longer a photographer. Put away your gear. Nobody has any use for your work anymore." How would I function in a world I see as a series of images to be captured and shared, left with the sensation of hitting the shutter time and time again, and not being able to do so? How will Michael function as a non-player when a player is all he's ever been? When it comes down to it, we're not talking just about a transition, we're talking about a major life change. And to be honest, I have no idea what we're in for. Sure, Michael has been battle-tested and proven strong, and it is by force of will that he has found a spot on that field each year. And I pray that his personal triumphs in life will continue. But it's not his success that I'm worried about. I guess I'm just worried about how he'll make it through the change. How will he deal with a life that will be so different from what he's known?

It is unfortunate that my fears are so legitimate. It is unfortunate that I know more friends and families that have separated after this change than have survived it. In 1989, a veteran wife, Kristy Hogeboom, told me that the post-NFL divorce rate was up to sixty-five percent. That was our third year in the league. If it's higher now, I don't even want to know.

I have always felt that life stories are the best way to learn. When a person is willing to share experiences of loss, or the triumph of overcoming loss, we can all benefit. This compilation of life stories is not only for my benefit, but for all those who have wondered what it must feel like to stop. What actually happens within the heart during that period of time between the old life and the new. That period of time when, more than ever, your actions will dictate your fate and the fate of your family. That period of time when the clock runs out.

LETTING GO
By Bill Lyon

Quit.

For every professional athlete, but especially for the professional football player, quit is the most loathsome of words.

Quit? It is an act of cowardice. It is unthinkable, unforgivable.

Quit? You mean, give up? Give in? Surrender? Concede?

Never! Never, ever, never!

From Biddy Ball on, it has been drummed into their heads: A quitter never wins and . . . well, you know how it ends.

So they play on. They play on, no matter what. They play on whether they're winning by six touchdowns or they're getting their brains beat in. They play on through tears and fractures and concussions, and in weather that careens from one extreme to the other, and all the while they are told it is simply mind over matter: If you don't mind, then it doesn't matter.

They play all the way through the last echo of the whistle. They are told to play every down like it was their last. Because one day, it will be.

Oh my God, what a dreadful thought. No. No. A thousand times no. I can't let myself think about that. This can't end . . .

But of course it can, and of course it will.

One day the decision will be made for them. A coach may make it. Their own body may make it. But someone is going to tell them that it is time to retire.

Retire? You mean quit?

Yes. It means you have to let go.

It is the single most difficult thing that any of them will ever have to do.

Let go?

They can't. Not completely. Oh, they will retire all right, but the glorious sounds of battle will clatter on in their ears and a part of them will always remain out there, and sometimes at three in the morning there will be a bone that never quite healed or a joint dull with the ache of arthritis that will prod them awake and they will remember what it was that caused the hurt, the crushing

1

block, the ripping tackle, the grand collisions. They will awaken and grunt with the pain, and the memories will come flooding back, and it will hit them that they still miss it so.

Let go?

The ex-pitcher Jim Bouton, in his seminal baseball memoir, *Ball Four*, wrote the epitaph for every professional athlete when he arrived at this poignant, bittersweet conclusion: "I spent my whole life gripping a baseball, and in the end I found out that all along it was the other way around."

Let go? Hardly.

Retire? Yes. Grudgingly, though. With wrenching reluctance. Kicking and screaming all the way out the door.

More than one of them has vowed: "They'll have to tear the uniform off me." Unfortunately, that can be arranged.

The athlete is the only member of our society who has to die twice.

The professional football player makes a Faustian bargain with society. He is given a glorious half-life and then just as he is coming into his prime he finds himself ripped from the protective, insular cocoon of a team and dropped, unceremoniously, into the real world.

Hero to zero.

Just like that.

The great hockey player Gordie Howe once said, mournfully: "They teach you how to play the game, but they don't teach you how to leave it."

That is one of the purposes of this book.

What's it like to be a jock? It's like you're on a scholarship through life.

You're singled out early on, and made to feel special. Maybe because you're big. Maybe because you're fast. Maybe because you're both. Maybe because you possess an inordinate capacity for punishment, for both administering it and absorbing it.

Once identified as special, doors immediately begin to open for you. The path is cleared. People fawn over you. They are eager to do things for you. They want to give you things. A passing grade. A deal on a car. A seat in first class. A patch of bare skin to autograph. A drink, a snort, a hit, a companion for the evening.

You never have to introduce yourself.

You never have to pick up the check.

You never have to apologize.

You never have to grasp the concept of cause-and-effect. No one presses upon you the notion of accountability or responsibility. That's what lawyers are for. And agents. And accountants. And hangers-on.

You never even have to grow up.

Of course, inevitably there will be a price for this terminal adolescence. When your playing days come to an end, the first jolt is to the ego.

"Hey, didn't you used to be . . . ?"

You are cut loose and now you stand in the lobby of the swank five-star hotel where the team always stayed and you are alone, terribly, vulnerably alone, and you turn in small circles of confusion, a little child lost, a child in a giant's body, uncertain of exactly how to go about managing the simple task of getting yourself home.

Someone else always made the reservations, someone else always checked you in, checked you out, paid the bill, took care of the luggage, arranged the aisle seat, picked up your discarded laundry. All you ever had to do was sign your name.

You became used to being told what to do. Always, there was "coach." Always there was someone pointing you in the right direction. You were like a soldier, trained for combat, conditioned to obey, to react instinctively, to never question a strategy, to never refuse an order, to never, ever quit.

And now you are on your own.

You knew this day would come, but you always assumed it would be tomorrow, not today. Wasn't it just yesterday that you were in college and being drafted? Wasn't it just yesterday that everyone had the hots for you? It was . . . what? Nine years ago? Are you sure? Nah, can't be. Nine years? Damn, where did it all go?

All your life, you looked out at the world from a helmet. It was like you had blinders on.

So the coddling ends. Or at least it slows to a crawl.

And the first thing you learn is that the world has almost no compassion for the ex-football player. For every one who idolized you, there were two who envied you and resented you and consoled themselves with the sneering assumption that, being a football player, you were roughly as smart as the lint in their pants pockets.

The first thing that occurs is the death of your identity.

"There is an undeniable, unavoidable grief process," says Dr. Joel Fish, a sports psychologist. "The reason that the emotional trauma is far greater for a football player than for other athletes is that football is different in terms of the toll on your body and the rhythms of the sport. There is bonding and there is the competitive rush, just as there are in other sports, but what separates football is the building to a crescendo once a week.

"The formula changes depending upon the player's circumstance. Is the retirement forced? Or is it planned? It's far different for a John Elway, for example, who chose how he would go out, than it is for someone who is cut and then goes unclaimed by any other team. One does it voluntarily, if a bit reluctantly. The other feels total rejection.

"What adds to the mix is that for most of them, football is a profession more than it is a job. A job is something you know you have to get up and go to every day. It's how you pay your way. A profession sustains you on several levels, not just financial. That's why it's always easier to retire from a job than it is from a profession."

Dr. Fish is director of the Center for Sports Psychology in Philadelphia. He has done work for all four of the city's major professional sports franchises—the Eagles, Phillies, 76ers, and Flyers. He agrees that football players seem to suffer the keenest withdrawal pangs. Whether they leave the game voluntarily or are pushed out the door, they face the same five-stage emotional catharsis as, say, a cancer patient who is given six months to live.

First, there is denial. *Hey, come on, I can still play. What do they mean, I've lost it? I've got at least a year left, maybe two if I really take care of myself.*

Dr Fish: "The ability to objectively evaluate yourself is compromised. You feel the same. You look in the mirror and you don't see any appreciable difference. Maybe you haven't even lost a step, but at that level only a minute slippage, maybe even two to three percent, is enough."

Then anger. *Why me? I'm still better than half the guys in this league at my position. I keep myself in shape, I work out all year. I eat right. I don't deserve this.*

Dr. Fish: "The fairness issue. I've held up my end of the bargain. I've given my all for my whole career. So don't I deserve better? Where's the justice?"

Then comes the bargaining. *All right, I'll quit feeling sorry for myself. But I need one more game. I've had a great career. If it's time for it to end, OK. But is it asking too much for me to go out on my terms?*

Dr. Fish: "God, let me play just one more year. Even just one more game. I'll do anything. You bargain with God, with your coach, your general manager, your agent. You try to strike some sort of deal that will keep you around. I once had a pitcher tell me: 'I'd cut off my right arm to pitch one more game.' And he was right-handed."

Then comes depression. *It really is over, isn't it? No more games. No more camps. No more practices. No more hangin' with the guys. I'll never pull on the colors again. The only way I'll ever be in a locker room again is if somebody invites me. And even then I'll still be an outsider . . .*

Dr. Fish: "Reality arrives and it is stark and undeniable. You can no longer ignore that it's over, so there is a certain coming-to-terms, and with that comes a measure of regret. I didn't really appreciate it when I had it. I wish I'd known then what I know now. The second phase of depression is grappling for a sense of identity. Now who am I? It's like a three-legged chair that's had one leg pulled out. You look at other men your age, maybe thirty or thirty-five, and they're still on the upswing. And me? I'm going to old-timers' games. There's a tendency to mourn wasted opportunity."

Finally, hopefully, comes acceptance. *It's time to move on. Snap out of it. You're a football player, for God's sake. Enough with the sniffling. Get a grip and get up and get a move on. You could always get up from a hit, you can get up from this.*

Dr. Fish: "This is my reality and I have to deal with it. No more wasting energy on regret. It's time to think in the future, on what will be and not what was. You may never reach one hundred percent closure, but it is possible to reach the point where you think about it only if someone starts asking you about it, and even then it's not a fixation. For example, if something triggers my memory and I start thinking about my old girlfriend, by tonight I'm talking, and thinking, about something else."

The tricky part is realizing that one ending can become a new beginning.

"The Chinese," notes Dr. Fish, "use the same word for crisis and for opportunity."

A professional football player is regarded by his employer as a depreciable asset.

Just like livestock. Except with half as many legs.

You have value as long as you produce. When you don't—whether because of injury or age—your employer will bring in someone who is swifter, stronger, smarter, and almost always younger, and you will be invited to leave.

Oh, but hey, wait a minute. Don't go just yet.

Yes?

Almost forgot. Don't forget to turn in your playbook.

It's business. That's all. Nothing personal. It's entertainment, yes. But it is unmistakably a business, too, and one with a bottom line. The bottom line is measured in dollars, sure, but also in wins and losses. And when you are not contributing to more wins than losses, well, it really doesn't matter how good you used to be or what a swell fellow you are at heart or how everyone sure did like you in the locker room.

You know this, of course. Because you talk about it with the other guys. You know you're livestock. Meat on the hoof. But that's OK. Because the money is good. But mostly because the game has got its hooks in you and you couldn't quit if you wanted to . . .

And one thing more: You're a stud. You're different. People have been telling you so for years.

You're a football player and you are young and strong and you are ten feet tall and bullet-damn-proof, brother.

You are the exception. To everything.

What applies to others does not apply to you. You can spit into the wind. You can tug on Superman's cape. You can work without a net.

When he was in college at North Carolina, the wondrous linebacker Lawrence Taylor was frequently spotted climbing around on residence halls, walking on ledges like Spiderman, clamoring up to the roof, and tip-toeing along the very edge like a cat burglar, seeming to invite disaster.

Asked why, he shrugged and replied that he just felt like it, that he liked the rush, liked the thrill, liked living on the edge, that he needed something to make him feel alive while he was waiting for the next football game, the next practice, the next hit.

He was known as LT and he redefined the position of outside linebacker. He was an assassin on the field, running down quarterbacks from behind, cleaving the ball from them with a chopping hand, and then collapsing them like the bellows of an accordion.

In one of sports' more memorable and chilling graphic quotes, he said of his favorite quarterback hits: "I love it when their eyes roll back in their head and you can see the snot bubbles coming out their nose. That's when I know I really laid 'em out."

And an eavesdropping boom microphone caught him on the sidelines exhorting his Giants teammates just before kickoff: "We gotta go out there and play like a pack of rabid dogs, baby."

But once the game is over, there are no switches to turn off the passion, the violence, the appetite for destruction. Lawrence Taylor had the perfect temperament for football, the ideal aptitude. But after he retired he was lost at sea, drifting, bewildered, cut loose from the game that had always moored him. He struggled to adjust, to cope, just as many who came before him, and many who will come after him.

His troubles began to pile up like his quarterback sacks had. He pleaded guilty to filing false income tax returns. He was arrested for possession of crack cocaine. His driving license was suspended for failing to pay parking tickets. He was charged with leaving the scene of an accident. And then, the incident that absolutely mortified him: He was picked up during a police sweep of deadbeat dads for lagging behind in child support payments. He was handcuffed and spent twelve hours in a cell.

The great LT, led away with his hands cuffed behind his back. Lawrence of the Meadowlands rousted from his own house at two in the morning and taken to a holding cell, dumped there with the flotsam and jetsam of the legal system. From afar, it was a jolt. Imagine what it must have felt like up close, to a man who had been led to believe that he was invulnerable.

"It was an embarrassment for him to be arrested and put in jail," said his attorney, Thomas Melani. "LT has a habit of not following up on things until later. He's just not making the money he was before."

In his last year in the NFL, in 1993, Taylor's salary was about $1,000,000. A tidy sum. Apparently almost all of it, and what he had earned before, just dribbled away. Alimony. Delinquent child support. Back taxes.

He tried the restaurant business. He tried selling memorabilia on home shopping channels. He tried making appearances. It wasn't as though he didn't try. It wasn't as though he just gave up.

It's just that what he was best at, he was no longer able to do.

He was, first and foremost, a hit man. On a football field, that can get you in the Hall of Fame. On the streets, it can get you in the penitentiary.

Shortly before he became eligible for the Hall of Fame, Lawrence Taylor was arrested a second time on drug charges. There was considerable speculation about whether he would be voted in by the writers after that. Typically, he was not only unrepentant and unapologetic, he was defiant.

"I'm sure there have never been writers who have ever done drugs," he said, during a conference call with the media, including some of the very same writers who would be voting for him. Or against him.

"I don't apologize for anything," he said. "There are some things in our lives we wish we could change. Unfortunately, we can't do that. But if guys are asking me to be remorseful for what I've done, I can't do that. There are some things I'd like to change, but I can't so I'm not going to worry about them."

His coach, Bill Parcells, said LT ought to go into the Hall of Fame "on roller skates." And Taylor himself said: "Based on the bylaws, it should be a no-brainer."

He was referring to the absence of a so-called morals clause in eligibility for the Hall of Fame. There is no citizenship criteria. Candidates are judged solely on what they did on the field.

Taylor spoke of himself in the third person: "Has he ever had problems? Guilty. Has he ever been through controversy? Guilty. Will he have more controversy? Guilty. I have that problem."

And then he got to the heart of the conundrum: "If you're going to start going into off-the-field problems, then you're going to have to kick half of the people out of the Hall of Fame now."

The breakdown of the voting is never announced, only the result.

In January of 1999, on the day before the Super Bowl, the result was that Lawrence Taylor was voted into the Hall of Fame.

———————————

Some of them prepare for the day that is unavoidable. Some of them anticipate life after football. Some of them realize that the ability to bust heads and tolerate great pain has a very short shelf life.

Alan Page is a shining example. His NFL career was one of valor and extraordinary service. He played fifteen seasons, most of them with the Vikings. He was a defensive tackle and in the off-season he studied law. Even before he retired, in 1981, he was a lawyer and a member of the Minnesota bar.

He was the exception—the game did not have the narcotic hold on him that it seems to have on almost everyone else.

"Actually, toward the end I was fairly bored with football," he says. "I realize that sounds strange, but I needed the stimulation that law school provided. I dreamt of being a lawyer long before I had dreams of being a football player. I didn't set out to be a professional football player, and it didn't dawn on me until my junior year in college (at Notre Dame) that I might actually end up playing in the NFL. I guess it would be accurate to say that I sort of got sidetracked by football."

Seven years after he retired from the NFL, he was inducted into the Hall of Fame. And four years after that, he was appointed to the Minnesota Supreme Court, becoming the first African-American to hold an elected state office in Minnesota.

Page used his Hall of Fame acceptance speech as a forum to decry the failure of society and our educational system to nurture young or student athletes with the same zeal they do other students. He noted that while many of his teammates had been college graduates, a depressing number of them were, in fact, functional illiterates. Their schools had wanted their bodies but had shamefully neglected their brains.

"They weren't prepared to do anything else, which was heartbreaking," said Page. "You must have ambitions that go beyond being a football star because there will come a time when you will not be a star anymore, and unless you are equipped with the skills to do something else, you will feel lost."

Page was able to make the transition because he didn't regard leaving football as a terrible loss, but rather as a launching pad for his second career. He didn't feel the need to mourn because he had given himself something to look forward to with great anticipation . . . and not something to look back on with a consuming sense of bereavement.

But he knows, and understands, how seductive the football life can be. He watched enough teammates retire and then struggle with the transition.

"You never really have the opportunity to grow up," he says. "It's like you're living in a candy store and nobody tells you that you'll ruin your appetite. Everyone wants to help you, everybody wants to be your friend. Everybody wants to do for you."

Then one day you find that you can't do for yourself. And to compound it all, the cheering stops.

And *that* can be the most jolting part of all.

When the great Joe DiMaggio, retired from baseball by then, was married to Marilyn Monroe, she returned from a tour of Korea where she had American GIs howling and yowling at every stop. Still flushed with the exhilaration of those receptions, still hearing the thundering echo of all those roars, she told her husband, breathlessly: "Oh, Joe, you never heard such cheering."

And he replied instantly, in a voice cold and hard: "Oh yes I have."

Joe Namath, who heard more than his share of cheering, asked: "Ever been cheered? Ever heard sixty-thousand people chanting your name? It's indescribable, man. Heck, even the booing doesn't sound bad. I know a lot of players who still hear the cheers. You've got to try to stop that, but I don't know that you ever can, completely. I understand why actors like to work in front of a live audience. The applause . . . the applause . . . "

Yes. It is heady, isn't it? The sound generated by two hands smacking together in approval, in appreciation, in awe. It is intoxicating, and, as Namath said, can become addictive very quickly. But when you have heard it again and again and then one day it is replaced by the sound of silence, well . . . sometimes a person will go a long way to hear that sound again.

While he was still a professional basketball player, Bill Bradley and the other New York Knicks checked into a hotel in the very early morning hours. The lobby was deserted, save for a lone figure seated on a couch in the far corner, his shadow cast from the glow of one light. The man sat there intently, staring at a large window, against which a savage rainstorm was pounding.

The man on the couch was leaning forward attentively, as though he were in a concert hall concentrating on the music, rapt, utterly and completely lost in the sound and the moment.

There was something about the figure that looked vaguely familiar. Quietly, Bradley moved closer. Recognition startled him. The man on the couch was Mickey Mantle. *Mickey Mantle!* The great

Mickey Mantle was mesmerized by the rain, by how it was hammering against the window.

Bradley, intrigued, listened himself for several moments. Gradually, it dawned on him: The rain beating against the panes sounded exactly like a large crowd applauding.

When the cheering stops, you take your applause anywhere you can find it.

————————————————

Some of them end up in court, before the bench. Some of them end up sitting on the bench.

Some of them end up homeless and sleeping in their car. Some of them end up estranged from family, enslaved to the bottle or pharmaceuticals. Some of them end up extracting molars and interpreting X-rays, running their own companies, and even helping run the country. Some of them are bright and actually informed about things beyond football.

Some of them reflect and grieve, and then find that the terrible, aching, hollow place that was left when they were pried away from the game has begun to fill in at long last. And some of them, tragic victims of unrequited love, never do find their way or their stride.

Some of them think they are forever young, forever able to tackle and block and run, not only indestructible but immortal.

What they all have in common is that one day they will be separated from the game, and when that umbilical cord is cut their pain will be far more intense than they ever imagined. They may or may not be ready for it. Likely, the latter.

One of the things this book is intended to do is serve as a guide for those still to come, from those who have already made the trip. What follows are visits with those who have let go and who have lived to tell about it. They spin war stories. They speak, with candor, of what they went through when they retired from the game.

What this really is, at heart, is a love story.

Because whatever may have befallen them, good or bad, they cannot, any of them, imagine their lives without the game.

"It's just too bad, you know, you don't tell a doctor he can't practice after he reaches a certain age. You don't tell a pilot he can't fly, you don't tell a football player he can't play anymore. He thinks he can go on forever, but then there's that time when he is in the twilight of his career, and it was the hardest thing in the world for me to accept the fact that I had to get out after fourteen years. But I had to and then you finally find out after you get out that it's not as bad as you think it is. I wouldn't have had it any other way, I would have played as long as I could."

Leo Nomellini, DT-OT 1950-63 San Francisco
NFL 75th Anniversary
NFL Films, Inc.

"I'm so happy that I got to play. People say, 'What was it like?' You know I had days where I was in the zone and what more could you ask for? I mean, what a wonderful opportunity. And athletics is something that I started doing when I was a young kid, I loved to do it, I thought it was fun. But . . . I said when it was time to go it really wasn't much fun anymore. And that's about as honest as I can be."

Don Meredith, QB 1960-68 Dallas
NFL 75th Anniversary
NFL Films, Inc.

"I think the thing all great players have in common is a passion for the game, a real love for the game, however you want to put it. But what that does for that player is it makes him do things out of the ordinary and perhaps play too long, but he loves the game. I mean what are you gonna do, you gonna quit doing something you love? And I think that's what I admired most about players like Unitas and John Brodie and Y. A. Tittle, was that they played for a long time and they played very, very well for a long time, but they never lost the desire to play. They loved the game 'til the end."

Dan Fouts, QB 1973-87 San Diego
NFL 75th Anniversary
NFL Films, Inc.

"You can learn in the game from the beginning, high school, college and pro ball, especially pro ball, what a teammate means. How to work together. What discipline is, because there's an awful lot of discipline. And all your life, if you never say another word about it, it gets in your heart and you know what happened, and you can always have that warm feeling. When you see an old teammate, it all comes out again. It's a wonderful thing to have been able to play the game."

Don Paul, DB-HB 1950-53 Chicago Bears; 1954-58 Cleveland
TNT Interviews

13

Cynthia Zordich

ROCKY'S ROAD
The Rocky Bleier Story

There never really is a convenient time to get shot.

But when you're lying in a rice paddy thirteen thousand miles from home, the heat merciless and the humidity worse, feeling isolated and sleepless for two nights, your thirst almost as bad as your fatigue, buddies dying all around you . . . well, that's about as inconvenient as it gets.

The bullet entered his body and passed right on through, and all he heard was this soft thump, like the sound of a newspaper being delivered on a front porch. Then his left thigh began to sting, and he thought maybe the jungle ants were making a meal of him again.

He looked down and saw two holes. They were astonishingly symmetrical—one hole where the bullet had entered, the other where it had left. Both were leaking blood. He remembers that he looked at those holes for a time, curiously, almost as though they belonged to somebody else.

And then the enormity of what had happened dawned on him.

"I'm hit!"

His buddy Dave, who was a few yards away, tossed him a dressing. Dave lobbed the sterile gauze while lying on his back. No one dared stand up. A North Vietnamese soldier was firing a machine gun at them from a distance of only half a football field away. He and Dave and the others clawed frantically at the soft, wet earth with their hands, trying to dig a sanctuary. And yet to stay there was surely to die.

"Rock!" Dave yelled. "Rock, can you walk?"

"I don't know," Rocky Bleier yelled back. "I've never been shot before."

Then, lying there in the muck and the swelter, watching his blood leave him, Rocky Bleier began to giggle. He thought about what he had just said and he laughed at the absurdity of it:

I don't know, I've never been shot before.

The rest of them, the surviving remnants of that patrol from Charlie Company, 169th Light Infantry Brigade, United States Army, tried to return fire. But they had no cover. Rocky Bleier crawled to a hedgerow. His weapon was an M-79 grenade launcher. The hedgerow blocked his view of the North Vietnamese soldier's machine gun, so Dave served as his spotter. Rocky began firing grenades. The fourth one was close enough to stop the machine gun.

He fired until he ran out of grenades, spending about three dozen in all. Then he laid there for almost two hours, bleeding, defenseless, isolated, certain he was going to die. He prayed. Whether his prayers were answered or it was simply chance, he and Dave and another grunt named Doc got away and back to a wooded area where more members of Charlie Company had gathered. Twenty-two were still alive, five of them wounded.

The enemy had followed them. The enemy attacked. A grenade came tumbling into their midst. Rocky Bleier flipped to his right, swinging his wounded left leg over himself, and then was lifted off the ground by the force of the concussion. His ears rang.

He looked back at the place where he had been.

He saw a smoking hole two feet deep.

He couldn't get up. He had his eyes closed and was trying to make the pain and the ringing go away. When he opened them, he saw the most horrifying thing—another grenade flying through the air, headed directly for an officer, Tom Murphy. Before Rocky could shout a warning, the grenade struck Murphy squarely in the back.

Incredibly, it didn't detonate.

Instead, it ricocheted off Tom Murphy and bounced directly toward a helpless Rocky Bleier, landing at his feet.

And then it exploded.

When he woke up, Tom Murphy was lying next to him, moaning in agony. Rocky Bleier looked down. His trousers were shredded, both his legs peppered with shrapnel holes. Later, the doctors would pick out more than one hundred pieces. Part of his right foot had been blown away.

For the rest of his life he would wear a size ten and a half left shoe and a size ten right shoe.

"People always ask me if football is really like combat," he says. "No, it's not, much as we'd like to believe it is. Combat is life and death, literally. It's all about surviving. In football, there's always another game. In war, there's no guarantee there's another tomorrow."

Rocky and the others were outnumbered four to one, and surrounded. A helicopter gunship was called in. It blasted away for half an hour. Still, the North Vietnamese Army pressed forward. Rocky Bleier crawled to an M-16 rifle, propped himself up into a firing position, and prepared to die.

But for whatever reason, the enemy backed away, and then left entirely.

A grateful Charlie Company hauled ass.

They tried carrying Rocky Bleier in a poncho liner, but it tore. Then they draped his arms over their shoulders and dragged him. He screamed in pain.

"And then," he remembers, "this guy said he'd carry me fireman-style, over his shoulder. With the dark and the confusion and me passing in and out, I never did get his name, and I doubt he knows mine. We never saw each other again. But I'll never forget his courage and his generosity. I'm white, he was black. That didn't mean a thing then, and it means even less now. War has a way of being the great equalizer."

The place was called Hiep Douc, pronounced Hep Duck. When they had started the patrol, there were twenty-five of them. By the time they had escaped the ambush, all twenty-five were either dead or wounded. Rocky Bleier would receive the Bronze Star for valor, the Purple Heart, and half a chest full of assorted campaign ribbons.

But all he really wanted was the chance to run with the football again.

About the time the chopper evacuated him, the day of August 20, 1969, was coming to an end. Back at an aid station, he got a shot of morphine, and immediately begged for another.

He asked the first doctor who examined him: "When can I play football again?"

And the answer was: "Never. We'd better concentrate on just getting you to walk again."

What followed was seven excruciating months of surgeries and casts, crutches and canes, the pain and drudge of physical therapy. And then one day he slipped out of bed and into some sweats and set out to run.

"I wanted to find out," he remembers, "if I was still an athlete."

He got less than a quarter of a mile before he collapsed. He pressed his face into the grass so that no one could hear him crying.

He limped back to his bed.

And the next day he left it to run again. He ran one step farther than he had run the day before.

He ran one step farther than that the next day.

And so on . . . and so on . . . and so on . . .

He was christened Robert Patrick Bleier. He was born in Appleton, Wisconsin, a workingman's town with workingman's bars. His father, Bob, and his mother, Ellen, ran one such establishment. Some of their customers would stop off in the morning to fortify themselves for a day at the mills with a shot and a beer. Bob Bleier would take them into the bedroom and proudly show off his sleeping new son.

"Look at the little son of a bitch," Bob Bleier would say fondly. "Looks like a little rock lying there."

Along around dusk, their shifts over, some of the same customers would stop by on their way home and wash down a day of labor with another shot and beer, and invariably some of them would ask the proprietor: "Hey, Bob, how's the little rock?"

With such a start, how could he have been called anything other than Rocky?

The little rock grew up to resemble one. Not so tall—not even the five feet, eleven inches the Pittsburgh Steelers would claim he was—but solid as a boulder. He played center on the high school basketball team, which won forty-nine games in a row. He was a running back on the football team, which ran up three straight undefeated seasons, twenty-seven wins in a row.

In 1964, Notre Dame University's Fighting Irish got a new football coach: Ara Parseghian. They also got themselves a new football player: Rocky Bleier.

In 1966, he played in one of college football's biggest games, the controversial 10–10 tie with Michigan State, when both were undefeated and ranked one-two in the country. He caught a pass over the middle in the third period and was speared in the back by a linebacker's helmet. After the game, standing at a urinal, he felt a rush of pain, looked down and saw that he was passing pure blood. He had suffered a lacerated kidney.

19

In 1967, his senior year, he was elected captain, and in a game at Georgia Tech he scored a touchdown just before halftime. He also tore the ligaments in his left knee. He played the entire second half anyway. On the following Monday, he had surgery. His college career was over.

His professional career looked like it might never get started.

He knew he was relatively small and relatively slow but he also hoped that the scouts might have noticed his work ethic, his grit, and the fact that winning seasons seemed to follow him around wherever he played. The 1968 NFL draft was held in late January. He waited and he waited and all he managed to do was work up a case of frustration, and a mighty thirst.

He decided to go drink beer. When the ten o'clock news came on, he thought he heard the television set telling him that he had been drafted. He had.

In the sixteenth round. By the Pittsburgh Steelers, who were just awful.

He was pick number 417. Out of 442. But he was a pro.

He would come to fall in love with Pittsburgh, and vice-versa.

"It's a working class town, with a Puritan ethic, and very ethnic, a lot like Appleton, and it had a comfortable small town feel to it," he says.

During his first scrimmage at training camp, he came babbling into the huddle, all aflame as befitted a former Fighting Irish football captain, and he clapped his hands and barked: "OK, guys, here we go now, here we go . . . "

The jaded veterans looked at him, only mildly amused by his enthusiasm, and one of them snarled: "None of that rah-rah college shit here, rook."

Near the end of training camp, the head coach, Bill Austin, sent for him. Rocky Bleier's heart thumped with dread. When the head man summons you during camp, it can only mean that you'll be told to leave.

But what Austin told him was that his student deferment had expired. The Steelers had just received notification from the Appleton draft board that Robert Patrick Bleier, one of their rookie running backs, had been reclassified One-A.

Austin told him the Steelers would take care of the matter. After all, he was a Steeler now. He had made the team. In the euphoria of that thought, it never occurred to him that he might end up in Vietnam.

The letter began: "Greetings, from the President . . . "

The Steelers tried to maneuver him into bureaucratic sanctuary. The Reserves. The National Guard. Special deferment. Anywhere they could hide him, using the influence of friendly congressmen and generals.

But through it all, he says, he felt something gnawing at him. His conscience.

"I was the eldest son. I was raised in a town that had American legion posts and VFW posts, and I was steeped in the American tradition of God and Country, and I believed in it, I believed that there are certain obligations and responsibilities that go with living in this country. And I also asked myself, if one day I got married and had a son, what would I tell him when he asked me what I had done during the war?

"Not that I didn't try to weasel out of it, not that at first I didn't try to evade the draft. I'd like this to sound heroic, but the fact is I was hoping I'd get hurt playing football and wouldn't have to serve. Once I knew I had been drafted, our next game was against Cleveland and I was on kickoff coverage and I ran down the field and just threw myself into their wedge. Three guys trampled me. One ran right across my chest and it felt like a car had gone over me. I remember I laid there for a minute actually hoping I had broken a couple of ribs, hoping I wouldn't pass the Army physical.

"Once I knew I was going in," he says, "I committed myself. I figured combat was like football, that when you held back, when you tried not to get hurt, that's when you'd get hurt for sure."

So he became The Reluctant Hero.

He got shot and blown up and put pretty much back together and then he came back to the Steelers, and he was a man missing most of three toes on his right foot, which doesn't sound like much until you try to accelerate.

He would lie in bed at night and curse his foot. He worked out fanatically but the pain was unceasing.

"They kept telling me to do something else," he says, "but there wasn't anything I wanted to do as badly as I wanted to play football. I can't say enough about the Steelers and their patience. God bless Art Rooney (the Steelers owner, now dead). The old man was so loyal and so caring. One year he paid for one of my operations and gave me a year's salary ($19,000) and suggested they make me a scout. He really did treat you like you were a member of his family."

He took a job selling insurance, and he worked out early in the morning and late in the evening. He took his workouts where he could find them, including running up and down fire escapes.

"Everyone," he says, "ought to have to sell insurance once in their life."

There were times he felt like a charity case. It was whispered, loud enough for him to hear, that he was a Rooney pet, that the only reason the Steelers kept him around was because the old man had a soft spot for him. These comments only stiffened his resolve. He used them to drive himself. He gained forty-five pounds over the years, all of it muscle, rebuilt himself, actually gained speed, and one day awoke to find himself a starter, just as the Steelers were becoming a dynasty. Terry Bradshaw and Lynn Swann. Mean Joe Greene and Jack (Fang) Lambert. Franco Harris and, yes, Rocky Bleier. The Steel Curtain.

His first Super Bowl check, which he received in January of 1975, was the winner's share—$15,000.

The ring meant more, and still does.

"All those years of trying to become a contributor, and then all of a sudden we win four Super Bowls in five years," he says. "It still boggles my mind. And it all seemed to go by so fast. One day you're at your first Super Bowl, and then the next, you're . . . "

Retiring.

He says he never really thought about it until after the 1979 season, which would end with the Steelers' final Super Bowl.

"I didn't start at the beginning of that season, and that required an adjustment on my part," he says. "Most coaches don't tell you anything . . . this is how we're going to use you, whatever. But when you look up and you see they have four running backs and there's only one ball, and the other backs are young, strong bulls . . . well, I became a backup at both fullback and halfback and a third down player.

"All players want an identity, and you take it where you can find it. But by midseason I was back starting and we go to the Super Bowl and I was thinking the old man has come back quite nicely, thank you very much. And during Super Bowl week the media started asking me if I had thought about retiring. I know that Dick Hoak, the running back coach, had told me before not to mention retiring out loud because in (head coach) Chuck Noll's mind, if you start talking about it, then you've already done it."

During the offseason, a movie about Rocky Bleier's life was being finished.

"The movie guy calls me and says it will be aired in December and it would be better if the guy the movie is about was still playing, so I think, well, OK, maybe we can defend our Super Bowl and maybe win three in a row. Nobody's ever done that. But that will definitely be it for me. Nineteen-eighty will be the last season.

"It helped that I had made that decision before the final season, and it helped that it was my decision. That gave me a real sense of closure, a sense of peace. I had no regrets. How could I? There was nothing else achievable. Oh sure, I'd like to have made the Hall of Fame, but I had played for some great teams. We'd had success like no other team, my career certainly wasn't being cut short, and I just felt like all my big needs had been fulfilled. That makes it a lot easier to walk away. I could enjoy that last season. Each town, I said my goodbyes."

He said his goodbye to Pittsburgh in the most melodramatic of ways. In their final home game of 1980, the Steelers played Kansas City at Three Rivers Stadium. It was a meaningless game and the Steelers played like it. They trailed 16–14 with only a couple of minutes left.

23

"We had eighty yards to go and for some reason Bradshaw decides to give me the ball six times in a row. I hadn't carried it six times in a whole game all year. Here I am, thirty-five, never fast and now real slow, beat up from twelve NFL seasons, and I get the ball six times in a row."

The crowd awoke. Fifty-eight thousand people began to chant his name: "Rocky! Rocky! Rocky!"

At the Chiefs' eleven-yard line, with thirty-two seconds left, Bradshaw leaned into the huddle and submitted his order: "Full left split 85 trap, on two."

Rocky Bleier: Off-tackle.

The right guard pulled. Rocky Bleier followed. Blockers flattened defenders. The hole was enormous. He went through it. One tackler hit him from the side, but ricocheted off. At the goal line, a defensive back was coiled. They both left the ground.

In midair, they collided, helmets clacking. Rocky Bleier, with ball, came down just across the goal line.

At the gun.

It was outrageously, extravagantly, hopelessly theatrical. Anything else, of course, would be decidedly anticlimactic. Yet, in fact, there was one game left, on the road, at San Diego. The plane ride home to Pittsburgh was worth the trip. It was very liquid.

"We carried on as much liquor as we could and we drank it all. Jack Lambert and Jack Ham and I sat together and toasted each other all the way home. And I sat in my car in the parking lot at 4:30 in the morning and that's when it hit me. It's over. My career, not the Steelers. I think it was a couple more years before any of us realized we had been part of a dynasty. I just remember sitting there in the car by myself and crying.

"It was good. It helped."

He had arranged an on-air job with a Pittsburgh TV station and went to work immediately, and when July came he did what he had always done—he went to training camp.

"That helped, not missing a beat in the routine you were used to," he says. "Then the regular season began and the very first play of the very first game they called quick trap up the middle. That was my play, only somebody else was running it. I could feel it in my stomach. I swear I could feel the hits.

"Guys would come up to me and say, 'Rocky, you look great. You could have played another year.' And I thought, yeah, and I would have been on the bench watching, and you know what? It's a whole lot safer watching from up here."

What he found was that changes came, gradually to be sure, but life-altering nonetheless.

He tried marriage and it ended in divorce. He tried running a business and it ended in bankruptcy. He repaid all his creditors. "A hundred cents on the dollar," he says, proudly. All those events were just as jolting in their own way as any Vietnamese hand grenade. But he survived, just as he had in Nam.

Appropriately enough, at the age of fifty, at a nice round half-century, his debts paid and remarried, he got to start out all over again in life. He appreciated the chance, and he appreciated his mother's favorite axiom: Too soon old, too late smart.

"You leave little pieces of yourself scattered around," he says. "Right after I retired as a player and the Steelers were struggling, wherever I'd go Steelers' fans would be saying, 'We need you back, Rock. You guys would never have lost like this, Rock.' You become larger than life to people, and they don't realize that you are no different than they are.

"We have certain expectations of our heroes. We don't realize they have feet of clay. We have health problems, we go through divorces, we have business failures, just like everyone else. Just because you play football doesn't make you immune."

No, not immune from life. If anything, maybe football makes you more susceptible to life.

"You have a fear of failure and that's what drives you on the field," he agrees. "When you're done, you still have that drive but where do you redirect it? You're going to stumble around for a while, searching, hoping you will find your niche.

"You'll always be a ball player. That follows you around. But that's OK. That gives you a common ground for talking with other people."

Talking is what he does for a living now. He averages 120 motivational speeches a year, mostly to corporate gatherings. He worked his way up, just like he did in football. He started at high school banquets and now he shows up fairly regularly on Maui, among other nice-duty locations.

"Life's a helluva journey," he tells them. "Enjoy it."

The journey down Rocky's Road certainly has been an extraordinary one. There should be several curves left yet. In March of 1999 he turned fifty-three. He still works out daily, almost as diligently as when he was playing. He runs, bikes, lifts. He is fit. He also has knees that bark at him and a left shoulder that makes grinding sounds due to degenerative arthritis.

But it is, he admits, a fairly short inventory of discomfort. He has, after all, been shot and hit with grenades, and has taken a dozen years of NFL hits.

"Yeah, all things considered, I'm very fortunate. I probably ought to hurt more than I do. And what does hurt, you don't know if it's from war or football or just plain age."

He watches games on TV from time to time and says he makes himself conversant with the game so he won't embarrass himself at social gatherings. He and his wife Jan will go to three or four Steelers home games a year. He pays for the tickets, parks with everyone else.

He has absolutely no urge at all to play, he says. But there are people who have urges for him.

"It's been almost twenty years and there are people in Pittsburgh who won't let go of the seventies," he says. "They'll yell at me, 'Hey, Rock, why don't you suit up?' "

And Rocky Bleier will smile in appreciation, and fortified with the wisdom that you can never live up to the glories of the past, he will respond with just about the best possible answer:

"Thanks, but I'd rather be a memory . . ."

Cynthia Zordich

Cynthia Zordich

CONCRETE CHARLIE
The Chuck Bednarik Story

Those hands. You cannot help but stare at them. They are hypnotic. Mesmerizing.

It is thought that the oldest living thing on the planet is a tree that dwells on a bleak, hardscrabble, windswept spit of desolation, and it is so cantankerously hardy, so unyieldingly stubborn that it seems to take root in rock. You can't kill it, and it won't die on its own.

Those hands, they belong on that tree.

The fingers are bent at grotesque angles, the knuckles hideously swollen. The pinky on the right hand wanders out at a ninety-degree angle, almost as though it belongs to another hand.

Those fingers have been stepped on. Chewed on. Twisted. Bent. Yanked. Cleated. Caught in the ear holes of helmets. Caught in face masks and violently shaken

31

about. All that, plus whatever other atrocities football players commit on each other when they are hidden from the view of the whistle-blowers and the yellow flag-throwers, down there at the bottom of the pile, when the rule is to grab hold of the handiest extremity and practice extreme sadism.

Those hands . . . imagine the stories they could tell.

Well, those hands are the property of Chuck Bednarik. He is beamingly proud of them, and he will gladly recount for you each dislocation, each firecracker pop that meant yet another fracture, each ligament torn, each muscle shredded, each bit of cartilage ripped loose from its moorings. He can give you down and distance and gruesome detail.

Arthritic? You bet.

Hurt? Only every minute of every day, that's all.

He says this with a perverse delight because those hands, those gnarled, callous claws, are befitting to a man who was anointed with the best nickname there has ever been in all of sports: Concrete Charlie.

"Like it? I loved it!" he thunders.

And it is obvious that he loves it still. He not only loved it, he lived it, and now, as a lion in winter, he tries to live it still.

Chuck Bednarik. Last of the Sixty-Minute Men. Iron Man. Concrete Charlie.

That's quite a load to be lugging around, quite a lot to live up to, especially when, on May 1, 1998, you have turned seventy-three.

He snorts at the notion of mortality.

"I'm up at six every morning," he says. "I can run ten miles, play eighteen holes, and mow the yard, before noon."

He winks, blue lagoon eyes twinkling to soften how harsh that all sounds. But you look at him there in the swivel chair in his kitchen, half a hoagie in front of him, not ten pounds off his best playing weight and his body yielding only the most grudging of inches to time, and you suspect that if there were money riding on it, if it really mattered to him, he might just do it, might just do the ten miles and the eighteen holes and the two acres of lawn, all in the same morning, and then ask what you've got in mind to kill the afternoon.

In 1960 a sportswriter named Hugh Brown wrote in *The Bulletin* that the middle linebacker and the center for the Philadelphia Eagles—who were both the same man—"is as hard as the concrete he sells." Chuck Bednarik sold ready-mix concrete in the off-season. One could not make a living playing professional football in those days.

Even if you were Concrete Charlie.

Even if you were the toughest, meanest, most versatile, most indefatigable, most steadfast SOB on the field.

"I was the No. 1 pick in the draft," he says, "and you know what I got? I got $3,000 for signing my name to an Eagles contract and I got a salary of $10,000. I bought a new car for $2,700 and a house for $14,500."

"I played both ways, offense and defense, and I kicked off, I punted, I snapped the ball on field goals and extra points. Now, you tell me, what was left that I didn't do?"

Uh, sell programs?

"That was about all. And when I say I played both ways, I mean there was contact on every play. You got hit! You got the stuffing beat out of you. Not like this pantywaist stuff today, where they'll say somebody like this Deion Sanders, ohhhhhh, isn't it wonderful how he plays both ways. Give me a break! He doesn't play both ways. He's just out there, doing a soft shoe. How often does a defensive back even get touched? He goes a whole game and never makes a tackle. That pitty-pat stuff, that's not two-way football."

His voice is a rising rumble. This is a sore subject. Concrete Charlie is not just proud of his name and his reputation, not just proud to have been the last of the Sixty-Minute Men, he is zealously protective of that title, more passionate about guarding it with each passing year, and determined not to concede it to someone who doesn't have hands like his, hands like the roots on the tallest, oldest tree in the forest, hands that got that way by honest, hard labor.

He looks at those hands, looks at the pinky that has set off on its own, and he laughs.

"The difference between me and Deion is, he's got diamonds on all his fingers."

Yes, Chuck Bednarik is bitter. Yes, he is resentful. Yes, he admits it, and eagerly it seems. Yes, he is blunt, and to a fault. As his wife Emma likes to say: "If you want to know what's on Charlie's mind, you don't have to ask. Usually you don't even have to wait ten seconds."

No, there is no diplomacy, no pretense. He is what he is, unashamed and unrepentant.

"Sure I'm envious of what they make these days," he says. "I see what they make compared to what I did and it makes me nauseous. Deion couldn't tackle my wife. I just scan the games on TV, only scan them. I know they're bigger today. Everyone goes three hundred pounds. But look at 'em when they come off the field. They're sitting there taking their last breath. They gotta have oxygen after one play! Think any of them will live to be fifty? So, yeah, they're bigger. Faster, too. But better?"

He shrugs, demands: "Show me."

The glasses he wears seem to be giving off sparks.

"Look, I don't want to come off sounding like a braggart. But I did what I did. It's like Ali said, 'If you did it then it's not bragging, it's fact.' "

And, yes, he did it. Oh my, yes.

When the Eagles won the pro football championship in 1960, Concrete Charlie played all but ninety seconds of the game. He had retired two years prior, but had come back. He was thirty-seven years old. And on the last play of the game, the Green Bay Packers' brutish fullback Jim Taylor caught a pass and was heading to the end zone for what would have been the winning touchdown.

Except Concrete Charlie got him, wrestled him to the cold, hard ground like a rodeo cowboy bulldogs a steer, and then sat on the squirming, seething Taylor until the clock blinked down to all zeros.

"You can get up now, Jim," Concrete Charlie told Taylor. "The game's over."

It became a line for the ages.

Also for the ages was Concrete Charlie's hit on Frank Gifford. It remains even now the definitive tackle in the sport of football. Coaches still scrounge around for the grainy black and white shot from November 20, 1960, to show their charges how to legally decapitate another human being.

It was in Yankee Stadium, the Eagles were winning 17–10 inside the last two minutes, and Gifford was running a pass route directly into the Bermuda Triangle, over the middle, into the Dead Zone, reaching back for the pass that was thrown behind him, snaring it with an elegant ease, the graceful nonchalance that was his signature, turning to head upfield and . . .

Wham!

If he'd been hit full with a baseball bat, he wouldn't have flown backward with such velocity. The ball flew forward. Gifford lay like a corpse.

"Chuck knocked him right out of his shoes," insists Tom Brookshier, who was Concrete Charlie's teammate.

That seems a bit overblown.

"No, look," says Brookshier as he walks to a wall in his den and points to a thirty-eight-year-old photograph of Gifford, motionless as a cadaver. And, yes, it does look as though his shoes are barely hanging to his toes.

Looming over the supine Gifford is Charles Philip Bednarik, in mid-hop, doing a dance of unbridled glee. For long, bitter years New York Giants fans have accused him of taunting, but Concrete Charlie looks you in the eye and says: "I can tell you word-for-word what I was saying to Frank.

35

"This f-----g game is over!"

Gifford sustained the king of concussions, and he was knocked out of not only that game, but the rest of the season . . . and the season after that!

And this is what Gifford has said: "It was perfectly legal. If I'd had the chance, I'd have done the same thing Chuck did."

At the card shows he does, Concrete Charlie has two stacks of 8x10 photographs ready for autograph seekers. They can select one that shows him crouched, poised to pounce on an unseen opponent. Or they can opt for the other one, that famous shot, Bednarik looking down at the unconscious Gifford.

"Nine out of ten choose this one," says Concrete Charlie, holding up the most famous picture in the history of professional football.

"There was a celebrity roast for Frank a few years ago and I was asked to be one of the roasters. So I told the guy in charge that right after he introduced me he should have all the lights in the room turned out. Total darkness. So he did, and I waited, five, six, seven seconds, and you can hear the crowd wondering what the hell is going on. When the lights came back on I looked at Frank and said, 'Does that ring a bell?' The place broke up."

But behind the gruffness and the bluster, behind the bitterness and the bile, there is a part of Concrete Charlie that is more marshmallow than concrete. In 1997, when Gifford made the front page of all the tabloids and was the centerpiece of all the TV trash shows, caught in a compromising and embarrassing position with a woman who was not his wife, he found himself at a banquet sitting all alone, shunned like a leper. No one wanted to venture within twenty yards of him.

Except for Concrete Charlie.

"He told me, 'I'm going to go over and speak to him,' " said Emma Bednarik. "He said, 'This isn't right. He's not a killer.' You never know what Charlie is apt to say, so I was holding my breath the whole time."

Concrete Charlie made sure the rest of the room saw him as he walked slowly and purposefully to the solitary man, sat down, and cheerily boomed: "Hey, Frank, good to see you. How you doing?"

Gifford's head was bowed. Even though he didn't look up at first he smiled and said out of the side of his mouth: "I made you famous, didn't I, Chuck?"

"Yes, you did, Frank."

"I'm still your friend, Chuck."

"And I'm still your friend, Frank."

There is a yowling commotion outside. Concrete Charlie sighs heavily. Spanky is bringing Concrete Charlie another gift. Maybe a mouse. Perhaps a mole.

As a scrawny orphan, Spanky was dumped at the bottom of Concrete Charlie's driveway. Spanky was barely alive, ribs showing, but he hissed and clawed and showed so much fight for such a tiny kitten that Concrete Charlie, the tough guy, couldn't help but take him in.

In gratitude, Spanky hunts down furry critters and delivers them, proudly, to the kitchen door, as a sort of tribute. Concrete Charlie pretends to be annoyed.

Concrete Charlie rises from his chair and walks with only the suggestion of a hitch in his get-along. He had knee replacement surgery (on the left one) in 1994. It was the first and only time his legs had ever been operated on. "To me," he says, "that's a miracle. Twenty-one years of football and never have to have knee surgery, that's a miracle."

He returns with a shopping bag full of letters. They're from East Moline, Illinois. From Overland Park, Kansas. From Pelham, New Jersey. He averages forty to fifty letters a month. They want his autograph. On collector's cards. On scraps of paper. Even on a helmet. It is amazing; he is nearly forty seasons removed from his last football game and yet the clamor for him is greater that ever. A new generation has discovered Concrete Charlie and they are agog, like paleontologists who have just dug up the remnants of the most frightening dinosaur of all. The Sixty-Minute Man.

"Dear Mr. Bednarik: Is it true that you played both ways? Could you please sign this? I am enclosing a pen."

All of the attention pleases him mightily, and he doesn't mind saying so.

"Thank God for grandfathers and fathers," he says. "They tell their sons and grandsons about me. They tell them: 'Now there was a football player!' And then kids see me on Classic Sports shows. And NFL Films has been very, very good to me."

The supplicants write to him in care of the Pro Football Hall of Fame in Canton, Ohio, and regularly the Hall forwards a full shopping bag to him, up there in his hilltop Tudor-style house, in Coopersburg, Pennsylvania, near his beloved Bethlehem. And he signs them all and sends them back.

No charge.

"I know there are guys who get fan mail and open the envelopes and if there isn't money in them, they throw them away. I could never do that."

No, he couldn't. Concrete Charlie has a code to live by. It is a code he began to form while still in his teens. He formed it while he was crammed inside those bombers he flew in combat missions during World War II. He was a machine gunner. He was only eighteen. So young, so very young to be introduced to death. Thirty times he took off, thirty times he landed.

Even now he can hear the flak pinging on the wings and the fuselage, deadly shards of jagged shrapnel knocking, knocking, knocking to be let inside. Even now, he sees other bombers in flames, men jumping from them, pulling frantically at parachute rip cords.

Some of the chutes open, billowing plumes.

And some of them don't.

Very quickly, Concrete Charlie got in the habit of going to the five o'clock mass.

"I have a lot of devotion in me," he says. "I go to mass every morning. I have a Virgin Mary monument in the backyard. I've had a lot of miracles in my life."

And those analogies we are always making, the ones equating combat on the football field to combat in a war?

"Yeah, they're a lot alike," he says slowly, considering his words. "But no matter how bad you might get hurt playing football, at least there's nobody shooting at you."

Back from the war, he enrolled at the University of Pennsylvania and almost instantly became an All-American. Franklin Field was stuffed full in those days, the glory days of the late 1940s. Penn played the big-name schools, and the bigger the names the harder Concrete Charlie hit them. He quickly became the biggest name in college football.

At a Croatian Hall dance he first laid eyes on his Emma.

"Look at her!" he commands. "She's still beautiful. Absolutely gorgeous. She's seventy-three. Doesn't she look twenty years younger than that? We are married 50 years."

As a matter of fact, she does. And her eyes sparkle as she recounts their first days:

"My brother pointed him out to me. I knew him from nothing then. I asked, 'What's an All-American?' I thought football was a dirty sport. My brother said, 'He asked for your phone number. But don't go getting cocky. He'll be like a sailor. He'll have a girl in every town.' The first time we went out, I sat up against the door of the car. I was going to jump if he made any kind of move."

Ten months later, on June 5, 1948, they were married.

They have five children, all daughters, and ten grandchildren.

Emma: "Charlie refers to them as Daughter No. 1 and Daughter No. 2, and I tell him: 'Charlie, they have names for heaven's sake.'"

Yes, they do, and when he speaks their names, when he speaks anything at full volume, they all jump. Except Emma. She knows how to gentle him. She knows how to be a horse whisperer to him. She can get Concrete Charlie to come around, every time.

"I couldn't stand the yelling," she says, "so I learned very early how to tell him little white lies. Never to hurt him. Never to deceive him. Just to keep the peace. Just to stop the yelling. Just to bring quiet into the house."

He listens to this and nods his head, in affirmation and agreement, and his eyes shine. It is a look of adoration.

"I have a violent temper," he says, contritely.

But Emma knows how to muzzle him, and also just how to keep him feeling good about himself.

"A man called me," says Concrete Charlie, "and wanted to know if it was OK if he named a race horse after me. I said sure. So he called me the other day and said Concrete Charlie had just run his first race. He said he got boxed in and he got tired and finished sixth."

And Emma looks at Concrete Charlie and smiles sweetly and says: "I told the owner of that horse that his horse can't get tired at the end. Because this Charlie never did."

Concrete Charlie beams.

He put in his years in pro ball and retired after the 1959 season. He was thirty-five years old and he felt every day of it. Of course, being Concrete Charlie, he never admitted that to anyone. They gave him a hero's send-off.

"They gave me a thousand dollars," he says.

That year, on the way to the championship, he played virtually every second of each of the last five games. He did so even though he had torn his right biceps so horribly that the entire muscle came loose and slid down his arm until it got to his elbow, where it col-lected in a sort of grotesque puddle.

The other players, tough men themselves, saw it and swallowed the bile that was rising in their throats. They looked on with wide eyes while Concrete Charlie pushed that mound of muscle back up his arm, nudged it into the approximate place where it belonged, and then tied it down with a large Ace bandage.

The legend of The Iron Man swelled.

Against Cleveland, he ricocheted out of a three-man pile-up and landed in a heap in front of the Browns' bench. The great coach Paul Brown looked down at him and snarled:

"Give it up, old man!"

Concrete Charlie scrambled to his feet and sprayed the patriarch of the Browns with defiant spittle and elaborate hyphenated profanities, and then made a point of putting a little extra mayhem into each of his hits the rest of the game.

He came back in 1961 to help defend the championship. But he was thirty-seven by then and the team was in decline.

So was Concrete Charlie.

And he knew it.

If you're going to be the Sixty-Minute Man all your days, then you have to be unsparing when you assess yourself. No alibis. No excuses. No rationalizations. Take it straight, without a flinch.

"I knew I was losing it," he says. "Thirty-seven—that's enough. You can't kid yourself. You know what you used to be able to do. When you get to where you wanted to be on a play and they've passed you by, then it's time. Oh, I could've kept playing, fooled them for another year or so."

But he couldn't stomach the thought of fooling himself. He could still play, but he couldn't be Concrete Charlie, and damn if he was going to tarnish the legend.

So he retired, this time for keeps.

"I was all right with it," he insists.

"No, he wasn't," rebuts Emma, softly and firmly.

He shrugs, saying wordlessly that, yes, she is right.

"I went to camp my first year out of the game, just to help out a little. I thought maybe I could wean myself away from the game."

And could he?

He looks at Emma, and she answers for him: "He tried not to show it, but I knew what was inside of him. Charlie has a lot of restlessness in him. It was very hard for him to be separated from football. I think they could have cut off a leg and he wouldn't have missed it as much as he missed football."

He does not disagree.

"In fact," says Emma, triumphantly, "he would play now if he could. Isn't that right, Charlie?"

Concrete Charlie fidgets in the swivel chair in his kitchen and blurts out his confession:

"Sure I would. Yeah, I'd line up right now. The money, the way it is today, I'd make more for one game than I made my whole career. Yeah, I'd line up and get the snot kicked out of me."

He smiles a fox smile.

"I could go in and snap the ball for a punt," he says, "only I wouldn't run down the field."

Sure he would. He'd give in, he'd give in to temptation and he'd give in to instinct and he'd do it, if they'd just give him the chance.

He'd bend over and assume that snapper's splay-legged stance and wrap those gloriously gnarled claws around the football and send it whistling back there to the punter and then he'd rise up and explode out of that stance and set off down the field, looking for somebody to crock. Seventy-three years old, running on a plastic knee, and looking for someone to knock ass over teacups.

And, oh, how grand it would be . . . The Last Ride of Concrete Charlie.

He looks at his Emma and smiles fondly.

And she looks at her Concrete Charlie and she gives him a big wink.

Cynthia Zordich

"I think it's a mixture of several things, one of them being it's a game of pain. It's recognized as pain, it's accepted as pain. When you go out there you know it's pain, you know it's not like basketball that hides behind that, you know, you don't touch anybody in basketball, it's a clean game. But football is a combination of accepting pain, tolerating pain, applying pain, you know, and that makes the difference. Now we all understand that fatigue and hard hits will make cowards of us all. Football separates the men from the boys and that makes the difference. I love it because I come from the ghetto, it was a natural for me. I had a lot of hostilities in my heart and soul because of circumstances that I was raised on. I had hostilities stacked up like dirty clothes in the corner when I came into the game. Had I went into baseball I still would have maintained all those hostilities inside me. Football allowed me the pleasure of releasing those hostilities 'cause I had the chance to go down there in the pit and hit something, and the harder I hit, the more I released those hostilities."

Deacon Jones, DE 1961-71 LA Rams; 1972-73 San Diego; 1974 Washington
When asked about the magic of football
TNT Interviews

"One time we were playing and there was a kid that I thought was a very good football player and he was cut and wasn't told that he was cut until we got to the city to play that day and, you know, how they do it up, they put your names on the lockers and his name wasn't on the locker, and instead of telling this man that he was not going to play and in fact was cut, they waited until he found out in Philadelphia and he didn't know he was cut until then. That's the worst thing you can do to a human being, so disrespectful. Well, I started yelling and screaming . . . the day before we had this meeting about camaraderie and team and here's a good example of how terrible things could be."

Alex Karras, DT 1958-70 Detroit
When asked about the reaction around the league after the Paul Brown firing and the idea that players are not robots but human beings
NFL 75th Anniversary

"But I guess football, as far as I was concerned, was always kind of a means to an end. Not the end in itself. The late commissioner Bert Bell, that's what he stressed, because my first signing, when he signed me to my first contract, he was part-owner of the Pittsburgh Steelers with Mr. Rooney. 'You know, Bill,' he said, 'You got to do something else. You can't play football all your life. You can make some decent money while you're playing, but you got to do something else.' And I always thought that football should not be an end in itself."

Bill Dudley, HB-TB-DB 1942-46 Pittsburgh; 1947-49 Detroit; 1950-53 Washington
TNT Interviews
75th Anniversary

"There never was and never could be the thrill, the camaraderie, the friendship, the smell of the grass, the cheers of the crowd . . . no matter how much success you may have in business, they'll never match the thrill, there'll never be the feeling of victory that comes in the lifetime of being a professional athlete. Particularly with the team that I was blessed to play with. The friendship, the feeling, the relationship was one for all and all for one. It was just that kind of team. But believe me, there isn't a day or month that passes where you don't think of that team and the boys on the team, and what they meant to you and what you meant to them."

Sid Luckman, QB-DB-HB 1939-50 Chicago Bears
Talking about the thrill of the 1943 Championship in Chicago

Cynthia Zordich

AMAZING GRACE
The Pat Summerall Story

His best friend deceived him.

For which, Pat Summerall says, he will be eternally grateful.

For long, riotous years, Summerall and his best pal, Tom Brookshier, had played Butch Cassidy and the Sundance Kid, microphone partners and night riders rollicking around the country, TV celebrities seen by millions, relentless and thirsty—unquenchably thirsty—seekers of pleasurable diversions.

They would finish their telecast of a football game or some other sporting event, and then repair to the nearest, most convenient upholstered watering hole. There, night tended to dissolve into dawn before they found their way back to lodgings, sometimes their own, sometimes not.

Their memories of those raucous times are mostly scraps and blurs.

"Between us, we could usually piece together bits of evidence, but we were never really sure about all that had transpired," Summerall reflects. "People would tell us we'd had a really great time, but there were so many gaps we'd have to take their word for it."

Having been professional football players, both assumed they were immune to the usual inevitable consequences of such reckless living. They were spared when their employer, the Columbia Broadcasting System, decided to separate them.

"If CBS hadn't broken us up," says Summerall, "I am convinced neither one of us would be alive today."

He wouldn't come to this conclusion until much later, however, and not until after he had time to analyze the situation soberly, dispassionately.

"Brookie was—is—the closest thing I have to a brother," Summerall says. "He's the only one who could have tricked me and gotten away with it."

From a distance, Brookshier had watched with growing alarm what his former partner was doing to himself.

"I was drinking myself to death," Summerall says, pausing for emphasis after each word. "Everyone saw it but me. That's how it always is. The only one who refuses to recognize that there's a problem is the one who has the problem."

Denial is always the drunk's first weapon.

He was careful; he never went on the air inebriated. His speech was never slurred. He never toppled out of whatever crow's nest he had been assigned, whether in a stadium press box or in a golf course tower or from some suspended aerie overlooking a tennis court. Super Bowl, Masters, U.S. Open . . . he always showed up for work coherent and reasonably clear-eyed. Viewers heard only the familiar sparse presentation, the soft, pleasing drawl, the economy of words, the utter lack of hyperbole.

But when the work was done and it was time to unstrap—well, then he made up for lost time. With both hands.

"Jack Daniels was my running mate," he says.

It was his former running mate who lured him into ambush early in the spring of 1992. Tom Brookshier waited until Summerall had concluded working the Masters in April. And then he called his pal.

"I was in Philadelphia, getting ready to do a voice-over for NFL Films," Summerall recalls, "and Brookie gets me and asks for a favor. He says he's selling luxury suites in an arena in Philly and he's got a potential client who's a big fan of mine, and if I could just meet with the guy for a few minutes that would probably be enough to seal the deal.

"I agreed, though I was less than thrilled, and Brookie says to meet him at the Stouffer's Inn in Camden, New Jersey. We meet in the lobby and he says the guy is in a room on the 12th floor. I guess I should have been suspicious but I just wanted to get it over with. And then when we opened the door and went into that room . . . "

His voice catches. Even after all these years, he can see the hotel room and the circle of chairs in it, each one occupied by a dear, and deeply concerned, friend.

It was an intervention.

The friends of Pat Summerall had gathered to save him from himself.

The late Pete Rozelle, the long-time commissioner of the NFL, was there. So was the president of the Mayo Clinic. So were marquee names from sports and television. So was Pat Summerall's daughter, Susan. They had been assembled there, he later learned, for two days, patiently waiting for him.

Now, from across the years, he sees that room through the mist of grateful tears. On the day of the ambush, however, he saw the room only through the red haze of anger. He didn't feel love or gratitude for those who had gathered; he felt betrayed.

Only later would he learn that there is usually a correlation, that the deeper the problem the greater the anger, the resentment. Friends are seen as enemies.

"Here they were wanting to save me," Summerall says, "and I was sure they were the ones who had the problem."

51

Each one in that hotel room had written him a letter, in longhand. One by one they stood to read.

"I didn't hear much of anything, I was so mad," he says. "I was so furious they practically had to tie me down."

And then his daughter stood.

"She said, 'Lately I've been ashamed to share your name.' "

That was the hit that took him to his knees.

As he relates this, Pat Summerall is sitting in Eden, in a lawn chair at one of the umbrella tables on the impossibly green grass of the Augusta National Golf Club veranda, in the shadow of two enormous oak trees thought to be two centuries old. It is a soft early April morning, on the eve of the 1998 Masters. The air is thick with the heady musk of spring and of rebirth and recycling and resurrection. Surely there cannot be another locale anywhere better suited for assessing and for appreciating and for offering up thanks.

His friends had arranged for a private plane. It would fly Pat Summerall across the continent, to California, to the Betty Ford Clinic. He would be admitted immediately.

He agreed. Numbly. His daughter's letter had sucked most of the resistance out of him.

Tom Brookshier, like a true friend, made the trip with him.

"Sometimes," Brookshier says, "you just need someone to hold your hand. I told him: 'Patrick, I'll go to the ends of the earth with you if that's what it takes.' "

The usual stay is twenty-eight days. Pat Summerall was there for thirty-three.

"I asked them why, and they smiled and said 'You were so mad and raving that you didn't hear anything anyone was saying for the first five days.' "

Gradually, his anger cooled. He listened. Sobriety took hold. He became one of the clinic's most famous triumphs. Very soon he was not only a testament to the wonders of rehabilitation, he was on the board of regents of the clinic.

In that capacity, he gives speeches from time to time. Invariably, he reaches into his pocket and brings out a sheaf of pages from yellow legal pads. They are wrinkled and worn from constant usage.

They are the letters that were written to him by those people who gathered in a hotel room to save his life.

His story has a happy ending. But it did not come without a crushing cost.

There was, as there always is with great trauma, damage beyond repair.

In Pat Summerall's case, sobriety cost him a marriage. He and Kathy had been wed thirty-five years. They had three children—Susan, Jay, and Kyle. And grandchildren.

"But my wife . . . my former wife . . . she had been in such denial for so long, she wasn't the same person. And, of course, sober, neither was I. It was inevitable, I guess, that we separated."

Four years into sobriety, he trusted himself to try again. He and Cheri live outside Dallas. She arranges his schedule, points him in the right direction.

"We're near the airport," he says. "I can get just about every place I need to get non-stop."

Pause. Smile.

"Except for Green Bay."

The entrance to their place is guarded by two large stone gates. On one is etched the address. On the other is etched the name they selected, with great care, for their homestead:

Amazing Grace.

As it does to most who play it for a living, football has left Pat Summerall with assorted souvenirs, reminders of the violence that is meted out and absorbed.

He is six feet, four inches tall but when he walks he is shorter because he tilts forward slightly. His body is avenging a career of physical indignities.

He has a slight crouch and a slight limp. When he sits, he takes his time unfolding. When he stands, he does so deliberately and slowly, as though he is carrying eggs in his pockets.

Let's take inventory:

*Six surgeries on the left knee. "One when I was playing, five clean-outs since."

*Nose broken eleven times; what is left is flattened. "I try to convince myself that it gives character to my face."

*A long, jagged scar on the front of the left forearm, an even longer one on the back. The arm was laid completely open to repair a compound fracture he sustained during a game. "The compensation is that it blocks out the hook in my golf swing."

On May 10, 1998, he turned sixty-seven. His hair is a mane of snow, distinctive and distinguished. Most of the whiskey glow is gone now from his nose. The spider webbing of broken capillaries has faded and his liver is on speaking terms with him. All things considered . . .

" . . . all things considered, I got off lucky. I see guys a lot worse off than me. Guys in wheelchairs. Guys hooked up to machines."

He was a natural. Strong and supple, sleek as a cheetah, he was good at any sport he tried. Not just good, All-State good. Tennis. Football. Basketball. Boxing.

He was born and grew up in Lake City, Florida. He is a true son of the South. His grandmother was named Augusta Georgia Summerall, his grandaddy Thomas Jefferson Summerall, and that Confederate heritage is evident in his courtliness and gentlemanly manner

His parents separated when he was young. They wanted to send him to an orphanage, but his aunt and uncle intervened and took him in. They lived a block from the

Columbia High School football field, where he would later star. Hour upon hour he kicked footballs on that field.

He kicked with a right foot that he came to regard as charmed. It was backward at birth, so deformed that a doctor broke it and reset it in the correct position. During a ten-season career in the NFL, that charmed foot kicked for 561 points, including 101 field goals and 258 extra points, 129 of those in a row.

He played before specialization came to the sport, before two-platoon football, before nickel packages and dime packages, in the era of the sixty-minute men. He was an end on offense and an end on defense, and he placekicked as a sideline. He played before the advent of soccer-style kickers and used a squared-off shoe, kicking straight ahead, with a high chorus line follow-through.

In 1958, playing for the Giants in a blinding snowstorm at Yankee Stadium, he was sent in to try a forty-nine-yard field goal against the Cleveland Browns. The score was 10-10.

The offensive coordinator of the Giants argued furiously against the attempt.

"You can't kick it that far, not even on a calm day," Vince Lombardi shouted at Summerall.

So much for the pep talk.

He kicked and the ball tumbled end over end through the howling wind and the swirling snow and the bone-deep cold . . . and fell just over the crossbar.

The 13-10 win enabled the Giants to tie the Browns for the Eastern Division title and forced a one-game playoff between the two the following week. The Giants won that, too, and then played the Baltimore Colts in the overtime epic—Alan Ameche tromped through a gaping hole and fell into the end zone—that did more to raise the public's awareness of professional football than probably any other game ever played.

And when Pat Summerall jogged off the field at Yankee Stadium after kicking the field goal that made the game possible, Vince Lombardi was waiting for him, his lips pulled back over his teeth in what might have been a smile or a baring of fangs.

"I thought he was going to hug me," Summerall remembers. "Instead, he was screaming at me: 'C'mon, you son of a kangaroo, c'mon, you know you can't kick it that far.' "

He ended up doing a lot of things that surprised people. He won a scholarship to Arkansas. For basketball. He not only got his degree there, he earned a master's degree there as well.

In Russian history.

He also taught junior high English and history.

"I fully intended to be a teacher," he says. "Football kind of got in the way."

Kind of.

He was signed, in 1952, by the Cardinals, when they were in Chicago. His signing bonus was $250, which just so happened to equal the bar tab he owed. He played five seasons for them and then five more with the Giants, and early in the 1960s, when his career was winding down as a player, he began working for CBS, first in radio, doing brief commentaries, then in television. That would enable him to make the transition from player to ex-player almost seamlessly, with none of the usual sense of separation and loss.

"I'd like to tell you that it was hard giving up football," he says, "but it wasn't. Not really. But only because I already had something lined up and because that something was the closest thing to actually playing the game. Plus, you don't get hit. And you don't have to have help getting out of bed the next morning."

"But if I hadn't been able to stay close to the game, I don't know what I would have done. I've never been in combat, but I guess football is as close to it as you can get. You develop a lot of foxhole friendships. That's the part you miss the most, I guess."

He was privileged to spend his broadcasting apprenticeship in the company of some of the profession's most luminous talents. From Chris Schenkel he learned the value of meticulous preparation. From Jack Buck he learned that the booth wasn't church, that it was permissible, sometimes even preferable, to laugh. And from Ray Scott he learned the precious gift of understatement and restraint.

"In six and a half years with Ray, I never heard him make a mistake," he says. "That was because he wanted to make sure he was right before he spoke. He wasn't in a hurry. And he felt that often the pictures spoke for themselves, and all we did was get in the way, clutter things up, speaking inanities."

That has become Pat Summerall's signature, the absence of speaking the obvious, the absence of the shrill and the shill. Over the years—thirty-three of them with CBS, then four and counting with Fox—he has been likened to Perry Como and Gary Cooper. He has won the public's trust and confidence. He has become to sports what Walter Cronkite was to news, a symbol of comfort and credibility and assurance.

In the words of Beano Cook of ESPN: "If I ever got cancer, I'd want Pat Summerall to be the one to tell me."

When this is repeated to him, Summerall winces. And also blushes. He recognizes the intense compliment that is meant.

"I was blessed with a voice that doesn't offend too many people. And I've always thought I was a pretty good listener. That comes in handy when you're sharing a booth with some-one else for three hours at a time."

Brookshier was his first on-air partner. Theirs was an easy, natural fit.

"But I never would have guessed we'd end up together," Summerall says. "Brookie was a very good defensive back with Philadelphia, and of course the Giants and Eagles played each other frequently. I remember one game, it was all over but the shouting, everyone kind of relaxed, just playing it out, and Brookie laid a lick on me so hard that he split my helmet. I was lying there, and I looked up at him and snarled: 'What's wrong with you, you blankety-blank? What'd you do that for?' "

"And he looked down at me, almost out of pity, and he sneered: 'Why, you're pathetic. You shouldn't even be out here. You're gonna get yourself hurt.' "

After Brookshier, he was partnered with John Madden. For almost two decades they have been sports television's most famous and most effective couple. Madden is the rumpled, unmade bed, a shambling Saint Bernard wildly gesturing, splotching his sentences with his own sound effects. Summerall is the ideal antidote, serene and controlled, elegant and eloquent, cleaning up his excitable mate's verbal clutter, the terse two-sentence counter-point. Madden will aim his telestrator at a tailgate pig roast and Summerall will remind you of down, distance, and score.

"He's the least affected broadcaster I've ever known," says Madden. "No ego at all. I'm very outgoing and disorganized. Pat is very controlled and organized and that really helps me. His strength in tying things together makes up for my weaknesses. He knows what everyone has gone through, or is going through, because he went through it himself."

"He's what we mean when we say less-is-more. He makes me comfortable and I know he makes viewers feel that way, too."

They meshed from the start.

"We never worked at it, never planned anything," Summerall says.

Which, of course, is precisely why they work so well together. Nothing is forced. Rehearsals or scripts would spoil their chemistry.

"Our first game together was at Tampa Bay and John had a suit and tie on, which of course looked like a straitjacket on him. He was sweating something awful, and I thought, 'Oh boy, if his nerves are this bad and we haven't even gone on the air, this is never going to work out.' Well, it wasn't nerves. It was height. John doesn't like heights and he's claustrophobic. That's why he doesn't fly. But when the game started he put all his phobias aside and by the end of the first quarter of our first game, I knew this was right."

It was so right that when CBS lost its NFL broadcasting rights, Pat Summerall and John Madden sat together in the empty stands of the Silverdome after their last game and pondered work without each other.

"I told John, 'I don't believe I can work with anyone else.' And he said, 'I don't think I can, either.' Fortunately, we didn't have to."

Madden: "Tell you all you need to know about Pat. My two sons were in college and they were going to play against each other in football—Mike at Harvard, Joe at Brown—and I wanted to go to their game. The problem was, Pat and I watch film on Saturday for our Sunday game. For me to get away for their game, Pat would have to come up early so we could watch film on Friday. Well, not only did he come in on Friday, he came in on Wednesday, so he could be at a dinner where they gave me an award.

"Do you know what was so special about that? The best gift any of us can give to each other is the precious gift of time. Our time. He gave me that, and what's even more amazing, he didn't bitch about having to do it. Me, yeah, I would have done it, but believe me I'd have bitched and moaned and complained the whole time, made sure everyone realized what a favor I was doing. But Pat never mentioned it. Not a word. Never held it over me. He just came in, did it, never made it seem like an imposition.

"You know, he tries to be always in control, the tough guy, the cool guy. Well, I know for a fact that when Ben Crenshaw won the Masters in 1984 . . . everyone was very, very emotional because Ben Crenshaw is such a great guy and everyone was happy for him . . . Pat was so choked up, so glad for Ben, that he had to hand Ken Venturi the microphone for a couple of moments."

Asked to verify this, Pat Summerall nods hesitantly that, yes, it is so.

And he turns away for just an instant. He seems to brush at his eyes. But no, he couldn't be . . .

Because as everyone knows, football players don't cry.

Do they?

Cynthia Zordich

Courtesy Cheri Summerall

THE FRIEND
The Tom Brookshier Story

The sound was the sound of a bite into a crisp apple.

Right away, Tom Brookshier knew his leg was broken.

Maxie Baughan, a teammate and a ferocious linebacker, trotted over.

"What'd ya do, Brookie?" he asked.

"Busted my leg, Maxie."

"Nah. You sure?"

Baughan bent over and leaned in for a closer look. He was a florid-faced man to begin with, and by the time the hitting had started on a Sunday afternoon and his engine was properly revved, his complexion would make a beet look pale. But when

63

he saw what was left of Tom Brookshier's right leg below the knee, he went ashen and turned away, feeling the nausea build.

The shin bone had shattered. A jagged end poked through the skin, and through Brookshier's sock and against the backdrop of mud it gleamed like an elephant's tusk.

The Eagles, the defending champions of professional football, were playing the Chicago Bears in Philadelphia. It was the eighth game of the 1961 NFL season. It would be Tom Brookshier's last.

Playing cornerback, Brookshier had been clipped from behind and at the same time whipsawed from the front. He was flung violently around, like a sneaker in a dryer. It was one of those times all players dread, when they are caught with no exit. Terrible injury is almost always unavoidable.

This play unfolded right in front of the Bears bench. Some of them heard the crunch of bone snapping. The legendary George Halas, founding father of the league, peered out from under his snap-brim hat, hunched his shoulders against a cold wind, and issued this staccato guttural sympathy: "Tough break, kid."

His words seemed to echo with an ominous finality.

"It was almost like the Old Man knew I was done," Brookshier says.

Thirty-seven years later, he sits in a chair in the den of his fashionable townhouse and pulls up his pants leg to reveal what the years and the scalpels have done. The leg is misshapen and gnarled, furrowed and dented, rather like the trunk of an old oak tree. And yet for all the insults it has endured, it remains astoundingly serviceable.

"I'll grant you that it looks uglier than a baboon's butt," Brookshier agrees. "But it works. Funny thing is, the knee on my bad leg is good and the knee on my good leg is bad."

His locomotion is mostly unaffected, however. He can walk eighteen holes without discomfort, and with only the suggestion of a hobble. He can still play his regular game of squash four times a week, with the usual opponents. They call themselves The Fossils. They do so with a pride that is pardonable, the pride that comes from having lived a long, eventful time and having lived to talk about it.

"This might interest you," he says, rising and walking across the room to the wall on which hangs an old green football jersey. The uniform number is 40.

"That's the one I was wearing when they carried me off for the last time," he says.

The statement seems especially revealing. Most of us want no reminder of anything catastrophic that has befallen us. We try to scrub disaster from our memory, hope that our subconscious will keep it buried.

But Tom Brookshier clings to this piece of cloth, embraces it, clutches this traumatic piece of his past, with an obvious, open affection. It is because it connects him to the game that was taken away from him so abruptly, so prematurely.

"Look at the bite marks on it," he says, laughing, remembering how each gouge, each puncture, was acquired. "And the repairs. Look how they sewed up the holes."

The mending was done crudely, by someone in haste. The replacement thread doesn't even match the jersey's color—it is a dirty gray, causing the mended spots to stand out like dried and dying dandelions on an otherwise lush lawn.

He only played seven seasons of pro ball; well, more like six and a half. So, understandably, he feels cheated. That was the most painful part of the shattered shinbone, knowing that it symbolized something that had been broken beyond repair. But there was a compensation, too. He was spared much of the agony of withdrawal—but most assuredly not all of it—that comes with forced retirement from the game.

"It was the only way I would have ever quit in a reasonable, sane fashion," he agrees. "I had to leave the game cold turkey. I would have always thought I could play. I would have always wanted to squeeze out one more year."

In fact, he tried to.

It took three surgeries for his leg to finally begin mending correctly. Three!

"They cut it the first time and then came back later and said, 'No, that's not right. We'll have to go back in.' So they did a second cut and that wasn't right, either. Third time was the charm. I was beginning to think maybe I should tell them to just put a zipper in and that way they could get to it easier."

As a result of all that cutting and rehabilitative work, and all that starting over, he was still in a cast when the next summer rolled around. But that didn't stop him from going to the Eagles training camp.

And not as a visitor.

He actually thought that he still might be able to play, casted leg and all.

"What a pathetic wretch I was," he says. "I mean, I was a one-legged gimp and there I was thinking I might make the team anyway. They ran me off, of course. But that I even went there, what does that tell you?"

That you were helpless? That the pull of football was so strong you were willing to try to play it on one leg rather than give it up? That the game meant more to you than you ever imagined, that it could turn an otherwise rational human being into a supplicant so prideless that he was willing to crawl and beg for the chance to keep on playing?

"Bingo!"

There is some consolation, though.

"You mean, because I'm not the only one who hasn't been able to let go without a terrible struggle?"

Bingo!

He gravitated, almost naturally, to the broadcast booth. He seemed to have the inate gift of gab. He was easy and natural before an audience. Nothing seemed forced. No fear, no uneasiness was detectable.

In fact, that was all a lie.

"I'm really a lot more shy than people have ever suspected," he admits. "I'm not an extrovert by nature. But I had to learn how to deal with strangers, learn to smile and make small talk."

His father owned a service station—you could remain in your car if you wished in those days because there were attendants who actually pumped the gas for you, and cleaned your windows and checked under the hood, all without charge and all without being asked. The station was in Roswell, New Mexico, where Brookshier was born, nine days before Christmas in 1931. He worked in the station, under the direction of his demanding father. The hours were long and dusty. The horizon seemed to stretch forever and every time he began to fantasize about what might lie beyond it, another car carrying people from far away would pull in.

"I had to greet people I didn't know. I'd flirt with the girls, of course. We had a lot of families, tourists, pass through. Our station wasn't very far from where that UFO was supposed to have landed in 1947, so a lot of people came through looking for Martians. We were more concerned about the Carlsbad Caverns cavemen that were supposed to be out and about every night."

His father, scarred by the Great Depression, believed you should be grateful just to have work. He wanted his son to understand that.

"I watched him work fifteen-hour days," Brookshier remembers. "The only time he ever let me go was for a ball game. But I never resented any of it. It made me appreciate not just what I had, but the memory of the Depression, of how everything could be taken away just like that, stayed with me and it's why even while I was playing football I was making investments and trying to set us up for life."

He played football in high school, even though he weighed barely 145 pounds. Basketball was his best sport, but he won a baseball scholarship to the University of Colorado. His first summer in Colorado he worked on a road crew and suddenly packed on twenty pounds. He became a defensive back and he returned punts. He wasn't especially fast but he had an aptitude and he certainly had the attitude. At least one professional team thought he had potential.

In the early 1950s the professional football draft was hardly the glamorous meat market that it has become. Word crawled westward from New York that the Philadelphia Eagles had selected, in a late round, a defensive back from Colorado named Tom Brookshier.

"I got back to the frat house after class one day and they told me there had been a phone call and I was now an Eagle. I said, 'No kidding.' And pretty much forgot about it. Vince McNally was the general manager. He didn't get around to calling me until a week or two later. He offered me $5,500. I thought, 'Hot damn! Now I can get married.'"

Which he did, on June 8, 1953. Barbara was a Teutonic blonde, with eyes like a mountain lake.

"First saw her in class in college. Still remember it. The History of Western Civilization. Somewhere between the Byzantine Empire and the Roman Empire I looked around and my eyes fell on her and I said, 'Who is that?'"

They're still married.

He and his new bride showed up for training camp and he asked which bank his money was in, and after the bankers stopped laughing they explained to the naive rookie from the sticks that the $5,500 was for the season, the whole season, and that it would be paid if, and only if, he made the team and actually began to play in games.

He did a quick survey of the competition in camp and felt the same sort of terror that must have seized his father when the banks had begun to fail.

"I looked around and counted ninety players," he remembers. "I asked them how many would they be keeping, and they said thirty-three."

A wolfish desperation set in.

"That afternoon I hit a first round draft pick harder than I knew I could hit," he remembers. "I mean I knocked him almost out. The head coach was Jim Trimble and he yelled my name, just screamed it, and I thought, 'Way to go, Dummy, now they'll send you packing.' But he walked up to me and looked me in the eye for a long time and then he kind of cocked his head sideways and said, 'I really liked that.' It's amazing what fear and desperation can do for you."

From then on he hit everything that crossed his field of fire during that first camp. No matter who they were, he hammered them.

"The veterans were telling me to ease up, it's only camp, and I'd tell them, 'Sorry, but no. Maybe next camp.' I was fighting for a job, for my life.

"One thing I did find out about football was, I was never the best player starting out, but the ones who were naturally the best tended not to work all that hard at it, and I did. I found that to be true at every level, high school to college to the pros."

He also learned that, in the pro game, there is a cycle of survival from which no one is spared.

"My rookie year in camp I beat out the starter at one of the cornerback positions. His name was Bud Sutton and he was a nice guy. He'd been in the league seven seasons. I really felt bad about it, and I went to him and told him that on the night he got cut. He was having beers with some of the other veterans who were telling him goodbye. It was a pretty emotional moment. But to his credit, he looked at me and said: 'Forget it, kid. One day there'll be somebody running you off.'

"That's when I understood this was the law of the tooth and the fang."

He got his rookie season in, then had to fulfill a two-year military obligation—he had achieved a commission in the Air Force through the ROTC program while in college. His duty was spent at the Air Force Academy, helping coach the football team.

When he returned, the Eagles won the championship in 1960. The statute of limitations never ran out on that glorious season.

"I had a man come up to me after a speech I made just the other day, and he was carrying this old hunk of splintered wood. He said it was a piece of the goal post from Franklin Field that his father had ripped off when the Eagles had won the championship. He was carrying this piece of wood like it was a religious medal. When you're playing, you never fully realize the impact that you have on some people's lives. And maybe that's just as well. There's enough pressure without knowing all the consequences."

69

When the shattered leg forced him into retirement, he began serving as the sports guy on one of the local television stations in Philadelphia. He did it for seventeen years. The money was good, the fame heady, and the cost high. He was a stranger in his own house.

"The kids would see me in that little box at night, and then they'd be in bed when I got home, and then I'd be in bed when they got up."

Enter Barbara.

"You need someone who will tell you the truth," he says of his wife. "Someone to keep you grounded. In TV, it's showbiz. Politics. No one will give it to you straight. Barbara always tells me when I'm absolutely crazy. If it had been anybody else except her, I'd probably have been married five times by now."

As if on cue, she comes up the driveway, dragged along by an eager dog named Rose. They have been strolling in the park. Well, Barbara has tried to stroll while Rose has been harassing squirrels.

"Rose is a Jack Russell Terrorist," Brookshier says.

Informed that she has been identified as the rock on which their marriage has been built, Barbara smiles. It is a look that says that her husband's assessment is indeed correct but that she is much too modest to say so out loud.

She will agree to this: "He needs someone to reel him back in when he gets out there in the deep water."

On a wall in Brookshier's den office is the advertisement that a local bank used to promote what was then a revolutionary new service—paying your bills by phone. The advertisement shows a lively blonde holding a Touch-Tone phone in one hand and making a fist with the other. The caption reads:

"Once a month Barbara Brookshier punches out everything she owes!"

The husband of Barbara Brookshier smiles with pride and says: "They only used one other person for that campaign. Joe Frazier."

70

His tone suggests that, heavyweight champion or not, Smokin' Joe would have met his match in Barbara Brookshier. Who would know better?

They were a combustible couple early on.

"I threw his engagement ring in his face a few times," she says. "I don't think anyone thought we would last six months."

With luck, it'll be more like sixty years.

They have two daughters and a son. Their son, Tommy, was born with deformed hands. Two fingers and a thumb on one, three fingers and no thumb on the other. No one is ever really ready for something like that. But it had an especially devastating effect on Brookshier. A football player, isn't he supposed to have only perfect children?

He tortured himself for a long time, believing he had somehow done something wrong. As though he had any control over something like that.

"Something like that," he says, "I think it either drives you apart or it pulls you together. It drew us close. We brought this soul into the world; we have an obligation here."

Tommy played some football. And caught passes. How proud that must have made his father.

He nods yes. And swallows several times. He doesn't trust his voice to speak.

When he broke into TV, the timing was perfect. The National Football League was just beginning to explode into the public's consciousness. Replays and slow motion, isolated cameras and *Monday Night Football* were all unfurling. From 1965 to 1974, Brookshier and another former player, Pat Summerall, teamed up to do a review-and-preview TV show called "This Week in the NFL."

"We were Frick 'n Frack," he says. "We had fun. And we fit. Pat can say something in two or three words, where I'll need two or three paragraphs."

In 1975, Summerall decided he wanted to switch from providing analysis to doing play-by-play. CBS asked him if he had a preference for a partner.

"I'd like Brookie," he said.

Among other events, they did the debut game at the Meadowlands, the stadium used by both the Giants and the Jets. It was built on reclaimed swampland in New Jersey, just across the river from New York City. It was also whispered that the site had served as the burial ground for a number of mob hits.

"Just before kickoff," Brookshier recalls, "the door to the booth opens and this enormous guy with a broken nose and cauliflower ears and a gravel voice and a cigar big as a baseball bat sticks his head in and says to Patrick and me: 'It's true what they're saying, you know. Hoffa's here. He always did love football.' And he closes the door. There's been a rumor forever that Hoffa is buried in the stadium. I swallowed and looked at Patrick and said: 'I don't think we're in Kansas any more, Toto.' "

They had a great run together.

"The ironic part," says Brookshier, "is that on the field we had been mortal enemies.

"Everywhere else, we clicked. Pat never left you hanging when you were on the air. And I'd need him to pull me back in off the ledge. I'd lapse into some stream-of-consciousness thing and wonder what was my point, and Patrick would decipher it all in a sentence. He was wonderful at filling in all my blanks."

In return, Brookshier served as the designated driver, sometimes symbolically and sometimes in fact, on their late-night or all-night forays that would become the stuff of legends.

"We lasted through '81. It was about all we could stand. Literally."

As their reputations for escapades swelled, some of it based on fact and some on exaggeration, Barbara became increasingly irritated.

"I loved Pat," she says, "but I'd tell Tom: 'You don't even drink that much. Why do you let all those stories grow and grow?' But he's very easygoing and loyal. Pat was a great friend, and Tom couldn't help but feel that he should look out for him, that that's what friends did for friends."

Summerall went on to team up with John Madden, in a relaxed, natural-fit partnership that has echoes of his work with Brookshier. And Brookshier has gone on to become an entrepreneur-rancher, commercial realtor, and radio station owner. ("We got out of the ranching business when we realized that the bad horses ate just as much as the good ones. We were lying there one night, listening to them going after the hay, and Barbara said: 'You know, your father told us never to own anything that eats while you sleep.' ")

In the spring of 1992, Tom Brookshier performed an act of friendship for which Pat Summerall feels everlasting gratitude.

"What it was," says Summerall, "was an act of salvation."

He had been drinking hard and steady in the eleven years since he and Brookshier had been disbanded. He came to Philadelphia for a banquet honoring his old bud, and though Brookshier concealed it, he was aghast at how his former partner looked, so bloated and puffy.

"I'd heard he had the limo driver stop one time and he got out and threw up blood in the ditch. I knew something had to be done, but I wasn't sure how to do it." Until Kathy, Summerall's wife of thirty years, called Tom Brookshier.

"Kathy said, 'We have to do something, even if it may mean that I'll lose him.' "

As it would turn out, she was prophetic.

Pat Summerall would be made sober. He would be saved. But in the process his thirty-five-year-old marriage would be ended.

An intervention had been arranged at Kathy's request. A dozen heavy hitters from the business and sports world, all friends of Pat Summerall, were summoned to a hotel in Camden, New Jersey, across the river from Philadelphia. It was Tom Brookshier's responsibility to lure Summerall to that hotel room. It was a daunting task.

"As soon as we opened the door, Pat started back out and I remember how Hugh Culverhouse (the late owner of the Tampa Bay Buccaneers) grabbed him and pulled him back in. A man from the Betty Ford Clinic was there, and he'd had everyone in the room write down what they felt about Pat. One by one, they stood up and read. His daughter . . . Susie's letter . . . it was unbelievable. Everyone in that room was crying."

A private jet took Pat Summerall and the man from the clinic across the country, where Summerall was admitted and where he stayed for thirty-three days. Tom Brookshier made the trip with his pal, feeling as though they were walking The Last Mile. But he dismisses what he did.

"Look at what Kathy did," he says. "What an incredible sacrifice she made. She gave up her marriage to save Pat's life."

"Boy, something like that ought to be worth a free pass through the Pearly Gates. Don't you think?"

He made it a question, but he didn't really want the answer. He was sure he already had it.

Phila. Inquirer/Phila. Eagles

"The worst thing that can happen to any ballplayer is that he gets hurt before he's hit the point where he doesn't want to play anymore, and it will stay with him the rest of his life. Because he'll feel like he could have accomplished more, just like myself. You know, when I got hurt, that year, even to this day . . . when I'm praying I ask God if he would show me what could have happened that year . . . I swear to God I have not run across anything since I left football that was tougher than that to deal with. I mean . . . major. And that's why I really think that when you see a lot of guys leaving before they really want to leave that it's easy to get in trouble."

Bubba Smith, DE-DT 1967-72 Baltimore; 1973-74 Oakland; 1975-76 Houston

"The pluses of playing in the NFL have been great just because of the friendships I've created. The respect that I've been able to get from the game, as well as the respect that I've been able to give to the game, to the people that I've watched, to the people that I've met, to the people who have played the game for so many years, to the guys that built this game. To all the people that have made this game what it is. They talk about other sports, how they love the game. Yet, this is the game. NFL is the game."

Ronnie Lott, DB 1981-90 San Francisco; 1991-92 LA Raiders; 1993-94 New York Jets

"I miss the game. I think it's a great game. I think there's a lot of guys who couldn't play when I played. I think there's a lot of guys we had that couldn't play today. They are stronger, bigger, and well paid and God let them make all the money they want to make. I don't envy that. I don't envy their life and what it turned some of them into. I don't know what a lot of their futures have because it don't go on forever. I don't really know if they play it because they like it. I really don't. We did. We sure didn't do it for the money."

Bob Snyder, QB-DB-TB-HB 1937-38 Cleveland; 1939-43 Chicago Bears
TNT Interviews
75th Anniversary

"Football's a very special way of making a living and those that do it best have the most difficult time leaving it, and in fact never do. It's very much like guys that fought in Nam. The guys that were most successful, that could go out into the jungle and would stay out there and . . . they could do that one thing very well, and then when you want to repatriate them back in society those skills didn't translate very well into being a stock broker or an insurance salesman. They couldn't take those skills. And football is very much like that."

George Starke, OT 1971-84 Washington
When the Cheering Stops
NFL Films, Inc.

Cynthia Zordich

HOLLYWOOD
The Thomas Henderson Story

He remembered later, when all the feeling was running out of his body like water running down a drain, how surprised he was at how easy it is to break your neck.

All he did was make one tackle, a violent, jolting act to be sure, but one he had committed a million times before without causing permanent damage. But this one was different. This one would almost cost him his life.

And, ultimately, give it back to him.

On a steamy night in Miami in late August, in the last game of the 1981 NFL preseason, a running back for the Kansas City Chiefs named Joe Delaney came slashing through the hole. He was led by the fullback, who was snorting like a rhino. Thomas Henderson, who was playing linebacker for the Dolphins and trying desperately to rid himself of an enslaving, consuming cocaine addiction, did a nimble little swivel and made the blocker miss.

79

Then Thomas Henderson came at Joe Delaney like a helmet-tipped missile. He hit him headfirst, like he always hit them. It was wrong, of course. Coaches had been telling him for years that his tackling form was all wrong. Hit with the shoulders, they said.

"But God gave me bad shoulders," he says. "He gave me a rock for a head, but bad shoulders. I didn't just tackle people, I tried to blow them up. I tried to run right through them, go in one side of them and come out the other, and leave a big hole. And every time I'd make one of those hits, I'd hurt my shoulders. They'd keep popping out of place."

Sooner or later, they'd give up trying to correct him, trying to change his form. He was so good that eventually they'd all let him do it his way. So he bore into Joe Delaney, head-first, and . . . his neck snapped.

"At first, I thought maybe I'd been hit by lightning," he remembers.

He suffered what is called the hangman's fracture. He blacked out. But his football player's instincts took over. He awoke and his first act was to stand upright. If I'm on my feet, he reasoned, then I must not be dead. As long as I can move, I'm alive. The football player's instinct is always to resume play. Go ahead, snap the ball. But now Thomas Henderson began to get a serious case of the tingles. Followed by the shakes. His entire body began to tremble uncontrollably.

"I felt like an accordion that was being squeezed shut," he says, "like my whole body was going to just fold up."

He stayed in the game for one more play. By then the pain was excruciating, bomb bursts ripping at his back and legs and neck. The agony was so unbearable that when the ball was snapped and the tight end ran to block him, Thomas Henderson turned and ran the other way. He lurched backwards for twenty yards, petrified that anyone might touch him.

Then he fell to the ground.

They took him to the locker room, removed his pads, and left him on a table while they went out for the second half. No X-rays. No hospital. They put a whiplash collar on him and told him to go home.

He went to a party instead. He remembers drinking two bottles of champagne to help wash down a handful of Percodan. That helped chase away some of the pain. But his body was stiff as a cadaver.

He was driven to his dormitory room, and there he lay in his bed for most of two days. The game had been on a Friday night and the players had the weekend off. He was alone. At about four in the morning on Sunday, he awoke to the feeling of somebody taking a sledgehammer to his head. He was unable to move. He remembers screaming for almost five straight hours until a maid finally heard him.

In the hospital they found that he had broken the C1 cervical vertebra and cracked the C2. Additionally, C5 and C6 were spurred. They wrapped his skull in pounds of plaster. He was in the hospital for three days. He spent every waking minute of it freebasing cocaine, which is virtually odorless. Whenever the nurses would come into the room, he would hide the pipe between his legs.

The Dolphins announced he would be placed on the injured reserve and would be released at the end of the season. He says he was never prescribed any rehabilitation, or any off-season therapy, or any medication. So he medicated himself. With bowl after bowl of coke.

The Dolphins said he would be paid his entire year's salary, $125,000. He calculated how much pure cocaine he could purchase with $6,000 and change each week for sixteen weeks.

"Enough to ruin three or four noses," he says, chuckling softly.

His supplier was named Ken. He got every one of Thomas Henderson's checks.

Every one?

"Every one," he says, in a tone that is flat and matter-of-fact. Not that he didn't, and doesn't, have regret. Time has eased it some, and in becoming a recovering alcoholic and a recovering addict he learned, finally, to let go of the past and the awful, self-destructive recriminations. The past is beyond retrieving.

It took him just four months to smoke up and snort up all of his money.

"I was hopelessly, powerlessly addicted," he says. "Nothing mattered to me except The Pipe and The Dope Man. Not food. Not friends. Not family. Not even sex. There are some incredibly wild sex parties when you're on coke, but if you're using it steady, then pretty soon you become impotent."

His ravaged nose bled constantly. He was nauseous all the time. He sold his house and smoked up that money. He pawned his Super Bowl rings to a friend for $7,500, and smoked up that money. The horrified question, of course, is: In God's name, why?

"Because nothing else matters to you," he says.

Not even the love of your life? Not even football?

"The truth is," he says, sighing, "I went from neurosurgeon to neurosurgeon, trying to find one that would do fusion surgery for me. I'd heard that if you fused them, the vertebrae, they'd be actually stronger than before you broke them. Every one of them told me they'd do the operation, but only to save my life, only to keep me from winding up in a wheelchair. They wouldn't do it if I planned on trying to play football ever again."

But of course that's precisely what he wanted to do.

"Of course," he says. "There was a time in my life when football meant everything to me. But it had become an enabler. It was what enabled me to get the drugs that I was living for. By the time I was in the pros, the only part of the game that I loved was the game.

"I hated the boss mentality and I hated going to work and sitting in a dark room watching film, and I hated practice. But I loved Sunday. I loved playing, but I despised the process that made playing possible. So when I broke my neck and I was lying there on that table in the locker room, all alone, I made up my mind. I resigned myself that I had to let go of football."

82

But he couldn't.

"No, I couldn't. But not because of the pull of the game itself. What I couldn't let go of wasn't football, it was coke. I don't even remember my first season away from football because I was wasted that whole time. I'd get my check and then buy crack."

The irony is, he avoided the bends, the withdrawal, that afflicts most of them that first year they are away from the game. But in return for missing that suffering, he endured a suffering that was ten times as great.

"Before I ever broke my neck, my spirit had been broken," he says. "If you've never done cocaine you can't understand its pull. I started out snorting but the nose that God gave me couldn't handle the volume I had in mind, so I started smoking crack, and when you inhale the vapors, well, it's like orgasms in your brain. All your pleasure centers light up like a pinball machine.

"You keep wanting to repeat that first hit, the way it rocks you. But after a while your systems becomes so overloaded, you can only get so high, and then beyond that, well, there's only death.

"I remember coming out of rehab one time and I'd been off the stuff for a while and I took my first inhale—I mean I really sucked it in, deep—and the next thing I knew I woke up on the floor, there was blood in the corner of my mouth, and I'd flown backward, clear across the room. It was like I'd had cardiac arrest. My first thought was: 'Ohhhhh baby, I've got to do that again!' "

When he didn't have enough money to buy cocaine, he turned to a liquid friend. Gin. He could do a quart of Tanqueray a day. He'd drink lunch, return for happy hour, and stay through the dinner hour to avoid all the traffic at rush hour. By two in the morning, the traffic tended to thin out.

Somehow, he never killed himself. Or anyone else.

He was twenty-nine years old, and a total wreck. Football was done with him, even though he didn't want to be done with football. It took a broken neck to stop him. It cut him off in his prime, cut his NFL career short.

"And it probably saved my life," he says, taking a long, deep inhale.

Only this time all he takes in is oxygen. And redemption.

Hard to tell which is sweeter.

On his birth certificate, he was identified as illegitimate. It would be twenty years before he would meet his biological father, the man who had abandoned his mother before he was born. Whenever he thought about him, it was in anger and befuddlement and in these defiant, testosterone-laced terms: I'll show you how well I did on my own—I don't need anybody.

Thomas Henderson grew up in Austin, Texas, in an area known as the Cut. It was a warren of pool halls and bars and alleyways where young street wolves could learn how to survive on guile and wile, and especially on speed. The ground was carpeted with broken glass and he thinks he developed his extraordinary speed by running barefoot—sometimes he had no shoes—across the shards.

"It was like I floated across those alleys," he says. "When you're running barefoot over broken glass you'd be surprised how long you can keep your feet off the ground."

Thomas Henderson's first mentor was a resourceful wraith of a man known as Go Devil. He showed the youngster how to scavenge through garbage behind the better restaurants, and how, with enough persistence, a man could extract half-eaten filet mignons and discarded T-bones and make himself a sumptuous stew. The young Henderson became adept at stealing bikes and stealing sodas and then redeeming the empty bottles. He made money shooting craps in the glass-littered alleys and he learned how to hustle at pool.

The man who lived with his mother would get drunk and beat her routinely. When Thomas Henderson was twelve, he decided to try to stand up to the bully. They were on the front porch, the man drunk and ready to batter his mother again. But before Thomas Henderson could do anything his mother shot the man. Gunfire will usually end a relationship, but they would stay together for ten more years.

The young Hollywood knew, instinctively, that he couldn't stay there.

"I was pretty sure I'd end up dead," he says. "So I begged and pleaded and finally got permission to move to Oklahoma City and live with Nettie Mae Higgins. She was my momma's cousin and she had raised my momma."

Thomas Henderson played exactly one year of high school football, during his senior year. He was a fullback and a defensive end. His talent was breathtaking. His speed—that run-over-glass speed—was astonishing.

"I had about sixty sacks that one season," he says.

No one could run away from him. And he couldn't run away from himself.

He was paid $2 for each sack. He used the money to buy marijuana and speed. He ended up at a small black college, Langston, located north of Oklahoma City. The school had an enrollment of eleven hundred. He was even more dominating than he had been when he played football in high school. Football financed his education and he supported himself on the side by selling pot. He also was introduced to LSD. Hallucinogenic heaven. He was hooked instantly.

"I could see the trees breathe, the grass crawl," he remembers. "I could see through my eyelids."

At 10:15 in the morning on January 29, 1975, the Dallas Cowboys, America's Team, a franchise with a reputation for finding pure nuggets in slag heaps, took Thomas Henderson with the eighteenth pick in the first round of the college draft. He celebrated with a bag of weed.

His first contract included a $60,000 signing bonus and a starting salary of $25,000 a year, with $5,000 raises in each of the four succeeding years. Such a sum could buy a man his very own pharmacy.

His introduction to Tom Landry, the Cowboys' stern and exacting coach, began not with a welcome or a congratulation but with a rebuke: "Thomas, we took a chance on you."

They would feud every step of the way for as long as he played for the Cowboys. Between them there was a generation gap and a yawning cultural gap. The coach was a demanding disciplinarian and the player was the freest sort of free spirit, as undisciplined as the wind. The coach saw the player squandering a great talent and the player saw the coach as a pious hypocrite, who applied a blatant and inexcusable double standard.

Anyone who watched them struggle for control over each other in those days would never have imagined that once he had become clean and sober, Thomas Henderson would say: "I used to detest everything Tom Landry stood for. Now I revere the man."

The Cowboys' systems was based on computer printouts of trends and tendencies. Thomas Henderson's system was based on intuition, a feel for where the ball would be. The Cowboys' playbook was thicker than many telephone books and players were given five different colored pens with which to write in them. The only colors that interested Thomas Henderson were the rainbows that drugs created in his befogged mind and the lingerie worn by the women he slept with.

The Cowboys knew they had a weapon here, an assassin, and the best place for such unthinking, hell-bent fury was on special teams. The impassioned Mike Ditka was the coach of the special teams. He would stomp along the sidelines on his bad hip like Captain Ahab. Thomas Henderson became his harpoon.

"He'd have me take an extra five-yard drop so I'd have a bigger head of steam and then he'd tell me to run down there and kill somebody," he remembers. "I get a hip pointer my rookie year, against the Cardinals, and I'd never felt such pain. I was paralyzed. I couldn't move. And that's when I got introduced to a new set of drugs. They shot me up and then gave me codeine and they asked me: 'Can you go?' See, there's a subtle little threat in there. 'Can you go?' That's football code for, if you can't go someone else can."

He went, and on a kickoff return he got the ball on a reverse and ran ninety-seven yards, all the way to the end zone. He flew down the field, hip totally numb. He finished with a flourish that would become his signature—he leaped up and spiked the ball, basketball-style, over the crossbar. Landry fumed. The other Cowboys winced at what was, in those days, thought to be the most flamboyant kind of hot doggery. Thomas Henderson landed triumphantly and noticed that his hip still didn't hurt. Boy, he thought, drugs sure are wonderful.

Nobody warned him that he wouldn't be able to walk on Monday. Or Tuesday. "The real pain comes on Wednesday," he says, his voice brittle at the memory. "If they have anesthetized some part of you, it takes a while for the Xylocaine and the cortisone shots to wear off. When they do, your body screams at you: 'You can't ignore me no

86

longer!' So they gave me another shot of Xylocaine and another one of cortisone and codeine IVs, and I got hooked. By the third week of my NFL career, I was hooked on drugs that would let me go through the day and not feel. It was great. I could play football and not hurt. And I had pot and Quaaludes and Percodan for rest and relaxation."

Cocaine came along shortly afterwards. It welcomed him with its silky, insidious embrace, and he hugged it right back.

"I read that coke was dangerous," he says, laughing in rich baritone, "so I did the smart thing. I quit reading."

He played on all the special teams and was used increasingly at linebacker, especially in passing situations, because he could neutralize running backs and tight ends. He began to live the life of jock royalty. He was turned on to the splendors of being chauffeured around in limousines during this relationship with one of the Pointer Sisters, Anita. He would emerge from behind smoked glass, with ruffles and flourishes, dressed grandly, sunglasses hiding his coke-inflamed eyes.

The days of limo-riding inspired his nickname. Players started calling him Hollywood. He decided it fit. It fit even better than the rocks of cocaine he was stuffing up his ravaged nose every day. He began to live the role. He would seek out the minicams and the tape recorders and make bold, outrageous statements, and soon enough he was a media darling.

"I never really got the attention I wanted until I started my Mouth of the South routine," he says. "Of course, once you start saying things that get you noticed, you have to keep topping yourself."

Before one Super Bowl, the Cowboys versus the Pittsburgh Steelers, Hollywood Henderson took on the Steelers quarterback, Terry Bradshaw. Bradshaw, Henderson crowed, was so dumb that he couldn't spell cat even if you spotted him the c and the a. Bradshaw passed for touchdown after touchdown and the Steelers won the game. Afterwards he said: "Ask Hollywood how dumb I am now."

Hollywood could barely answer. He had become the first player in Super Bowl history to get stoned during the game, on the field. He had fixed himself a little nose cocktail— liquid cocaine in an inhalator—that he secreted inside his pants.

He lasted five years in Dallas, and by his own estimate had sex with more than one thousand women. There always seemed to be an orgy somewhere, and he was either visiting or hosting.

"I could talk a cat down off a fish truck," he says. "I could talk just about any woman out of her clothes, and drugs only made it easier. This is not something I am proud of now. At the time, I flaunted it. I was a sexual showoff, an exhibitionist. All I can say is that I heartily repent, and the man who did all those disgraceful things no longer exists. I have buried him, as deep as I know how."

The road to redemption, however, was long and hard and filled with overturns and flips into ditches. He fathered a daughter, named her as close to himself as he could— Thomesa Holly—and while he waited for her to be born he curled up on the floor of the hospital room and laid out cocaine lines fifteen inches long and rolled up a hundred-dollar bill and snorted himself into a blissful oblivion.

In an impulsive, coke-fueled rage, he retired as a football player. It took him only nine weeks to smoke up his salary of $110,000. The Cowboys still owned the rights to him and were only too happy to trade them. He drifted to San Francisco and Houston, freebasing in locker room commode stalls, his life revolving around cocaine, to the exclusion of all else. He reached bottom when he was arrested in the company of two underage girls.

Perhaps fittingly, he finally decided to seek salvation while he was watching a football game. He had gotten a chance with Miami but the broken neck had prevented him from playing even one down in the regular season. Six months later, he sat on a bed watching the 1981 Super Bowl between Oakland and Philadelphia, and the TV camera found Charlie Jackson, who was the head of NFL security. Thomas Henderson called the hotel where Jackson was staying in New Orleans and pleaded for help.

"I need help, I know that," he said. "I'm sitting here smoking my brains out right this very minute."

He spent forty-two days at one detox center, sixty at another. He learned to introduce himself as an alcoholic and a drug addict. He began to feel good about himself. And then he went to jail. He served time for the bust with the underage girls. He went to two meetings a week every week he was in prison. And it was in prison that he celebrated his first year of sobriety. That year became a second year, and then a third. And then a whole decade. Since November 8, 1983, Hollywood Henderson has been dead and

Thomas Henderson has been clean and sober. At 10 AM on October 15, 1986, Thomas Henderson walked out of the Susanville Correctional Facility, a free man.

While in prison, he qualified for a certificate that enabled him to teach reading to convicts. He realized that by helping others he could help himself. He has made eight inspirational films. He opened a string of rehabilitation centers.

"I have forgiven myself," he says, "and I've asked God to do the same, and whenever I have a chance to apologize or make amends to people I hurt, I try to do that. If I could live my live over . . . but I can't. None of us can. All we can do is try to learn from it. A very wise man told me a long time ago that anything is possible in sobriety but nothing is possible if I use."

He has two daughters and now he has become a grandfather. His trademark beard is sprinkled with gray. He is 6-feet-2 and his walking-around weight is 265 pounds. He is imposing.

"I look good," he says, pridefully. "I sleep normal these days and eat right and work out. My body has responded. I think it's grateful that I quit doing all the horrible things to it that I was doing. I still get tingles in my arms and fingers because that neck fusion never really healed. But, all things considered, medically, it's a miracle that I'm alive. But I feel like I got a mulligan in life, and this one I hit two-eighty right down the middle."

He moved back to Austin in 1990.

"You really can go home again," he says. "But only if it's OK with you. You have to feel good about yourself. It took me a long time to get over what I had done to myself. But I'm not who I was. I'm not my mistakes. I'm who I have become."

Every saint, it is said, has a past. And every sinner has a future. "I'd say I'm living proof of that last part," he says.

The other day he was driving along and he telephoned one of his daughters to tell her that he loved her. Shortly after he hung up, he had to pull over to the side of the road and put the car in park. He wept.

"It finally hit me, how grateful I was. I realized," he says, "I was where I'd wanted to be all my life. At last I was able to give unconditional love."

Chance Brockway

Cynthia Zordich

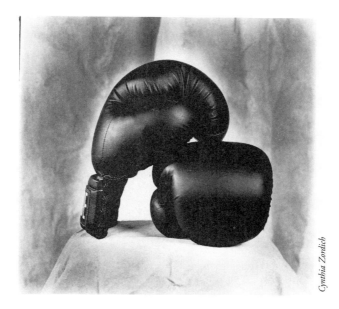

Cynthia Zordich

THE AMERICAN DREAM
The Vai Sikahema Story

He was five years old when his father taught him how to make a fist.

How to circle and stay just out of harm's way and to throw a jab like a little jack-hammer.

How to bob and weave and feint and dance away from danger, laughing.

Always, the same lesson over and over—how to avoid getting hit.

That, Loni Sikahema would tell his son again and again, is the secret. Make the other man miss. Everyone else will work on their hitting, their punching, but you, you will be the one that they cannot hit. You will be the one that the fists cannot find.

And the son would nod dutifully and obediently follow the choreography that his father would draw out with his feet on the dirt floor of their grass hut.

93

Around and around the boy would circle and shuffle, rolling his shoulders, bending from side to side, swaying like a cobra coming out of its basket. And the father, a stern man, would make corrections as they circled together, linked by blood, yes, but linked too by the dance of the ring.

They didn't know then, either of them, that one day the boy, grown to manhood, would make large, menacing people miss him. They would close in on him, hurt on their minds, and he would offer them a part of his body to hit and then snatch it away and they would be left flopping on the ground, like boated bass. Make them miss, the father would say, and it would turn out that, sure enough, the son would.

But not in a boxing ring. On a football field.

Tonga was where it all began. Tonga? A clutch of 150 tiny islands sprinkled on the Pacific like bits of frosting on some enormous cake. Tonga? Maybe five hundred miles south of Samoa. Still no help? Thirty-two hundred miles beyond Hawaii. From the mainland? Who knew for sure—eight thousand miles, maybe nine thousand.

In Tonga, America was on the other side of the world.

But one day, the father told the son, we will go there.

In the meantime, they moved up. They built a house. The neighbors helped. It was a wooden frame and not much else. No doors. A wire ran the length of the room and at night the mother would drape a cover over it for privacy.

"But we were the talk of the town with that house," Vai Sikahema remembers. "We were the Clampetts moving into Beverly Hills. No one on the island had ever seen a wooden floor before. We were poor, but I don't think we ever realized it because we were so isolated we didn't have anything to compare it with. And everyone else was in the same boat. If you don't have something and you've never had it, then how can you miss it?"

When the son was seven, his parents left him and his siblings with the grandparents and moved to Hawaii. It was piecemeal migration. It took three and a half years to get everyone relocated.

When the son's turn came he got his first pair of shoes. He put his feet in them, not sure what to expect exactly, and wiggled his toes experimentally, stood on the balls of his feet and bounced up and down, and then, holding his breath, he began to circle and weave and do the dance of the boxing ring.

They worked! The shoes worked! He could wear these things and still they wouldn't be able to hit him. He could still make them miss.

Hawaii was a stepping stone. From there the family would move on to Mesa, Arizona.

"I still remember how shocked I was that people didn't ride horses and carry guns," he says. "All we knew about America was what we saw in the movies we got in Tonga, and they were all Westerns . . . Audie Murphy and John Wayne, those were Americans as far as we knew."

The boxing lessons never stopped, no matter where the family was. On Saturdays, the father would take the son to the library, where he was the custodian. The two of them would have the place to themselves, and the father would read to the son. In a magazine, there was a boxing picture that would become famous. It showed Muhammad Ali standing over Sonny Liston, screaming at Liston to get up off the canvas.

Years later, Vai Sikahema would hang a copy of that photograph on the wall of the office in his home. When he looks at it, he remembers his father reading to him: "For three minutes, Muhammad Ali made $100,000."

The father would recite those numbers over and over, hushed awe in his voice, and the son would swallow hard and know that this was the way out, as his father would tell him. Boxing would be his ticket.

There was only one problem. The son didn't want to box.

By the seventh grade he weighed 150 pounds and that meant he was matched against boys seventeen and eighteen. It meant that he got used to tasting his own blood.

It did not escape his notice that the girls all seemed attracted to the football players. So he tried football.

He was a natural.

95

He could run, but not so fast that some of the others couldn't catch up to him. But when they did they couldn't hit him.

He had a knack for making them miss.

"You know where that came from," he told his father.

But the father only scowled.

"He didn't know a football from a gourd," the son remembers. "And of course that was perfect as far as I was concerned. My father was old school and he pushed me like hell, but with football, all he could do was show up and watch practice."

The father didn't get to see the games. Not at first. He was working in a bakery, which meant he was sleeping when the games were being played. But the son was so good that there was a story about him in the local paper and it mentioned that the father never got to see the son run and make them miss, so the school officials made Loni Sikahema a security guard at the high school.

Then the letters began to arrive from the colleges. And the recruiters began to call.

"My dad was twelve feet tall," he says. "Here we were, this immigrant Polynesian family, and there were universities that wanted to give me scholarships to come and play football for them. He and my mom still have a box full of the letters. Education mattered a lot to both of them, and now they saw that football could do things for me. My dad started watching every football game they put on television."

The son went to Brigham Young University. He was there in 1980 and 1981, and then he went on the mission that is required by the Mormon church. He served almost two years in South Dakota and then returned for his last two years of college. When he was a junior, in 1984, BYU went undefeated in thirteen games and won the national championship.

Vai Sikahema was 5-feet-8, 190 pounds. A running back. He never started. He did return punts and kickoffs, for which he had a natural aptitude from the very moment he arrived on campus. All the coaches agreed on one thing—that kid has a way of making tacklers miss him.

He wanted to try professional football, but he was also a realist. Most people who get inside a ring learn not to deceive themselves. He was sure that he would have to go from training camp to training camp, pleading for an audition.

And then, to his utter astonishment, he was drafted. The Cardinals, then located in St. Louis and two years away from relocating to Phoenix, took him in the tenth round.

He reported to camp with great expectations, and with a traveling companion—Keala. Kay-ala.

He saw her for the first time at a dance when both were at BYU, he a junior, she a freshman from Hawaii. He felt like he had looked directly into the sun. She was blindingly beautiful. He asked for an immediate introduction.

"We met on December the 12th, 1983 and we were married on July the 21st, 1984, which means that it was only—what?—six months."

He is grinning ear to ear as he does the math. Even after all these years, he can't believe his incredible good luck. They have three sons and a daughter.

He made his professional debut on the grandest sort of stage—in Canton, Ohio, in the annual Hall of Fame game. First football of the year. Broadcast on national television. The opponents, the New England Patriots, were stopped on the first series of the game, and punted.

Vai Sikahema fielded the ball and ran it all the way to the other end of the field.

Ninety-one yards.

Touchdown.

"I made a couple of people miss," he says. "And then from mid-field on there wasn't a soul near me."

He ran fast anyway, the adrenaline surging through him like jet fuel.

"I found a gear I didn't know I had," he says. "First time I ever touch a punt in the pros and I take it all the way back. I mean . . . "

His voice breaks off. Three time he gets a forkful of pasta near his mouth and three times he is overcome and has to lower it back to the plate. The best part is yet to come.

"My father was there to see it. I had told him that I might get cut at any time so he better get to that first preseason game. It might be his only chance to see me in an NFL uniform. I've still got the videotape of that game."

It is an acquired art, this business of standing under a kicked ball, tracking its arc, calculating exactly where it will come down, and then drawing the imaginary intersection in your mind, the path that will take you to it. And then once you have caught it—no mean feat considering all the variables, such as treacherous and capricious winds, blinding sun, slashing rain, bone-numbing cold—there is the matter of holding onto it and then running with it. Even as those who want to enfold you in an especially physical embrace are racing towards you under a full head of steam.

If you are a kick returner, you understand that you work without a safety net.

The early practitioners of this skill called themselves javelin catchers. It requires nervelessness and reckless abandon and a momentary loss, a temporary suspension, of all sanity. Vai Sikahema realized early on it was the only way he would make a living in the pros.

"The strange thing is, I get scared. Scared of lots of things. But I was never scared standing under a punt. I'm not sure why, exactly. I'm grateful, I do know that, because if you're scared you're dead in that business.

"I never realized how noisy it was, all those big bodies crashing into one another, until after I had quit playing and then started watching the game from the sidelines. But when you're out there, playing, it's like you're in a vacuum. When the play is over, then you hear all the noise and the screaming and the confusion. And you think to yourself: 'Boy, it sure did get loud all of a sudden.'

"But while you're running, there's no sound. It's like someone hit the mute button on the TV. It's almost an out-of-body experience . . . you're in the top row of the stadium looking down at yourself running down the field, and you're yelling at yourself: 'Go! Go! Faster, faster! Uh-oh, look out . . . ' "

There were a lot of high-speed collisions over eight seasons, hundreds of smash-ups. But he walked away from them all, partly because he never gave them a square-on shot at him. All those hours of doing the dance of the ring with his father . . . he knew how to make them miss, and those times when they didn't miss, he knew how to deflect the impact, how to divert a kill shot into a ricochet.

Of them all, of all those return-to-sender moments, one shines still. It glistens in his memory bank and lives still on tape that is played again and again on local television stations. He played five seasons with the Cardinals, one with the Packers, and two with the Eagles, and his best moment came on a cold and windy day in 1992, his next-to-last season. Philadelphia was playing the Giants in the Meadowlands, and the Eagles had fallen behind early and had scuffled to catch up. They finally had, and now the Giants were punting.

He brought it all the way back.

Eighty-seven yards.

Untouched by human hands.

His route had taken him along the Giants' sideline—their bench had screamed obscenities at him as he raced past—and now in the end zone he wheeled and flipped the ball and started to trot to the Eagles sideline. As he neared the goalpost, he noticed how thickly padded it was, and at that precise moment he was impaled by a bolt of emotional inspiration.

He knew just enough about showmanship to realize that the cameras would linger on him, hoping for some snippet of celebration that would make the evening's highlights.

So he ran to the goalpost and began to punch it. He worked it like it was a heavy bag. He dug vicious hooks and thunderous uppercuts into the padding. Lefts and rights. Body and head. The Eagles went ballistic, his teammates laughing and whooping and waving towels to urge him on. Eighty thousand Giants fans booed lustily.

And he kept whaling away.

"I knew my father was watching and I knew he was going nuts and I knew that he would know what I was trying to tell him with each punch," he says, and now Vai Sikahema has to lower his fork one more time because it is not so easy to eat when your eyes are filling.

"I mean, I was already juiced with adrenaline and with the incredible emotion of the moment, and then the more I thought about my father, what I was doing, the faster and the harder I punched. I wanted to knock it down, all of it, the goalpost, the whole thing."

The Eagles returned home from that game by bus, down the New Jersey Turnpike, and it was after three in the morning when Vai Sikahema walked through his front door. The first thing he said to Keala was: "I don't care how late it is, I've got to call my father."

They had developed a ritual, the father and the son. Each night before a game, the son would phone the father.

And his wife smiled at him and said, softly: "Are you kidding me? He's called four times already."

He left the game without much of the usual pain that accompanies such separation. It was because he had prepared himself, and because he had not deluded himself.

"I hadn't had a very good season in 1993. They were bringing in younger, faster kids. It wasn't like I'd lost a step because speed was never much of a factor with me anyway. If I'd been speedy, I might still be playing. But you can only make them miss for so long. The salary cap was coming. And then there was my family . . . the kids had been dragged around the country and now they were getting to an age where we needed to stay put and we needed stability."

He had made sure before he ever jumped that he had a soft place to land. One of the Philadelphia television stations, WCAU Channel 10, a network affiliate, had offered him a full-time job. He would start as their weekend sports anchor. He had impressed them with a segment he had done on the weekly "Randall Cunningham Show," called "Vai's Guys."

And the way he figured it, he had already outlasted all the actuarial charts.

"After my eighth year, I realized that I had probably played seven years longer than I should have, given my size and lack of speed. So how could I possibly have any regrets at all? What you worry about isn't the past, but the future. I'll guarantee you, secretly every guy who's playing longs for something that he can walk into after football. You don't want to admit it, but you're afraid. You wonder if anyone will want to hire you.

"To make it to the NFL, you have a streak of arrogance in your personality, some tolerance for pain, at least a passing familiarity with violence, and absolute fearlessness. None of this is exactly the kind of stuff you find on the typical job resume. All during my career I watched teammate after teammate try to assimilate himself into the real world. I saw a lot of them lose their money, their marriages, their children, and that was frightening.

"I worried that I might lose everything I had worked for. I had always been driven by the fear of going back to the poverty where I had started. And, let's be honest, you become accustomed to a certain lifestyle. It can be intoxicating.

"My first year in the league I made the rookie minimum, which was $60,000. I was married, I had an eight-month-old child, and every week I would pick up my check, for $3,200, and we would go to the bank and convert it into cash and my wife and I would stand there and divide all these crisp new hundred-dollar bills between us and then head for the mall. We wanted to look like, feel like, spend like, the millionaires that our friends and family thought we were.

"But you get caught up in a vicious cycle. Camp rolls around and you've got no money and now you're haunted by this: 'What if I don't make the team? What do we do then?' We lived like this for my first four years in the league—spend first, worry later. And all the time you're watching teammate after teammate get terminated and then left to fend for himself in a world that has no use for a Sunday warrior once he's no longer a warrior."

He broke the cycle, finally, and began to save and think about the future. Or, more accurately, he was forced to break out of the cycle.

"I was lucky—I married a woman who was even more fearless than me. It wasn't like she'd come along after I had already made it. She was there from the start, when we didn't have two nickels to rub together. She encouraged me to retire and pursue television. She said we could live for a while on what we had saved and she would get a part-time job if we needed it."

101

Keala says: "He was always willing to take a risk and I was, too. We took the attitude of let's dive in and do it. We both sensed that we were meant to be together almost from the moment we met, and we got that same feeling about him retiring from football.

"He had gotten everything out of the game he had wanted, and more. We made list after list of all the pros and cons. I admit the first year or two I missed going to the games and watching him play. It's really quite emotional, a very heady lifestyle. But eventually I realized how fortunate we were to be able to walk away."

He made his TV debut in the spring of 1994 and his very first event was the NFL draft. It seemed to close a circle.

He made a conscious decision not to "hang" in the locker room, even though the camaraderie was what he missed most.

"We used to sit around in the trainer's room and bust on each other," he says, smiling.

"That was the best part of the whole game, really. We were like kids. Behind closed doors, you forgot about being politically correct. It was hard making that break, but if I was going to be a journalist I had to do it. I couldn't be a hanger-on. It felt weird at first, like showing up at a family reunion and being on the outside. Now, I am an outsider. Hardly anyone's left from when I played.

"I never longed to be at training camp, so I didn't miss that. But the first couple of Sundays . . . well, I had been conditioned to play football for seventeen years, and you don't just drop that without some regret. Then I stood on the sidelines and watched those behemoths crashing into each other and I knew I didn't miss that.

"But you have to have the right attitude about retiring. I always thought it would be sad if those eight years were going to be the high point of my life. It was just a chapter. You finished it and you went on. It's like getting out of high school . . . you have some great memories and you look back on it with a certain fondness, nostalgia, but you're hoping the best years of your life are ahead of you."

At the same time, he acknowledges a debt to the game that is beyond repaying.

"I wake up every day and pinch myself to make sure this is really happening to me," he says. "Somebody asked me if I believed in the American dream. Believe in it? Are you kidding me? I'm living it."

"It was a wonderful camaraderie that we had amongst the players. My dearest friends, and some of them are still my dearest friends, were the guys I played with . . . We have a little fraternity that I don't think exists anymore, certainly not like the one we had, but there's something that was so unique about it and when I was hurt in 1960, laid out in '61, I'm not all that intelligent but I made a great decision to come back and play, because there are few things in life that you are given and it was a real blessing to be able to physically be able to do what I did and to be able to go out there week in and week out, I was really blessed to do that and not ever seriously be injured, to maybe more that anything else have the awareness to appreciate how important that was in my life. To be able to take my two sons in the locker room with me, and after a football game to come back out to escape the crowd in front of Yankee Stadium, to walk out of the dugout, the first base dugout, and walk across the field to the exit in center field and pass all those monuments out there, Babe Ruth, DiMaggio, and all those wonderful old names, Lou Gehrig, that are out there, and stop, maybe as your boys are wandering around and jumping over and up and down those monuments throwing tape rolls that Sid Merrett the trainer has given them, and just to sit back, and just before you leave to smell; it was only New York, there was booze, there was popcorn, it had this wonderful aroma to it and I don't think I'll ever forget that. Stand there and just take a deep breath and be young enough to do it and old enough to appreciate what I've done, whether it was for good or for bad, it was a wonderful experience."

Frank Gifford, HB-WR-DB 1952-64 New York Giants
When asked what it was that he missed about the game when he sat out and what it was
that he wanted to go back for
TNT Interviews
75th Anniversary

"Football is still a part of my life. A major part of my life. It's meant learning to deal with sadness, with pain, with injuries. It's learning to have to deal with success. Football has been a basis of my everyday existence to this day. So many ups and downs in the game. Learning how to get along with other people. Football convinced me that life is a team game. I had people help me. It's realistic. It's factual that football is a team game. Life is a team game to me. I've been able to deal with my life away from football in a more organized, disciplined manner than I would have been able to otherwise. There's nothing easy about football. And life isn't always easy. Football, I still love."

Joe Namath, QB 1965-76 New York Jets; 1977 LA Rams
TNT Interviews
75th Anniversary

"What generally happens is . . . when you go into your next field you're ten, fifteen years behind your peer group, you know, whatever field that is, I mean how do you go out and suddenly become an effective person in marketing or sales when you've been tied up in one career all your life?"

Ron Mix, OT-OG 1960 LA; 1961-69 San Diego; 1970 Oakland
When the Cheering Stops
NFL Films, Inc.

106

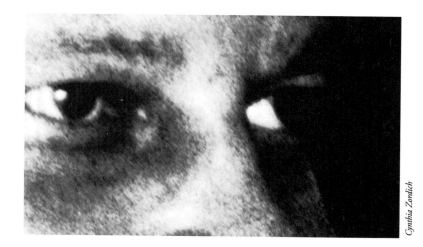

Cynthia Zordich

THE ZEN WARRIOR
The Ronnie Lott Story

He still remembers the first time he made himself disappear.

He narrowed his eyes and scrunched his face in concentration. He slowed his breathing, made his pulse throttle down. He took a big, deep inhale. Held it. Took a slow, deliberate exhale. Again. Again. He uncluttered his mind. Emptied it of all distractions. Felt his heartbeat slow . . .

Ka-whump . . . ka-whump . . . . . . ka-whump . . . . ka-whump . . . . ka-whump . . . .

He picked out a spot on the horizon. A focus point. He stared at it. He would transport himself to that place. He would will himself there.

Well, he couldn't, of course. Not literally. Not physically. But what he found was that he could make a part of himself disappear into himself. And from his center, his spirit center, he could draw energy. When Ronnie Lott put that energy into a hit, it looked like the light from a thousand suns. Most times, the man being hit was vaporized.

Ronnie Lott considered himself a Zen warrior. This unsettled a few people.

"Yeah, they think that maybe you made one too many tackles without a helmet," he concedes, laughing. "They look at you sideways and they take a step back and you can see them thinking, 'Man, let me move away from this guy. He's weird.'"

Yeah, Hall of Fame weird. In all, he made 1,161 tackles in a star-spangled 14-year career in the National Football League. Most of the recipients of those hits wobbled away roundheeled and unable, until ammonia caplets were cracked open under their noses, to recall their own names.

He may not have invented the position of strong safety but he surely perfected it. His became the standard by which hits are measured. Before Ronnie Lott, the game of defense was neatly compartmentalized—you had the mastodons up front, the saber-toothed linebackers in the middle, and the velociraptors at the corners. Lott was T-Rex.

He had the best of the two continuums, time and space. He could get a running start and the proper angle for maximum destruction. A butterfly of a receiver would fly carelessly into Lott's crosshairs and there would be this distinctive sound, somewhere between thunderclap and sonic boom, and then the trainers and the medics would be running from the sidelines, and those up in the booth would be chortling gleefully while the replay unspooled in violent slow motion.

In the NFL's *Crunch Time!* videos, Lott would talk in graphic detail of the sensation of a jolting tackle. He said his eyes would roll back into his head and assorted bodily fluids would come spraying out of his nose. He wasn't only a devastating hitter, he was uncommonly articulate and freely forthright about his profession.

You do, of course, receive a bill after you have made your deliveries. The cost of playing football is never one-sided. By his reckoning, Ronnie Lott sustained at least a dozen concussions. He also was sent on uncounted journeys to that special place where everything seems to have a liquid quality to it, to hang in suspended animation, almost as though someone has called time-out on life. He referred to this brief stopover as never-never land. It only occasionally occurred to him that he might be paralyzed. Or worse.

"Do race car drivers think about crashing?" he asks. "They can't afford to, or then they'll never get behind the wheel, right?"

He also sustained, among those things worth mentioning, torn cartilage in his left knee, sprained ligaments in his right knee, a broken fibula, a dislocated finger, and a slashed lower lip. And at least once, he elected to finish what someone else started on him. During the 1985 season, the pinkie on his left hand was crushed, and he was told he would have to miss the playoffs.

"Why?" he asked.

"Well, Ronnie, you just won't be able to play until that thing heals."

"How about if we just cut it off, then?"

His logic seemed, to him, unassailable: If something doesn't work, get rid of it. So they did. They amputated the tip of the pinkie so that it would not interfere with the performance of his duties. When word of his elective surgery got out, even his most testosterone-fueled teammates regarded him with awe: "The man let part of himself get cut off just so's he could play! Is that some serious balls, or what?"

He says trauma is part of the game, and there are two options: "You either get used to it or you just don't think about it."

But really now, is it actually possible to dismiss it from your mind?

"The mind is the key to everything," he says.

Which brings us back to the time he first learned to make himself disappear. As early as pee-wee football he had tried on what he called his Bobo Scowl. He contorted his face with as much ferocity and fury as he could muster. It was supposed make him concentrate and scare his opponent.

Then, in junior high school, he read a book about the basketball legend, Oscar Robertson. The Big O described in detail how he would try to expand his peripheral vision so that he could see more of the court. He made vision exercises part of his daily practice, same as dribbling and shooting. The key, of course, was concentrating on a point outside your sightline.

Ronnie Lott, who already had an aptitude and a respect for the powers of concentration, dutifully did what Big O had prescribed. Eventually, he could immerse himself so completely in his concentration—almost to the point of self-hypnosis—that he could shut out the world. To practice, he asked his brother and sister to try to distract him. Being siblings, they didn't need to be asked twice to stand within inches of him and scream and shriek. Lott the Zen Warrior swears that when he was really, really on, he couldn't hear them.

Thus Ronnie Lott ventured into that mystical, mythical, magical spot of rhapsody known reverently to athletes as The Zone.

In The Zone, he created havoc. In The Zone, he could slow the game down. In The Zone, he could line up the target.

"I'd try to visualize a spot on the other side of him, and then I'd run through him. That way, I was accelerating even as I was hitting him."

You nod. You say that, yes, you understand, and Ronnie Lott chuckles softly and replies, politely: "With all due respect, no, you don't. You don't understand. Not really. You can't. Not totally. Not until you've been there. Not until you've splashed somebody. Or been splashed yourself."

The game is played in a state of rage, some of it pharmaceutically induced and enhanced by piping potent pregame cocktails of amphetamines and caffeines directly into conduits that already have rivers of adrenaline surging through them. Ronnie Lott says he confined his use of assorted medicinal dosages to those that would hasten healing, not produce fury. He was already naturally wired with the thought of making himself disappear and then reappear on the other side of the man he hit.

"But I always watched out for the droolers," he says. "You never knew what they might do."

He speaks of kinetic energy, the force that crumples bumpers and caves in front ends. A good jolt of kinetic energy will leave you feeling like a swarm of mosquitoes is buzzing 'round your head. "If you can pound someone long enough, hard enough, eventually you make something give," he says. "It's really pretty basic. A lot of guys can make hits like that, but not all of them do. It requires making a decision without any room for compromise, an absolute total commitment, and then at the last moment you sell out, you risk everything for those last six inches of impact."

Considering his imposing resume, the significant wreckage he left in his wake, it is surprising to learn from Ronnie Lott that, more than once, he has had some severe doubts about his ability to play.

"When I was a freshman at Southern Cal, I got my first look at college linemen and I mean, I was intimidated. They had arms bigger than my legs. I knew right away the only way I could survive was to hit bigger than I was."

He became a two-time All-American and was the Trojans' MVP in 1980. Then he was drafted by San Francisco, and promptly was reminded of the difference between playing for the scholarship and playing for money.

"We were playing Atlanta. They had this punishing running back, William Andrews. It was like running into a tree, trying to tackle him. Well, they threw him a screen pass and I saw it coming, and I got a ten-yard head start. I had a kill shot all lined up. I accelerated into him and it looked like I had blown a tire. I slid off him like butter.

"I remember thinking, 'That was your best shot and you still couldn't bring him down. How in the world are you ever going to make it in this league?' "

Isn't that ruinous pessimism?

"I'm a natural-born pessimist," he replies. "I was thinking if that was my best, then I'd better get better. I think you can make pessimism work for you, motivate you. I don't mean sink into depression or give up. I always look at the downside of my life, at what I have to improve. My glass is usually half-empty. That old philosophy of if you expect the worst then you're never disappointed. It's a lot easier looking at life without expectations rather than thinking that something will happen if you don't make it happen."

Ironically, he says all of this quite cheerfully. Of course, he made it work handsomely for him. In his NFL career, he made sixty-three interceptions. He made the Pro Bowl ten times. He was four-for-four in the Super Bowl. He was involved in an estimated two hundred thousand full-speed collisions and then won an Emmy for talking about them.

And to think that the ball he was first crazy for was round and meant to be bounced . . .

He liked football, loved baseball. But the basketball felt best in his hands. He was born in New Mexico but grew up in California, moving because his father was in the military. California was a fortuitous move—it meant he could play sports, outdoors, every day of the year.

He was lean and sinewy. His legs were skinny and never would get big. But from his father he got a fierce work ethic. When he was in junior high, Ronnie Lott read that Pistol Pete Maravich, the wondrous basketball player who died much too young, came by his ball-handling wizardry by taking a basketball with him wherever he went and dribbling, dribbling, dribbling. So Ronnie Lott wore out basketballs, wore the grain off them until they were smooth and without seams, dribbled them on pavement and floors, off walls and doors, and even sometimes, it seemed, off ceilings.

Playing football in high school, in Rialto, California, he sprained his left knee. He wanted to play anyway. The coaches wouldn't let him. So he put on another player's jersey and sneaked out onto the field. As though they wouldn't recognize him the first time he delivered a hit.

In college, he still dabbled for a time in basketball. In one game, Southern Cal against arch-rival UCLA, he played with such abandon and ferocity that not only did he foul out, it took him only the first nine minutes of the game to do so. It was the ultimate affirmation—he was destined to play football because he played every sport like it was football.

The player who struck a cord in him while he was young was Larry Brown, a running back for the Washington Redskins in the early seventies. "It was the way he ran with the ball," Ronnie Lott recalls. "He just threw his body around. He wasn't very big, but he sure played like he was. You could tell, he had heart. I wanted them to say that about me.

"I never played for the money, though it sure was nice. I never played for the rings, though I'm very proud of them. What I played for, and what I think most guys play for, is respect. That's the one thing that you carry around with you all your life through. What drove me was that when I stopped playing football, I didn't want anyone to say, 'Well, yeah, he was good but if he'd given everything he had, he could have been better.' "

He spent his first ten seasons with San Francisco. After the 1990 season, he says they offered him a salary cut and the opportunity to be a sometime player. In other words, they thought he had used up his body and was pretty much done.

The pessimist in him was thrilled by such an evaluation. It motivated him to prove them wrong. Which he did, with the Raiders for two years, and then for two more with the Jets. In the 1995 preseason, having joined the Kansas City Chiefs, he sustained a fractured fibula during a game against Phoenix in one of those freak accidents that cannot be avoided nor completely understood afterwards. He did nothing more than bang his leg off a thigh pad, but, on the ricochet, the viciousness of the torque snapped the bone. It was as though he had been the end-man on a high-speed game of crack-the-whip.

He didn't take it as an omen that he was supposed to retire, not initially. But the first doctors said three weeks, maybe four. The next doctors said no, more like six weeks, maybe eight. Maybe, although no one wanted to say so out loud, never. He accepted the probable finality of it with amazing calm.

"I had decided before going to camp that this was going to be it, my last season regardless," he says. "My attitude was, if I go out in a blaze, great. If not, so be it. Having decided that probably made it easier. The Chiefs put me on the injured reserve list, and that was it."

In March of 1996 he made it official. He announced his retirement. He did not do so with dry eyes.

"Joe Montana and I used to talk all the time about how you can't play forever. We used to tease each other about staying on scholarship until we had qualified for Medicare. But it finally runs out some time. It runs out on everyone."

His body made the decision for him. His body decided it would like to go lie down in the shade and watch instead of hit.

"Every day was a tough day, but for a long time in my career even when just getting out of bed on Monday morning hurt some, I'd still have played on those Mondays if I'd had to. But my last year, I began to feel that, physically, I didn't want to do this anymore."

He had run out of ways to lie to his body. He had made a thorough study of it, had spent time and money researching creative, holistic ways of healing. He had experimented with all manner of ointments and balms, teas and herbs, acupuncture and anatomical manipulation . . . whatever would hasten the healing without putting the machinery at risk. Lord knows, there was always more than enough risk on Sundays.

113

He thought he had made a clean getaway from the game. He thought he had prepared himself for retirement, thought he would negotiate the transition to civilian life without suffering withdrawal.

"I used to talk all the time to guys who had retired, asking them how they felt, how it felt to be out of the game. I have the philosophy that you should never assume that life is going to be what people think it is. So that season when I was on IR (injury reserve), I watched games on TV. I probably went to nine games, maybe a dozen. And I was fine. No withdrawal symptoms whatsoever." Turned out, the pain of withdrawal was just lying in ambush, waiting until the season was over. He went to the Super Bowl in Phoenix. Dallas played, and beat, Pittsburgh.

"The atmosphere got to me. Big time. I was thinking to myself, 'Oh man, would I like to be doing this again.' I mean, the pull was huge. I wanted to line up one last time and lay a lick on someone. I got through it by reminding myself that I had no regrets, and I had no reason to have any regrets. I was satisfied that I had squeezed all that I could out of football. So let it go. Let it go."

It's not quite that easy, though. So Ronnie Lott took his mind off the game by over-whelming it with work, by not giving the memory bank a chance to click on. Less than four months after he retired he joined FOX Sports as a studio analyst.

"You try to exhaust things in life, do everything to the fullest," he says, "and then maybe you won't have time for regrets. I was fortunate, too, that I didn't have to completely cut my ties with football. I'm actually paid to talk about football. So that keeps me keeping myself immersed in the game. If you're going to have an opinion and express it on national television, you'd better be prepared."

In addition to working, he founded All Stars Helping Kids, a nonprofit charity to raise funds for various youth organizations through celebrity golf tournaments and a benefit black tie ball. He is committed to the national Stay in School program, owns a fitness club in San Jose, and also owns Dream Sports, a marketing company. He and his wife, Karen, have three children and live in Cupertino, California.

Some people have a full plate; he has a buffet line. It is intentional. The thought of an idle moment terrifies him. The thought of just living on his reputation, of going through life on perpetual scholarship, is abhorrent. He is not emotionally equipped to become a golf bum.

"Those guys who played in an earlier time, guys like Chuck Bednarik, they had to work for a living outside football. Why should I be different? It's not about being able to maintain a certain lifestyle. That's too shallow. I think we have an obligation to be productive members of society."

He knows exactly why he feels that way. "My father. He's my hero, my role model. He has a double retirement, from the military and from the post office, but every day he gets up and goes to work. He works at a home for boys. He hopes that he can make a difference in their lives, and that if he helps them then he is, in some way, helping all of us. He gets out of bed every morning figuring out what he can do to make his life better.

"An athlete should be able to blend in, find something he can do. We know how to take orders. We know how to communicate. We know how to adapt and how to adjust. I think when a player retires he ought to start turning over rocks until he finds something that interests him.

"You need a reason to get up every day. Otherwise, you have this feeling of being empty. Football leaves, and when it does it leaves a hole in you. If you let it happen, you'll start feeling sorry for yourself."

And is there a way through all of this?

Ronnie Lott says that there is, that it is as simple and direct as running through a tackle, and it is this: "You have to find a purpose for living."

Cynthia Zordich

RAY BOB AND THE .38
The Ray Rhodes Story

The gun goes wherever he goes.

It is a revolver. A .38. Chrome plated. So bright and shiny you could hang it on a Christmas tree.

It's fully loaded, of course. And cocked. Always. The safety is never on and the gun is never not cocked. The trigger has been filed so that if a feather so much as brushes against it . . .

KA-BLAMMMMMM!

Ray Rhodes smiles at the thought. It's his gun. Only he doesn't keep it in a holster or in his glove compartment or under his pillow or tucked in his trousers.

No, he keeps it pointed at his head. In between his right ear and his right eye.

In fact, the .38 doesn't exist at all. Except in Rhodes's head. But he sees it every moment of every day. He imagines it until it becomes real.

"That's the way I've always gone through life, like somebody's got a loaded .38 and it's pointed at my head and they're telling me I've got no choice, none at all. I have to succeed and if I don't . . . "

He sighs and swivels slightly in his chair and changes the position of his legs, crossing the left over the right. The heels of the cowboy boots he favors thump off the desk tip. He fixes you with an accusing gaze. It requires considerable effort not to look away.

"Don't be thinking I'm crazy. I mean, I know I am, my wife tells me so all the time"—he smiles—"but don't think I'm hearing voices and seeing things. I'm not like that guy in that show—what's his name? What was that movie about the guy who saw the invisible rabbit?"

Harvey?

"Yeah. I don't see twelve-foot rabbits. But I see that .38. I make myself see it. That's my prod, man. That's my motivation. Fear. Fear of failing. It's not money that drives me. Not fame. It's fear. The fear that I'll get my butt kicked. Be embarrassed. Get whipped. Fail.

"See, I think that kind of fear is healthy. At least it is for me. It's good for me to be walking around in a cold sweat all the time. I'm one of those people who walk through the graveyard whistling, but my head is always moving, looking around. You never know what's in the shadows. Something could jump on your back at any time.

"You want to get to the Super Bowl? You play like someone is threatening your life. You play like they've got a loaded .38 pointed at your head."

It is difficult to dismiss this as hyperbole because Rhodes himself has been to five Super Bowls. And he has been on the winning side every time.

During Rhodes's rookie season as a head coach in the NFL, a man listened to Rhodes go on and on about revolvers and graveyards and then said: "I get the distinct feeling that if you were guaranteed that the only way you could get to another Super Bowl would be to jump out of an airplane without wearing a parachute, the next word we would hear from you would be: 'Geronimo-o-o-o-o-o-o-o-o-o-o!' "

Rhodes laughed heartily and agreed that that was exactly what would happen.

"I'm accustomed to being the underdog. In fact, the truth is, I enjoy that role. It's when I'm most comfortable, when my back is up against the wall."

And if no wall is handy, he will invent one.

The genesis of this consuming desperation to succeed, this pathological fear of failure, can be traced to the tiny, dusty, hardscrabble central Texas town of Mexia. Pronounced Ma-HAY-yah.

Mexia is a ninety-minute drive south of Dallas. Weeds grow in the road. Discarded oil equipment rusts in the sun, mute testimony to too many dry holes and not nearly enough gushers. Storefronts are boarded up. Other buildings, gutted by fire, stand like charred skeletons.

Thirty-five years ago, Raymond Earl Rhodes, third of four children born to Thedford and Tommie Smith Rhodes, a slender youngster built like a projectile, always seemed to be running. That is, unless one of the Southern Pacific trains was bellowing past. Then he would stop and stand there, chest heaving, listening to the seductive steel-wheeled promises of places far away, and allow himself to dream grandly. Even then, the .38 was a part of the dream.

He grew up in a one-story bungalow about a football field away from Limestone County Highway Fourteen, the only way into the city.

And the only way out.

"Everyone dreams, don't they? Me, too. And, you know, when you're young and you have all these dreams, it always seems like people are telling you you can't do this and you can't do that. But my father, he was my best friend, and he told me don't ever let anyone else tell you what you can't or can do. He would tell me to always create my own dreams, don't let other people dictate your life, what your life's gonna be.

121

"You have to figure out what works for you, what will keep you motivated, what will keep you hungry."

He found out early on what would work for him. Fear of failure made him run faster. No matter what sport he played, he excelled in it. But football was his best, because he always seemed to run like somebody, or some thing, was chasing after him. In fact, people often remarked how curious it was that when that Ray Rhodes was on his way to another touchdown, running like a cat that had got its tail caught under a rocking chair, he kept looking back over his shoulder, even though nobody was within twenty yards of him.

He was so good so early that to circumvent a state law designed to prevent underage kids from playing high school football he took on an alias. For his seventh and eighth grade years, Ray Rhodes became Walter Potts. Initially, he played for the town's all-black Dunbar High School and led the Black Cats to two consecutive state championships.

But in the summer of 1967 officials from the all-white high school approached Thedford Rhodes about having his son transfer. They saw him as a young Jackie Robinson. He would help break down barriers. Of course, there was an ulterior motive—he would give the school the best athlete around, and other great black athletes would follow him.

"There were a lot of tears and there was a lot of soul-searching," Ray Rhodes remembers. "My father said keep your dignity, keep doing the things that you know are right."

He did. And he kept the image of the loaded .38. He was anointed "King of the Rhodes." His running style was likened to the great glider, Gayle Sayers.

But the incident that seemed to define him came during a game in which he was gang-tackled. His mouthpiece became dislodged and the force of the impact caused him to bite clear through his lower lip. Blood streamed through the hole and splashed his uniform. He retreated to the sidelines, bent over. He took a drink but the water poured through the hole in his lower lip.

So he spat scarlet and put his helmet on and ran back onto the field.

Of such moments are legends made.

He started college at Texas Christian University, but said he was so horrified by the cruelty of a coach there—the cruelty was directed not at Rhodes but at a teammate—that in his second year he transferred to the University of Tulsa. For his two years there he excelled as a running back and receiver. Still, he was told that by transferring to a smaller program he would end up costing himself a lot of money down the road—his stock would drop in the NFL draft. He replied that some things simply were not for sale, starting with his self-respect.

The Giants drafted him in the tenth round in 1974. He tried not to let his jaw drop when he got his first glimpse of the Big Apple. He turned to his young wife, Carmen, and asked: "Big, isn't it?"

She swallowed and agreed: "It's not us, baby. But you'll knock 'em dead anyway."

Like her husband, Carmen was from Mexia and was accustomed to small town living. They had met in high school.

"He always says I had the eye for him," she says, smiling, "but it was the other way around, and he knows it."

Under cross-examination, he grins and does not deny the charges.

They settled in the North Jersey suburbs. Rhodes was quiet and stayed to himself. He avoided the media. At the highest level of the sport, he was no longer the projectile he was as a boy. Others ran past him. In three seasons he caught just fifty-one passes. But the coaches could not bring themselves to cut him.

They loved his work ethic. He was the ultimate overachiever. He was one of those players you want to keep around, and they desperately searched for a position for him.

They decided to switch him from offense to defense. He already had the pugnacious, hyperaggressive attitude of a defensive player, and having been a receiver for so long he knew all the tricks, all the routes, all the short cuts.

"A week before the 1977 season they called me in and said I was being switched to cornerback. And, oh by the way, you'll be starting, too."

For once he didn't need the image of the loaded .38 to motivate him.

"I must have gone to the bathroom thirty times before kickoff. We're playing the Washington Redskins in the season opener and my man is Charley Taylor, who's going to the Hall of Fame as soon as he retires. Billy Kilmer is their quarterback and he gets down under center, ready to call the first play, and he's looking right at me and he isn't even polite about it, he just breaks out laughing.

"Well, I start cheating back. Kilmer's just beginning the call and I'm already backpedaling. I know who they're going after and I decide that Charley Taylor might beat me but he sure ain't gonna beat me deep. So he runs about a ten-yard out and he catches the ball and I make a dive—I'm pretty sure my eyes were closed—to get him out of bounds and my helmet hits him and he gets a hip pointer and has to leave the game. I thought maybe I'd bought myself a break with that luck."

But they kept picking on him anyway. He was fresh meat. It's always open season on the new or the hurt in the NFL.

He didn't have the natural speed or the natural size so he had to find a way to compensate. He tried to distract the receivers he had to defend. He would talk trash and jive. He hit as hard as was legally permissible, and sometimes just a little bit harder.

"He was right on the edge of being dirty," recalls Beasley Reece, who played in the same defensive backfield with Rhodes. "What he may have lacked in skill he more than made up for by halfway cheating. He grabbed receivers and got in their faces and verbally took 'em out of their game. He was an intimidator, and I fed off his intimidation.

"He was like two different people. Away from the game he was so peaceable, and then in a game he turned into someone else. We'd have these family barbecues and there would be Ray bouncing his little girls on his knee, such a gentle soul. But you brought out a football and he became a killer. The word got around the league quick enough—if you were looking for a fight, go see Ray and he'll oblige you."

He admits to being an instigator in the locker room.

"I was one of those guys who would walk around the room just before kickoff, when it's real quiet and all you can hear are the toilets flushing. And I'd stop in front of guys and look 'em in the eye and ask, 'Are you scared?' Cause if you're scared, I've got me a big ol' mean guard dog out in my car and I could go get him and bring him in and sit him right next to you, you know, if you feel the need for some protection.' "

If he got a snarl and a curse for an answer, he would smile and move on to the next locker.

"I would do things like that, mess with guys' minds, try to get 'em jacked up for the game."

Rhodes played three seasons like that until the Giants changed coaches and he got traded to San Francisco. He played one season, 1978, and that turned out to be his farewell. It wasn't so much his decision as that of the Niners' coach, Bill Walsh.

A studious, thoughtful man, on his way to becoming proclaimed a football genius, Walsh was struck by Rhodes's single-mindedness.

"I remember I thought at the time that he would have made a great field general in war," says Walsh. "Men respect him, almost from the start. He's totally committed. He's demanding of you, but he demands even more from himself. And he doesn't get bogged down in the extraneous or the irrelevant. He gets right to the heart of the matter."

Walsh's instincts were right. Rhodes squeezed more out of himself as a player than anyone thought possible, and he demonstrated quickly that he could work the same wonders as a coach, wringing maximum effort out of others.

Still, he did not leave the playing field without great reluctance.

"You know what I missed most, and kind of still do?" he asks. "The way it smells when you're playing. The grass, the fear, the equipment. They've all got their own special smell. And I miss the way it feels when a guy is coming at you, making moves, trying to get you to bite on a fake, and then you're locked up, the two of you, and you look into each other's eyes.

"I always hoped my man would have fish eyes. You know what I mean, all bulged out?"

125

He does a remarkably accurate imitation of the bug-eyed surprise and panic of a freshly-caught bass.

"Fish eyes meant they were scared. There was some fear there. I liked seeing that. You can hear the guy breathing. And if you nail him just right, he just kind of goes flat, like you let out all the air."

He looks into space, out toward a distant horizon that only he can see, trying to bring the game back, the smell and the sound.

This is how much he misses the game: He keeps a handful of ammonia caplets in his trouser pockets, the kind that boxing cornermen and football trainers use to snap woozy athletes back to the land of the living. Sometimes standing there on the sidelines Rhodes the coach will get so carried away that he'll snap one of those caplets and put it under his nose and take a hit, his head ricocheting.

"Want one?" he'll offer.

No, no thanks Ray. We're sufficiently alert as it is.

"Turned out, I liked coaching. It's the next best thing to playing. But I don't know if I could have just walked away from the game . . . I'm not sure what I would have done if I hadn't been able to stay in football," he admits.

"Oh, I know," says Carmen. "I know exactly what he would have done without football. You take football completely away from him and he'd have gone crazy. And he'd have taken all of us right along with him."

She is just kidding, of course.

Isn't she?

She hears the creaking of the floorboards at three in the morning and she knows he isn't sneaking in, he's creeping out.

To watch more film.

To sit and stew in the juices of defeat if they have lost, or to sit and worry about the next game if they have won. There never seems time to savor a victory. And even if there were time, he wouldn't permit himself the luxury. If you celebrate, see, maybe the loaded .38 goes away, and then where would you be? What would you have to drive you?

After the 1995 season, his rookie debut as a head coach in the NFL, he was acclaimed as Coach of the Year. The trophy was huge, and buffed to such a gleam that whenever he looked at it he was blinded. He took that as a symbol, he interpreted that blinding gleam as a reaffirmation of what he had always believed—if you take time to celebrate a success, then all you succeed in doing is taking time away from preparing for more success. So keep driving. Don't get distracted.

He put his Coach of the Year award down in the basement. In storage. Out of sight, out of mind.

So the floorboards creak in the middle of the night and Carmen Rhodes knows exactly where her husband is going. Sure, she tries to keep him home, and he will give in grumblingly and they will go to bed. But he will lie there in the darkness and twist in the sheets for a while. When he gets quiet she knows exactly what he is doing.

"He's watching film in his mind," she says. "So I figure he might as well go to the office and do the real thing. At least one of us can get some sleep then."

They have four daughters. When one was in college, she brought a boyfriend home. Daddy didn't say anything to his daughter, but he asked his wife in frustration: "What's she see in that boy, anyway?"

Carmen smiled patiently and told him: "Ray, don't you see it? That boy is you. The spittin' image. She's found a younger you."

Of course, she worries about him, worries as only a wife can worry. Worries about his blood pressure. Worries what the self-imposed stress of an imaginary loaded .38 will eventually do. But she has struck a compromise, however disquieting and unsatisfying it may be.

"Having football is better than not having football. If you take football away from him, then you might as well just go ahead and shoot him."

Well, at least we'd know where to find the gun.

She smiles thinly and nods her head. Her Ray-Bob can't go halfway. He can't even let up just a little bit. The throttle always has to be wide open.

He served his apprenticeship and he served it well. In San Francisco, he coached the defensive backs for Walsh, and what a band of assassins they were. They were led by Ronnie Lott, one of the most fearsome hitters in football history. Rhodes felt like he was in command of Ninjas. And he gloried in the violence they created.

"They delivered what we'd call splatter-dash tackles," he recalls. "They'd just cave in guys. And then they'd send some off the field after they'd really knocked a guy loopy and they'd kind of sidle up to you and say: 'Hey, coach, I got a present for you. Put these in your pocket. These are that guy's (testicles).' "

Lott especially liked him, liked how he was as direct in his dealings with the players as they were in getting to the ball carriers.

"Ray knows if you're jive or if you've got heart," he says. "It's like he looks inside a player. It's not so much physical ability, it's what will a guy do when they're shooting real bullets. Ray would always say he didn't want to hear how tough you had it, he wanted to know how you were going to get out of the mess you were in."

San Francisco won four Super Bowls while Rhodes was coaching the defensive secondary, but he burned to be a head coach. He moved to Green Bay and was the Packers defensive coordinator for two years. But his family never did feel comfortable and he didn't much care for the cold. He had a chance to return to San Francisco, as defensive coordinator there. The result was a fifth championship ring.

And an interview for a head job.

He wasn't the first choice of the Philadelphia Eagles. Or the second. Or even the third. But as long as he got the job, the rest didn't matter. In the winter of 1995 he became the third African-American head coach in the history of the NFL.

Publicly, he waves off talk about race. But privately he admits: "You ask me why I take losses so hard and it's because when we lost I'm not only letting my team down and myself down, I'm letting down a lot of people in life who are out there depending on somebody to make a spark, start a fire, open a door, make somebody proud, give somebody else a chance."

His first two teams made the playoffs. By the start of his fourth season, only three players remained from the roster that he had inherited. And all his players swore by him. Several free agents came to the Eagles, for less money than they could have gotten elsewhere, because they wanted to play for the man who always has a loaded .38 pointed at his head.

He would ask them, frequently, to point it at themselves. Usually just before kickoff.

His pregame speeches became the talk of the team. They were salty and profane and riddled with graphic, occasionally horrifying images of assault and pillaging. He would have his players believing that the men who were going to line up across from them were breaking into their homes, ravishing their families, looting their houses.

In the beginning, he would light those fires in a Saturday night meeting, but he had to switch his speeches to Sundays because his players were so fired up they had trouble sleeping.

But then sleeplessness is a condition that Rhodes long ago came to take for granted. Now he is sleepless in Green Bay, fired by the Eagles after his fourth season, a three and thirteen meltdown. He wasn't unemployed for long—within days he was hired to coach the Packers. He will tell them what he has told all of his teams, what his father told him all those long, dusty years ago in Mexia: "You should always shoot for the moon. And even if you miss, you can always reach for a star as you go by . . . "

Cynthia Zordich

"If you learn from it, the game can really help prepare you to deal with a much bigger game, and that's living. Living's tough. This world is not an easy place to exist."

Brian Sipe, QB 1972-83 Cleveland
When the Cheering Stops
NFL Films, Inc.

"Preparation is the key and the lessons learned in football . . . how to prepare . . . the mental disciplines that it takes to get that job done . . . those lessons learned are going to carry over in anything else that you want to do."

Chuck Knox, T 1937 Philadelphia
When the Cheering Stops
NFL Films, Inc.

"Once the playing days are over, you still have to have a purpose in life. You have to have a reason to get up in the morning. And that's why I've prepared myself off the football field. Because I didn't want to be forty-five years old and talking about, 'Oh yeah, twenty years ago when I was somebody.' I want to be somebody all the time."

Councilman Reggie Williams, LB 1976-89 Cincinnati
When the Cheering Stops
NFL Films, Inc.

"Basically when I came to the track to be a trainer, I didn't bring to the racetrack the idea that I had been in professional sports and someone owed me anything. No one was going to give me anything, I had to get out and earn it."

Thoroughbred horse trainer Junior Coffey, RB 1965 Green Bay; 1966-67 Atlanta; 1969 Atlanta/New York Giants; 1971 New York Giants
When the Cheering Stops
NFL Films, Inc.

132

Cynthia Zordich

FALLEN
The Ron Wolfley Story

He fires up another Lucky Strike, unfiltered. Never mind that one is already burning in the ashtray.

He scrapes at the label on a longneck beer with one fingernail and studies it intently, like a man scratching at one of those instant lottery tickets. Watching him, you cannot help but think that if ever there was a person overdue for a winner, it is The Wolf Man.

He has a knack for cutting to the quick of the matter, and so in one poignant, haunting question he sums up the excruciating challenge that confronts every football player, past, present, and future:

"What do you do after you did what you were born to do?"

A long, long silence. This is a heavy rock dropped in a big pond. The ripples go on and on forever.

Uh . . . cope?

He smiles, appreciatively.

"That's the Cliff's Notes answer," he says.

The long answer is far more complicated, far more involved, and far more torturous. Few know that more acutely than Ron Wolfley. In a matter of a few wrenching months, he was ripped away from his three reasons for living:

His wife.

Their four children.

Football.

Having been a special teams specialist, he is accustomed to purposely entering into collisions and then analyzing their aftershocks. Special teamers don't sugarcoat things. The Wolf Man is brutally blunt about what has befallen him in the three years since he lost everything that had given him purpose:

"I've been drowning in a black sea."

He sounds almost relieved to say this. It's as though he has reached down to rummage inside one of his boots and has found a pebble that has been tormenting him, and now at last he is able to pull it out and set it on the table and stare at it. And if we want to look, we can. Special teamers, after all, are exhibitionists at heart. They are used to spilling themselves in public.

For coping with the losses of his family and career, he chose alcohol.

"A bottle of Jack a night," he says, "so I could at least sleep some."

But alcohol can only hold back another dawn for so long. The blessed numbness never lasts. The thirst is beyond quenching.

Wolf Man had become that old vaudeville routine:

Patient: "I'm drinking to forget."

Doctor: "What are you trying to forget?"

Patient: "That I'm drinking."

What we forget is that under all the armor, even the toughest football players have the same parts as we do, parts that can be squashed. Ron Wolfley played four years of college football and ten more of professional football and never suffered more than one separated shoulder.

But then, having survived all those years of football, he had his heart steamrolled twice by nothing more than words. Just two sentences devastated him, one from his wife, one from his coach:

"I want a divorce. Sorry."

"We're cutting you. Sorry."

He staggered around like a punt returner who has been high-lowed.

"For about a year and a half, it was me and Jack. Devastated doesn't begin to do justice to my condition."

And then?

"I started passing blood."

One morning he looked at the water in the toilet bowl turning crimson. Then he looked in the mirror, and he said to himself:

"Choose now. Choose right now. Live or die?"

The survival instinct won out.

"Yes, and I think that instinct's got staying power," he says, smiling. "I think I'm going to be all right."

In a nervous burst of anything-to-keep-my-mind-occupied energy, he dunks a couple of french fries into a small bottle of ketchup, swallows them, reaches for a chicken tender from another plate, puts out the cigarette that is smoldering in the ashtray, drags deeply from the one in his hand, and then cups the longneck and brings it closer. Clearly, this is a man who likes to juggle a lot of balls.

"Still trying to sort things out," he says.

On the football field, that isn't necessary. The sorting out happens predictably, almost instantly. Each snap of the ball answers the primal question: Can I measure up?

Wolf Man sensed from the very beginning that football could fulfill him like nothing else. He first sensed it while he was growing up in Orchard Park, a suburb of Buffalo, New York, where the winters with their white-out storms teach you to be hardy. During the football season, from his house, he could see the lights from Rich Stadium, home of the Buffalo Bills.

Those lights, he promised himself, would burn with his name one day.

There were five kids. Two girls, three boys. The father, Ron, was a trucker. He hauled gravel, wrestling with an eighteen-wheeler, the most honest sort of blue collar employment. He died, much too soon, of leukemia. The mother, Esther, was the greatest mom ever, according to Wolf Man.

"She fostered a pack mentality. She brought us close together and made sure we stayed that way. She was always saying, if you can't count on each other, who can you count on? If you fought amongst yourselves, she'd be the one to make you go hug each other."

The three boys played football. Craig had a twelve-year pro career and Ron had one that was almost as long.

"Dale was probably the best of all of us, but for some reason he never got a chance in the pros."

Wolf Man went to West Virginia, playing from 1981 through 1984. The Mountaineers went to bowls all four seasons he was there. He was six-feet tall, but always said, and still does, that he was a half inch taller than that, because there's just something about six-feet-and-a-half-inch that sounds bigger. He weighed 228 pounds and needed every ounce of it because he played fullback.

Mostly, he moved people. Violently. Forcefully.

He had an obvious aptitude, and an equally obvious fondness, for blocking, goal line situations, and short yardage downs, for all those moments when coaches look around for anyone who wants to participate, willingly, in train wrecks.

He was drafted by the Cardinals in the fourth round.

"The 104th player taken," he says, "and to this day I thought my friends were playing a joke on me when they called to tell me. I never thought I'd be drafted that high. I mean, I was a blocking back. Come on . . . "

But he possessed something that cannot be coached.

"Yeah," he says, grinning a crooked grin, "I liked to get in the way of people. Who knew you could make a living doing that?"

And quite a handsome living, as it would turn out. His first three seasons were with the Cardinals in St. Louis. He played four more with them in Arizona, then two with the Cleveland Browns. He finished up with one season with the Rams, who had relocated to St. Louis. He had come full circle, the only player to play on both St. Louis teams.

He had no illusions about the job description:

"Cannon fodder."

But like most of them, he gloried in it.

"It defined who I was. What football gives you is the chance to test your inner extremes, push the envelope all the way to the edge. The best part is you don't have to die. Most other things that test you like football does end up killing you."

He was good at what he did because he wasn't the biggest or the fastest or the strongest, and he compensated for that by raising his hand every time they asked for volunteers to walk into hell wearing gasoline suits, and by letting the warrior spirit in him ride with the wind.

"I wasn't playing on a level field. I was too small and too slow. I tried to make up for that with a kamikaze attitude. And I have to admit, when I'd see a guy who was just a little too perfect and he didn't measure up, I got a real jolt of satisfaction out of that.

"I think we all have a savage side. Everyone has a violence button. The thing is, I never knew, I never realized, that mine was on. When I did realize it is when I realized: Where do I test myself now?"

It is a question for which there is no ready answer. Each man has to supply his own. Wolf Man is still searching.

"But I feel like I'm about to get it surrounded."

He fires up another smoke and exhales a milky plume and some unabashed nostalgia:

"Every day, in football, you got to find out where you stood. You could find out where you were in relation to your peers. And, in a way, where you stood in relation to the cosmos. It told me where I was, not so much a macho kind of reinforcement, but I knew I'd never quit, never back down."

And where did that come from?

The answer, as so many of his answers seem to do, revolve around a woman. It is a thread that weaves a pattern through his life.

"My mother, she was one resilient lady. From her, I think I got the trait, that once you hang on you don't let go."

138

Even if it destroys you? Or those around you? Or both?

He exhales more smoke, more self-destruction: " 'Fraid so."

As a special teamer he was a demolitions expert. The best ones blow themselves up cheerfully.

"If a spaceship landed on earth and you wanted to show the aliens what this game of football is all about, just show them kickoff coverage," he says.

Let's see, the formula for that is: Velocity times mass equals . . .

"Chaos," he answers. "Little mushroom clouds all over the place. I played the absolute best part of the game. You get to run fifty, sixty yards and then, when you've got the throttle all the way back, you put your head into a guy who's roughly the size of the third ring of Saturn."

He found it exhilarating to the point of being a kind of religious experience: "It was Zen-like. I've never, not in my life, felt so free as I did running down under a kickoff."

"See, a lot of guys don't play the game correctly. They're too civilized. To play the game correctly, you have to behave contrary to everything your mother ever taught you. 'Don't walk against the traffic. Don't jump on your bed.' Your brain has to shut down. No thinking allowed. Just react. Rely on your instincts. The animal instincts. Pure animal. Those are the instincts that will get you safely back to the cave while all your poor look-before-you-leap neighbors are out there getting themselves eaten by the dinosaurs."

So where do you find a substitute for that rush? What takes the place of football?

"I'm still working on that one," he says. "I'm having a hard time finding it. Ultimately, it cost me my marriage . . . "

Her name is Kathy.

Not surprisingly, given his penchant for total immersion, he fixated on her.

She didn't become just his wife and soul mate, she became his obsession.

"Only girl I ever dated," he says, proudly. "She was my high school sweetheart. She was everything to me. She meant everything to me."

Eventually, she came to mean too much. Not for him, but for her. That's a lot to pile on one person.

"I think, now that I look back, that it's possible to love someone too much," he admits. "I don't feel like I smothered her exactly, or suffocated her. But I sure did just about worship her. I had her up there on a pedestal, that's for sure."

And from such a great height, there is only one possible direction to go.

In retrospect, maybe it was something of a miracle that their marriage lasted as long as it did—sixteen years, from the time they wed when he was a sophomore in college until the summer of 1998. They have two sons and two daughters.

"The oldest and the youngest were both born on our anniversary," he says. "December 21st. Shortest day of the year."

He says that as though it is somehow symbolic.

"The way my life was, if the sun didn't come up, as long as I was with her I was OK," he says.

He picks at the label on the longneck, stubs out one cigarette, starts up another. This is a man always peeling a label along with several layers of skin and soul.

"Now that I think back, that's an awesome responsibility that I laid on her. And when I didn't have football there for a while, she looked real high."

He was forced to sit out the 1994 season with a cranky back, caused, amazingly enough, not by football but by a spill he had taken when he was twelve. That one year of enforced idleness turned out to be a foreshadowing of all that was to come. Denied football, his need for her became even greater, and pathologically so.

140

"I fell into a huge depression. And all she saw was a guy falling apart right in front of her. I didn't know there was any trouble, though. I guess I was standing just a little too close to the forest, and I couldn't see the trees."

Football was restored to him the next year. He had nine seasons of wear on him, plus one year out of the game. He was viewed as damaged goods. No one answered his knocking, except the Rams. They gave him the tryout for which he begged, and then the opportunity to go out the way he wanted to.

On his shield.

"I couldn't stand for it to end with me on my back, with the bad back, not able to play. I wanted to go out the warrior's way. And I know a part of me felt that as long as my personal life was in order there wasn't anything I couldn't do on the football field. My marriage, my kids, they were my foundation."

He played ten games before they let him go. The last one was against San Francisco, and just before the game Kathy told him that she wanted a divorce. He could have been shot and it wouldn't have hurt as much. Then, right after the game, the Rams cut him.

Two bullets for the price of one.

"Actually, it was kind of a relief to be cut. At least I'd gone out dying on the battlefield. But I had seen my athletic mortality that year I had to sit out. I was pulling muscles right and left; my body was telling me it was over. All over."

Ten seasons on the demolitions squad and nothing more than a separated shoulder? How was that possible?

"I know," he laughs. "I felt like a guy who'd done two tours in Nam and never got shot. I was standing in the rice paddy and they were shooting at me and for some reason it all just whizzed on past."

The cruel irony—that he was spared great physical harm only to end up having to endure great emotional anguish—is not lost on him.

Kathy and the kids moved back to Buffalo. Wolf Man bayed mournfully at the moon, pouring out his torment and pouring another drink at the same time. When he was unable to kill himself with the bottle, despite determined efforts, he decided to go back to the desert, back to Arizona, back to the Valley of the Sun.

And how symbolic was that? Retreat to the desert, where survival is a daily test, where only cacti and mesquite trees and the tough and unyielding can survive? Could that have been a subconscious decision?

"Maybe," he allows. "What I do know for certain is that it was a sober decision, and I hadn't been making many of those."

"For a while I kept thinking we could work things out with the marriage, but I see now that it was mostly denial on my part. Meanwhile, my savings were all melting away. I was pretty much up against it. So I called a buddy in Phoenix, got a room. I had good memories there. I figured it was a place I might be able to land a job."

He did. On the radio. KMVP. Four hours each weekday, from six to ten in the morning. Sports talk. Getting the job was so easy, it was like stealing. He can bring the warrior's perspective to the conversation, and the artist's soul as well.

On his own now, he tries to wean himself emotionally. He paints. He sketches. He writes, mostly free verse. It is hardly surprising that his favorite color is black, or that his poetry is often dark and laden with confused questions.

But he has distilled all that football players endure, once they become former football players, into one eloquent poem title: "A Warrior's Heart—With No Battle To Fight."

"Just having some purpose, some direction in my life, I can begin to express my creative side," he says.

Ultimately, that may be his salvation.

He goes to the Cardinals games. He sits up on the roof of the press box. Mostly so he can smoke.

142

"I tried sitting in the stands, but I couldn't bear to listen to those know-nothing dumb-asses and what they were saying about the players. The game itself? I don't think it's changed. But the players aren't the same. It's for the money. We always used to say: 'You think you can play, huh? Well let's go out there and see you kick some ass.' And if you could, then we said: 'OK! You can play!' "

His former wife and his children are more than two thousand miles away. He says that he has come to understand that he can't drink his way across that distance.

"We are trying to make our divorce as loving as our marriage was," he says. "If I ask, 'Hey, can I take the kids here or there?' . . . well, she's real cool about that. And her parents, they're like my own. I wish we were still together, but I look back and . . . she had her reasons."

He swallows.

Fallen

Does anyone know what the newly dropped see
...when gravities of blood and bone come down?

Did anyone hear what the Battle King said
...when fighting flesh he fell and so his crown?

Won't anyone acknowledge that power's perception
...when the tethered see status as erect?

Did anyone notice the smiling sire of sadness
...when his mistress showed her aging defect?

Fall
like a King,
who can't rule,
bound here by gravity:
Through the dirt,
Through the stone,
Through longevity.

Does anyone know the right of North or South of wrong
...when the skull's grey compass reads sin?
Has anyone the cognition keys of the captures
...when solitude's soldier turns have been?

Could anyone see the days of the daze occurring
...when what's taken place is a place now taken?

Can anyone speak the fallacious tongue of chance
...when the directions of the directed are shaken?

Will anyone challenge the forecasts of the felicities
...when the lot in hand has no inheritance?

Would anyone choose division's sick pluralities
...when singular's song shows intelligence?

Fall,
into loss
past its pain
and ride over reality:
over this,
over that,
over their duplicity.

Can anyone feel the sudden tumble of loss
...when the upright collide with confusion?

Will anyone explain that specified condition
...when the presence becomes an intrusion?

Can anyone give fate's conscious path contour
...when reality's citizens seem declivitive?

Does anyone see weakness in original's state
...when adoring eyes frown at its derivative?

Fall
like they will,
as we all
with great complexity:
be precise,
be obscure,
behold polarity.

R. P. Wolfley

144

He is wearing a short-sleeved shirt that conceals half of a tattoo on his right arm. He had it etched into his flesh two years ago. The design is his, and he can explain all of its meanings, hidden or otherwise. Basically, it is a tribute to Kathy.

Besides the shirt, he has on jeans and boots and rings on each of his right-handed fingers. There are none on the left.

"Took about half the rings off, and also the bandanna," he says. "Didn't know if I'd scare you."

He was born a generation late. He is a flower child at heart.

This assessment delights him.

"I'm a walking paradox. Lot of people think I'm a biker. Or an outlaw. I'm a conservative. I'm a Republican. I'm spiritual. I love God. I don't think my way through life, I feel it. I'm a giver. But I kept to myself. All I ever wanted was respect. From my coaches, from teammates. It's why I played the game. I was a poor kid who grew up in a rich town, so I always felt I had to prove myself."

"I'm OK with who I am. I know that I'm different and I don't apologize. I choose to celebrate that. I'm going to be OK. It may take me a while, but I think I'll eventually get there."

Then his voice gets an edge to it, for the first and only time. And he says:

"I won't allow you to judge me."

And it occurs to you that no one needs to because no one could possibly judge Wolf Man as unflinchingly, as harshly, as he judges himself.

Cynthia Zordich

THE NATURAL
The John Brodie Story

John Brodie used to get his nose broken as often as other people bring in their cars for an oil change.

In seventeen professional football seasons, he sustained a busted beak eighteen times.

He came to regard them as annoyances, more nuisance than anything else. Some exuberant pass rusher would swing his forearm like a baseball bat and it would find its way inside John Brodie's face mask and smash against his proboscis and then his nose would begin to leak crimson again, and he'd kneel in the huddle and sprinkle the grass red while he called the next play.

He waited until he retired from the game to have it permanently fixed. He didn't think it logical to have the surgeon's careful work undone every season.

149

"It didn't seem to make much sense to get it repaired if it was only going to get broken again," he says. "I mean, once it's broken, it's broken. It just meant I couldn't breathe."

He relates this as simple fact, as you would talk about a recurring case of athlete's foot. But he isn't trying to pass himself off as uncommonly valorous.

"Lord no, there were guys who played with far more serious injuries than that," he says. "I was more fortunate than most of them. I mean, I'm fine now. I got my nose fixed and I breathe great these days. I get out of bed and everything works reasonably well and nothing much hurts. I still get around the golf course."

He pauses. The Florida rain thrums against the motel room window. It may affect tee times—he has flown across the country for a celebrity charity golf tournament, one of about a dozen in which he participates each year. Every time he takes a divot, he offers silent thanks.

"I see a lot of my pals now," he says, sadly, "and some of them are pretty well butchered. But I'm lucky. I guess my youth outlived my age."

He sips at his morning coffee. The caffeine goes down fine. So do most of the memories.

"When I played, the big money hadn't yet entered in. We understood the risk of injury, understood the game was conditional violence. Football was your passion as much as it was your job. Even though it was your employment, you understood that it was a lot more than that, something not easily put into words. But we knew . . . we knew . . . "

He played in three different decades in the NFL, starting in 1957, ending in 1973. In this era of free-agent nomads, perhaps the most remarkable part of John Brodie's career is that it was all spent in the same city, and all spent with the same team. San Francisco. The 49ers.

Outside of the repeatedly broken nose, he remembers only one other injury worth mentioning, and he remembers it because he wasn't able to play in a game and it stopped quite a run.

"Separated my shoulder and I missed one week and Tommy Davis, our place kicker, had his streak of 264 in a row broken, and I told myself, that's it, I'm not going to get hurt any more. It was the mindset of that time.

"Everyone was hurting but there was no rule then that a team had to report its injuries. You'd tape what hurt, get it shot, and play. I remember Y. A. Tittle telling me soon after I joined the team: 'If you want to get traded, all you have to do is go in there.'

"And Y. A. was nodding toward the trainer's room."

He pauses and gets up for refueling from the coffee pot, and then, when asked about his tolerance for hurt, responds:

"No, I didn't have an especially high threshold of pain. Mostly what I think I had was a survival instinct. We all do, to some degree. I remember how the view of the game from the sideline was so much different than when you were actually out there. Listen, from the sideline, that's a very scary-looking game.

"I remember that I hurt my ankle in '72 and I came out of the game for about five plays, and it was so noisy, so loud, all these bodies flying around, and I told them they'd better let me back in there because if I stayed out much longer I might change my mind about playing. A guy could get hurt out there.

"Adrenaline is a wonderful chemical. It kicks in and you begin to do things and you're not completely aware that you're doing them."

The survivor in him learned to adapt.

"You learn to create a kind of safety net for yourself and you try not to do things that you shouldn't. Because that's when you're at the greatest risk. That's when you almost always get hurt. I called a play one time that was going to work but it also was going to take four seconds to develop and I knew I was only going to get two and a half seconds. But we needed it to win the game, so . . . "

So he took the extra time, the extra second and a half, and then he took the shot that came with it, and even as the pain jolted through him there was the tingle of great satisfaction as well. It's the rush you feel when you have succeeded on guile and guts against a physically superior opponent.

151

"I already knew that the guys I was playing against were tougher than me," he says. "I took my satisfaction in figuring out a way to beat them. The game evolved and you had to learn to adjust. When I first started, you were booed if you ran out of bounds. But by the end of my career, getting out of bounds or getting down before you got clocked, that was the thing for a quarterback to do."

Quarterback always has been the position of fantasy. Who among us has not pictured himself standing tall in the pocket, cool and clear-eyed as chaos swirls all around, inspiring and leading, performing all manner of the heroic and the unbelievable?

"Tell you the truth," says John Brodie, sighing, "it was wonderful playing. Nothing else quite like it. But there is a long, l-o-n-g learning period. There is an apprenticeship that you have to serve.

"So much of it is a sense of feel that you develop over time. I never met a good quarterback who was introduced as a guy who can really run. Or a guy who's really big. Or a guy who's really strong. I want the guy who can throw it accurately. Velocity is fine, but the game is all about being able to get the ball to the right spot at the right time, while a bunch of other people are trying to take your head off."

Sometimes John Brodie threw spirals, tight and ballistically perfect, and sometimes he slung it sideways, just improvised a throw when it looked like none was possible because three large, bellicose tacklers were tearing at him. There were faster, more nimble quarterbacks than he. There were more impressive guns. But as the ultimate survivor, John Brodie served himself and his team by being able to speed-read a defense and get rid of the ball as fast as . . . well, as fast as the kid who could hit the light switch and still be in bed before the room went dark.

His release was as quick as anyone's in the game. When it came time to recite the list of fast draws, his name was mentioned in the same breath with Joe Namath's and Norm Van Brocklin's.

"One of the nicest compliments I ever got was from Deacon Jones. He said: 'No sense in rushing eight or nine guys cause you ain't going to get him before he gets rid of it anyway.' "

And the release, says John Brodie, starts not in the arm, but in the head.

"It's a decision-making process," he says. "It's not just knowing where you should throw the ball, but where you shouldn't throw it. You take a guy like Norm Van Brocklin, he couldn't run the hundred in three days, but he had a release that was a blur. It was because he recognized things quicker than most others.

"But that comes with time and experience. Once you assimilate all the variables, your confidence improves. But when you're first starting out . . . whew. You know that there are things that you don't know, but you don't know what they are."

The essence of a quarterback is leadership. Can you rally a team, get them to believe, follow, execute, keep them listening, following, executing when they are bleeding and behind?

"There used to be a saying that you haven't really arrived as a professional quarterback until you can tell the coach to go to hell," he says. "Now that didn't mean you did that literally, it meant that you could stand up and then get others to follow you. You don't do that with words. Words don't lead; words deceive. People lead."

John Brodie led the 49ers longer than anyone, before or since. Even now, no one has played for them as long as he did.

"My whole life, when I think about it, has been completing cycles," he says. "I've made it a habit of finishing whatever I get involved in. Commit yourself, then see it through to the end. I guess that comes from genetics, from values you get from your parents."

That also suggests a certain persistence that borders on obsessive.

"If you're saying I'm stubborn, you're right," he says.

He mentions loyalty as being important, too.

He mentions that he tends to be independent.

And that he can be something of a contrarian.

All of these traits, it strikes you, go into making a person who stands apart.

A quarterback.

153

The ball just seemed to fit his hand. Any ball.

From a very early age, John Brodie would pick up a ball and it would feel like it was a natural part of him, an extension of his fingers.

Some hands are made to perform surgery. Some hands are made to crack safes. Some hands are made to lead orchestras.

John Brodie's hands, everyone agreed, were made to make a ball, any ball, sit up and speak.

When he was only eight, it became obvious that his hand-eye coordination was special, advanced, destined.

"I could throw a ball, and the rest of it you learned," he says. "I lived and ate sports. I suppose I had to play because I could."

He was born in San Francisco on August 14, 1935, and moved to Oakland when he was still young. His father, a man with a quarterback's vision and sense of anticipation, created the Kaiser Foundation Health Plan. Even then, John Brodie can remember his father telling him that one day professional football would become enormously popular, that there would be huge stadiums all around the country, and that the games would appear on television.

Directly across the street from the house in which John Brodie grew up was a spacious park. Unlike the stereotypical playground of modern times, this one featured constant, attentive organization, structure, and supervision. You never had to wonder if there was a game going on.

"It was a good time to be a kid," he says, fondly, of the forties and fifties.

It was *Happy Days*, a time of *Ozzie and Harriet* innocence, a simpler time. Temptations were few. Sports beckoned with each change of season. And the kids John Brodie played with and against were incredibly athletic. He took his skills, and theirs, for granted, but only until he could measure his and theirs against the skills of others.

"I didn't fully appreciate how good they were until after we'd grown up and they'd all gone on to become stars," he says. "There was Bill Russell. And Frank Robinson. And Curt Flood. I first got an inkling of how lucky I'd been to grow up against that kind of competition when I first got to Stanford. I looked at the football team and I thought: 'Geez, our high school team could beat these guys.'"

That wasn't nearly as far-fetched or boastful as it sounds—seven players from his high school football days went on to play in the National Football League.

He was a good tennis player. He was a good basketball player. He was an even better baseball player. He was tall, graceful, with the powerful slope-shouldered build that identified him instantly as an athlete, and a good one. The Philadelphia Phillies watched him play third base and offered him $35,000 to sign with them. For the time, that was a lot of money.

His mother had a one-word answer.

She insisted that her son go to college, and she had scouted the possibilities as thoroughly as the Phillies had scouted her son. Stanford, she decided, was the perfect fit.

But her son's grades left him lacking. He could qualify for Stanford but only if he managed to make straight A's his senior year in high school. Somehow, he did.

"I took my English teacher to my senior prom, I did whatever I had to do, and I got those A's," he remembers, laughing.

He got to Stanford without a scholarship, and he was the eighth-string quarterback. By his third day, he was the starter. He was six-feet-one and by then he weighed almost two-hundred pounds, the dimensions of the ideal physique in those days.

And, of course, he could put the football on a gnat's eyebrow from thirty yards away.

There were no problems whatsoever for him on the football field. There was a problem in the library, however.

"You could see the golf course from one of the windows," he remembers.

It called to him. He answered the call. Frequently.

Yet he still managed to make sufficient academic progress to remain eligible, and to confound one coed in particular.

"I had an English class at nine in the morning and one day I woke up late and didn't have time to dress. I showed up in my pajamas. We had to write a theme. I did mine in only about twenty minutes and I got a B on it. This one girl got a C-plus on her paper and she was fuming. She said she wanted to read mine. And then she asked the teacher why there was that difference in grades and he told her, and she pretended to be angry.

"I guess she had already picked me out. Anyway, I invited her for coffee. She said yes."

Three years later, on June 15, 1957, he asked her something else, and Susan Brodie said yes again. Forever.

He got $3,000 as a signing bonus from the 49ers and he spent most of it on her wedding ring.

They have five children and nine grandchildren, and some of them live next door and some of them live only two blocks away, and the rest come back often. The newest grandbaby, a girl, is named Brodie. At the mention of her name, John Brodie tries to clear the huskiness that suddenly appears in his throat. But it takes more than one swallow of coffee to do it.

The 49ers drafted him and then casually called sometime later and wondered if he intended to play and he said that he did and they said that, well, in that case, maybe he ought to come on over and sign some sort of contract. So he got in his car and did.

He double-parked.

They asked him what sort of a salary he had in mind. He swallowed and said, oh, he figured around $20,000, and they said, slyly, why didn't he take some and leave some, and he knew they already had Y. A. Tittle and Earl Morrall, and he knew that there were only a dozen teams in the league and each kept just two quarterbacks . . . So he agreed to a salary of $13,000, plus the $3,000 bonus, and they shook on it, and John Brodie, now officially a professional football player, ran back to the car and to his fiancee and pulled away before he could get a ticket for double parking.

Most of the rest of the bonus went for rent. They got an apartment in Los Altos for $103 a month. In the ninth year of his career, when John Brodie became an All-Pro quarterback, his salary had gotten all the way up to $25,000.

His career was extraordinarily long and equally meritorious. A million kids grew up pretending to be John Brodie. His last game was at home, against Pittsburgh, in December of 1973. Earlier in the season, the coach, Dick Nolan, had said he intended to sit John Brodie and go with younger players.

"I said, in that case then, I think I'm through," he remembers. "Once you think about quitting, then you're already closer to doing it than you realize. Because most of the time players only talk about playing. I could feel my enthusiasm for the game draining away. I'd gotten weary."

Warming up before that last game, he tore a muscle in his right arm. His passes were impotent flutterballs. But he got shot up with painkillers one last time and came out to make his farewell one last triumph of guile and guts. He produced one touchdown drive before the other team discovered his arm was gone.

He came off the field for the last time.

Two weeks later he signed with NBC-TV. He would have a splendid twelve-year career in the broadcast booth.

"So leaving football wasn't traumatic for me," he says. "I was going to be doing national TV games, there was no reason for me to feel bad. I didn't have any separation anxiety. I didn't miss football."

Ah, but there was still a vacuum. There was still something he missed mightily.

157

"Competing," he agrees. "Yes, I missed that. Badly. I thought The Big Hurt about football doesn't apply to me. But, yes, I still needed an outlet."

Not surprisingly, he was drawn to competition that required mental acuity. He became a ferocious bridge player. And a killer at backgammon. And he even became a world champion domino player.

"Of course there's only one tournament and it's held in San Francisco and I picked the best player in the world to be my partner," he says, laughing.

But one competition held more allure for him than all the rest.

Golf. The one sport almost all professional athletes try. They find its ability to humble them irresistible. And John Brodie was no different than the rest.

Just better.

He got good enough to become a professional when he turned fifty and was thus eligible to try and make the Seniors Tour. He left the broadcast booth to devote himself full-time to golf.

"I think it's good for you to, every ten or twelve years, do something different," he says. "It replenishes you, recharges you, keeps you from getting stale or feeling bored."

He wanted not only to make the Tour as a regular, to prove that he could master two sports, but he wanted to win a tournament. In 1991, he did. In all, he played in almost three hundred Senior tournaments and made about $800,000, and as soon as he won that tournament, it was as though his golf game went away. Oh, the sweet swing is still there, but the passion has cooled.

He needed new goals, new challenges.

"I still like to play in the charity events," he says. "Golf is . . . well, you can't ever say, 'I've got it at last.' Because you don't and you never will. Golf's a lot like life. And I guess it's a lot like playing quarterback—your weaknesses keep you from being what you want to be."

It is the contention of John Brodie that the NFL is not furnishing the help for quarterbacks that it should. He sees the young, strong arms come into the league, with mechanical flaws and no real grasp of the game, and too many of those who are supposed to coach them are hung up on stereotypes.

John Brodie: "It's like Darrell Royal used to say, 'I don't know all that goes into making a quarterback, but when one walks into the room I can tell. I can pick him out.' "

So can John Brodie, and to that end he has become a tutor of sorts, a fix-it for those quarterbacks who want to come to him for consultation. That number increases each year. His best-known pupil is his own son-in-law.

After a checkered career of bad teams and injuries, of frustration and gnawing unfulfillment, Chris Chandler landed with the Atlanta Falcons and quarterbacked them all the way to Super Bowl XXXIII in 1999. He spent that week before the game telling the media how his father-in-law had suggested a couple of changes in his mechanics—one had to do with his footwork, the other had to do with his arm motion—and how it was as though the sun had come up.

Under John Brodie, he blossomed.

All this time, John Brodie thought he had quit football. But once a quarterback, always a quarterback.

Probably all the way to the grave.

He drains the last of the coffee.

"Probably," he agrees.

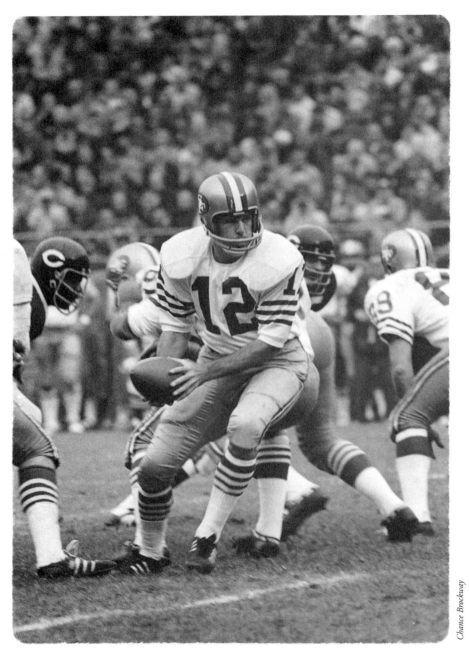

Cynthia Zordich

"Before I knew it the game was over. I was retired and now my past has run away from me faster than any running back had ever done. If I could I would have recorded every waking moment only to know if I wanted to I could relive it all over again, but only without the pain. Life has been good but also difficult. There will never be anything to equal the thrill of being there. Although it's over I thank God for letting me be a part of the team."

Walker Lee Ashley, Jr., LB 1983-88 Minnesota; 1989 Kansas City; 1990 Minnesota

"As a ten-year vet of the pre-59ers group I just received an increase in my retirement. I now receive $100 per month for each year played. This exceeds the amount I received for a player's salary in 1955, not bad considering . . . lost teeth, two knee replacements, one shoulder arthroscoped, and a series of shots in my spine to try to reduce the swelling in disc pressing against the sciatic nerve . . . if they don't help, then surgery will be needed. But, you know what, I would do it over again if I had the chance."

Mike Jarmoluk, DT-OT-DE-DG 1946-47 Chicago Bears; 1948 Boston; 1949 New York; 1950-55 Philadelphia

"You start playing the game on the hard slippery asphalt in your neighborhood, two-hand touch, that was the game. Choose sides, the fastest and the biggest would always win. I would always be the last chosen. You like the game and you continue to play in junior high, but again you were always the last chosen. In high school things change, you grow, you excel, and you win a scholarship to college. You continue to improve and finally the pros beckon. In your mind you can't believe that you have an opportunity to do something that very few people in the world get an opportunity to do. You ride this joyride for eleven years, and finally one day you awaken and realize that the end is drawing near. Something you have been doing all your life is gradually being pulled from you. Your skills that you worked so hard to develop were slowly waning, this could be devastating. However, having played on a team that won a ring, and later being a part of a team that was building, and would eventually win four Super Bowls, was really very rewarding to me. Retirement was easy because of those opportunities, but I had prepared three years prior to retirement for retirement. My last game was Franco Harris's immaculate reception, this was grand. I left with no regrets."

John Brown, 1961-66 Cleveland; 1966-1972 Pittsburgh

"A football player is not only who you are, it is what you are. People who never played will undoubtedly never understand this."

Mark Duda, 1983-88 St. Louis

Cynthia Zordich

LIFE SENTENCE
The Johnny Sample Story

He had been sneaking peeks at the clock all morning. Time hadn't exactly stood still, but it sure was crawling on its hands and knees. Now, finally, mercifully, kick-off was at hand.

He retreated to his little study down in the basement and noticed how there seemed to be a squirrel running around inside his stomach. He reached to turn on the television set and his fingers began to tremble. The tremors spread, through his hands, up his arms. In no time he had a violent case of the shakes.

The game came on and he sat there in squirming agony, pulse racing, heart palpitating, sweat streaming off him. His body would twitch and convulse. His wife came down, took one look at him, and rushed over.

"Are you OK? My God, I think you're having a heart attack. I'm calling the doctor."

163

"No, Baby," said Johnny Sample, "I just need you to talk me down."

An interesting choice of words: I just need you to talk me down . . . Isn't that what they do to someone who is suffering through withdrawal?

"I believe it is," says Johnny Sample, smiling. "I didn't OD but I sure did have a bad case of withdrawal." Withdrawal from football. Withdrawal from the game that had consumed him for twenty-one consecutive years.

And there, on a September Sunday, in 1972, Johnny Sample confronted the first day of the rest of his life without the game. It was Opening Day for the National Football League, and they had the nerve to go ahead and try to play the season without him. It was Sample's first game in retirement.

"Yes, and it liked to kill me," he says. "Getting over football? It's damn near impossible. Football gets under your skin and it stays there. For life." He snorts. And he squeezes the tennis ball that he holds in his hand. The ball is yellow and "US Open" is printed on it in red. He never lets go of that ball. He is in a restaurant, drinking orange juice (orange juice only because they don't have papaya juice, which had been his first choice) and he clings to that tennis ball like a child clings to the last tattered fragments of a favorite Binky.

This thought occurs to him: There is comfort in that ball, reassurance. It is the umbilical cord that tethers Johnny Sample to the game he has not played in more than a quarter of a century, a game that he still pines for. As long as he holds onto the tennis ball, he holds onto his past.

"It's not the money and it's not the lifestyle and it's not the fame. Those aren't the things that you really, really miss," he says. "You crave the competition. After football, I took up tennis. And sometimes I'm ashamed of myself, the way I play. Here I am, a grandfather, a man sixty-five years old, and I play every game of tennis like it's the Super Bowl. I'm jumping up and down, beating myself up when I miss a shot. Isn't that something?"

Yes. Yes, it is. But perfectly understandable.

"I understand boxers," he says. "Why they're always unretiring and coming back.

"My best friend lived in Oklahoma City then. He knew what I was going through and he'd call me every football Sunday, once before the first game on TV, and then again during the second game."

That's a true friend.

"Yes, it was like he was holding my hand long distance."

And when did he finally trust himself to end his self-imposed exile from the game?

"It was seven years before I could bring myself to actually go to a football game in person. I went down to Baltimore and watched the Colts play the Raiders. What an eerie feeling. I stood on the sidelines and my body felt—I don't know how to describe it, exactly—but it was a funny sensation. Even now, almost like an electrical shock, like my body is having its own little flashback . . . "

He had quite a run. He played from 1958 through 1971. He played in the two most famous professional football games in history. First, as a rookie with Baltimore in the 1958 overtime championship between the Giants and the Colts, the game that was the sport's breakthrough, and then for the New York Jets in Super Bowl III, the game in which his quarterback guaranteed a win and the game that remains, even now, one of the standard comparisons people offer when there is a memorable upset and a debate as to where it fits in sports history.

He played until he was thirty-six years old. He played until his body told him that it didn't particularly care what he planned on doing but that it was planning on shutting down. Now!

"I was really getting tired of getting hit," he says. "Not so much the contact itself because that's what I had always lived for, but it was getting harder and harder to recover. You start out and you're young and maybe you limp a little on Monday after a game. You get a little older and the hits pile up and pretty soon you're crawling out of bed. I mean, you're on your hands and knees to get to the bathroom.

"And then you get older still and you notice that it's Thursday and you still hurt like you used to on Monday. And you got to spend part of Friday in the whirlpool just to be able to get to practice. Plus, by then I was set up in business. I had a ticket agency and a sporting goods store. I decided that it was time to walk away while I could still walk."

He walked, and because he walked then he can walk just fine today. In fact, he can run, if that's your pleasure, although what he'd rather do is play tennis, which he does every day. And if you want to hoist a little iron, he can do that, too. It shows. His arms, roped with muscle, are, as the lifters in the weight room like to call them, "guns." His shoulders are thicker still. He wears his T-shirt purposely tight, and with the sleeves rolled up. Vanity? Ego? Sure. Why not? You go to all that trouble to sculpt a physique, and then to keep it preserved—why not show it off?

At two hundred and twenty-one pounds, he is only eight pounds over his playing weight. He doesn't drink, doesn't smoke, never has. He eschews red meat. The gray that flecks his eyebrows and his hair are the only hints that he is well into his sixties. The T-shirt that fits him like sausage skin advertises: "Tennis You Can Love."

Ever since 1982, Johnny Sample has run charity tennis tournaments, in LA, Newark, Washington, and Philadelphia. The money is used to set up inner-city programs. This isn't photo-op lip service. Almost three thousand kids sign up.

"And," he says, "we encourage dreams."

Probably because he still remembers his dreams . . .

He dreamed of outrunning the wind.

"I was going to be Jesse Owens," he says. "Track and field, that was for me. That's what my father wanted for me."

He was an only child, born in 1933, in Cape Charles, Virginia. His father was a barber, his mother a secretary. When he was eleven, he took on an idol. Jackie Robinson.

"He was the only idol I've ever had. When I was twelve, my dad took me to Ebbetts Field and I met Jackie Robinson. We shook hands and I don't think I washed that hand for a month. I still remember what he told me: 'Do what you want to do, not what anyone else wants you to do. Be your own man.' "

By the time he was in high school, Johnny Sample could run the one-hundred-yard dash almost as fast as you could say Jack Robinson. "I was running nine-seven," he says. Without the benefit of a starting block; he just crouched, like a cheetah cocking itself for the pounce.

He ran on tracks whose surfaces were made of crushed cinder, which made for tricky traction and for nasty scrapes if you happened to fall.

His sophomore year, he tried football. And fell in love with it. He played both ways, brilliantly. His father swelled with pride. His mother would have worried and fretted that he would be hurt. That is, she would have if she had known.

"My father said, 'We won't say anything to her. We'll just keep this our little secret.' "

Of course when he scored four touchdowns in one game and the local paper screamed his name in the headlines, keeping that secret was impossible. His mother pretended she didn't want to know what was happening. She didn't relent and come to watch him play until his rookie year in the NFL.

He went to college. Maryland State. Total enrollment: three hundred and twenty students. The team traveled by bus and the coaches drove. Twenty-eight players got uniforms; the other six did not. They were invited to the Orange Blossom Classic, to play Florida A & M.

"We flew to Miami," he remembers. "That seemed like the lap of luxury. We came out first, all twenty-eight of us. Then A & M came out. It seemed like they passed by us forever. They dressed 101 players. The heat and their depth destroyed us. We got beat fifty-something to fourteen. But I scored our two touchdowns and I guess that helped me get enough attention to get drafted."

By the Colts. In the seventh round. He was also chosen to play in the annual midsummer charity game that matched a collection of college all-stars against the defending pro champion.

"I got $500 for the game," he says. "I didn't know there was that much money in the whole world."

And then he found out there was even more. The Colts offered him $8,000. He accepted. They wrote him a check for $500. He thought it was a signing bonus. But later they deducted it. He was a math major in college and was practice teaching at Bates High School in Annapolis, Maryland. The way he got to work was to park his jalopy on top of a hill—the only way to get it started was to push it down the hill, run alongside it, jump in, and turn on the ignition.

"I took that check from the Colts to the bank and cashed it. I was very specific. I asked for one one-hundred-dollar bill. Ten twenties. And the rest in fives and ones. Then I called my parents to tell them. My mother said, 'Be sure you put that money in the bank.' I said I would, but of course I didn't."

Then he was backpedaling in Yankee Stadium—Yankee Stadium!—and the ball was spiraling over his head, a pass from Charlie Connerly headed for Kyle Rote, the great New York Giants receiver. The Colts and the Giants were playing in overtime, in one of the greatest football games ever, and his parents were there. The ball was over his head and all he could think of was that he would never catch up with Rote and it would be a touchdown and he would be in all the headlines the next day, the ultimate goat.

Only the pass was overthrown.

When he looked at the film later, Johnny Sample saw that he had been right on Rote after all, had him blanketed. In the emotion of the moment, his fear-fed imagination had created a disaster that never really existed. But then that, too—the pure rush—that was part of the allure of the game. The Colts won that game and the championship game the next year, in 1959. He had two interceptions in that game, one of which he ran back for a touchdown, and he also returned punts and kickoffs.

For 124 yards.

He knows the precise yardage because he has the film of that game. From time to time, he will go downstairs and take it out and sit there in the darkness and watch the grainy black and white images, watch himself being great. When his children were young—he and Andrea have two sons and two daughters—they would climb up on his lap and watch the film and pretty soon they knew all the plays by heart.

"Here's where you make that interception, Daddy."

His chest would swell until he thought it would burst.

His winner's share from that first championship game was $4,883. He was in a hurry for it. He needed it to make a down payment on a house, in the Cobbs Creek Parkway section of Philadelphia. So he called the commissioner of the league.

"Bert Bell was the commissioner then," he remembers, "and the league office was right down in Center City. He told me to come on by. When I did he handed me an envelope. The check was inside. He'd written it himself. Can you imagine something like that happening today?"

He bought that house. And though he doesn't live in it any longer, he still owns it.

"And I'll never sell it," he says, fiercely. "It was our first house. It means too many things."

The Colts showed no such loyalty. They traded him, to the Pittsburgh Steelers, where he labored for three long and frustrating years. The Steelers had some very good individual players, but they never seemed to blend as a team.

"We never won anything to speak of," he says. "Bobby Layne was the quarterback, and all the stories you've heard about him were true. He'd breathe in your direction in the huddle and the fumes would knock you over. He'd always look at me and shake his head and say: 'I don't know how you can play football and not drink.'"

The Steelers sent him to Washington for one season, and then he was traded to the Jets. He understood why. Eight years in the league. Thirty years old. It could mean only one thing.

"They thought I was through. I understood that. I didn't have any bitterness. Of course it turned out to be an enormous break for me."

The Jets got to Super Bowl III and then upset the Colts, who were eighteen-point favorites.

"As soon as we saw film of the Colts, we knew we would win," he says. "I don't mean we thought we had a good chance, I mean we knew we were going to win. What they did on defense matched up perfectly with what we did on offense, and vice-versa. We were really confident, but everyone was saying, 'Don't let anyone know. Don't say anything . . . s-s-s-h-h-h-h-h-h . . .' "

So of course Joe Namath went out and publicly guaranteed a win. Johnny Sample almost did the same thing.

"Just before we went to Miami for the game we went out to dinner in New York with two other couples, and the owner of the restaurant came over and said: 'I'm picking up the check and I'm buying you champagne because you guys are going to get killed.' One of the men with us, he was a b-i-g bettor, he offered to make a wager with the guy. I got up in a hurry and went to the men's room. I had my hands over my ears. I didn't want to know what they were doing or saying.

"But after the game I was supposed to fly to New York to be on the Johnny Carson show and my friend says: 'Hey, I made enough to buy you a plane to get you to New York.' He said he bet on the Jets and didn't take any points. But he did get 7-to-1 odds. I asked him why in the world would he make a bet like that and he said: 'Well, you told me you were going to win.' "

Johnny Sample had an interception and made several other big plays in that Super Bowl. He says the entire game felt like an out-of-body experience.

"I was seeing everything before it happened. It was like they were in slow motion and I was on fast-forward. The interception, I knew where that pass was going and I got such a big jump on it that I actually had to wait for the ball. On another pass play, I left my man to go cover the big Colts tight end, John Mackey. That was a risky thing to do but it was like I could see the play developing. I just got the tip of my fingers on the ball. But that was just enough."

Which, of course, he immediately told Mackey.

"Yes, we were both on the ground and I said: 'Big fella, I believe that may be your last chance.' "

Sample was a talker. A pleasant enough conversationalist, but with a hidden motive. His incessant chatter tended to distract opponents.

In the fourth quarter of that Super Bowl, the desperate Colts, trailing, brought in the injured and aging Johnny Unitas, hoping that somehow he could wring one more puff of magic dust from his weathered genius. Sample strolled over to chat.

"I told him, 'John, this isn't 1958. There are no more miracles.' He laughed. He was a great competitor."

Takes one to know one. Sample was so manic about his preparation, so passionately intense, that at first his wife thought she had married Mr. Hyde rather than Dr. Jekyll. They met at a banquet in Pittsburgh, corresponded for a year, and then wed in 1959, the year after he started playing pro ball.

"I guess not many people date by mail like we did," he says. "But I knew she was the one. She was, and still is, my best friend. We share the same values, the same commitments. A marriage is like anything else in life, you usually get out of it exactly what you're willing to put into it. She understands me."

But she didn't at first. As Sunday would near during the football season, he would sit there studying his playbook, so absorbed, so immersed, so oblivious, slowly transforming before her eyes into this engine of destruction, his grip on the playbook tightening until the pages began to shake. She could see his face twisting into a mask of homicidal rage. She had to say something.

"John, it's only a game, for goodness sake. You shouldn't approach it like it was life or death."

He can tell that now and laugh. But at the time he would stare at her and say: "But it is life or death for me."

He went into every game refusing to yield even a yard.

"I hated for anyone to catch anything against me, even if it was for a loss."

He fanatically kept himself in shape, lifting and running and, in the off-season, playing basketball exhibitions with a barnstorming team led by Wilt Chamberlain.

When he retired from football, he found tennis. It was a competitive outlet at first, until one day during a professional tournament when he was rushed into emergency duty as a linesman after a ten-minute crash course. He loved it, and promptly attended the United States Tennis Association school for officials. For five years he officiated tournaments all over the world, often working as many as fifty in a year.

"It wasn't for the money," he says. "It was because I could stay around competition. I guess it was my surrogate football. I'd come out early in the morning and hit with the players. That'll sharpen your game in a hurry."

There was one memorable confrontation, with a tennis player who was every bit Sample's equal when it came to losing oneself in the game.

John McEnroe.

McEnroe's temper was volcanic and legendary, and at the U.S. Open one year he objected—strenuously, profanely, and loudly—to a ball that had been called out by Johnny Sample.

"He yelled at me, 'We all know football players can't see.'"

Officials are taught never to risk responding with more than a word or two, never to engage in debate. Later, when the match was over, Johnny Sample met up with John McEnroe and told him: "Next time you do that, John, I am going to take hold of you and choke you until the life has gone completely out of you."

McEnroe paled and swallowed and retreated.

"Then some years later, during a Masters tournament in Madison Square Garden, I made a call he didn't like and he came toward the chair. We stared at each other. And he shook his head and walked away."

When Johnny Sample walked away from football, he had strapped himself into a financial parachute. He had invested in property, buying three large houses which he converted into apartments. He had the sporting goods store and ticket agency. These days he also hosts a sports talk radio show three hours a day, three days a week.

172

"Nobody had agents or advisers or lawyers like they do now," he says. "My father had always advised me to be my own boss, to get involved in situations where I was the one running things. He always said nobody will treat you as well as you'll treat yourself.

"I made $112,000 my last two years, mostly from big incentive clauses. That sounds like nothing today, but it was good money then. And I used it.

"I was lucky, I never had any serious injuries playing all that football. I guess the law of averages never caught up to me. I know now that the average career is four to five years and I was fortunate to have one that lasted three times as long as that, though that was something not many of us thought about when we were playing. You didn't want to let yourself think that it's going to end some day.

"We had a thirty-year reunion of that Super Bowl team, a golf outing, and some of the guys were in a bad way, either physically or financially," he says, glumly. "It's easy to fall into that trap, to think that you're going to play forever, that you'll always have football, that somehow you can hang onto it."

Johnny Sample has found a way to hang onto it, though. He and Andrea have three grandchildren now. That's a whole new audience to take down to the study and show the film of that glorious 1958 overtime or that glorious Super Bowl III, a whole new audience to scramble up in his lap and watch raptly and say:

"Here's where you make that interception, Grandpa . . . "

Cynthia Zordich

Cynthia Zordich

JAWS
The Ron Jaworski Story

"Thirty-two."

Thirty-two? Are you sure?

"Yeah. They showed me. It was on my medical records."

You sustained thirty-two separate concussions?

Ron Jaworski, former National Football League quarterback, nods his head in the affirmative. He wears a grave look. He is properly solemn, befitting a man who has survived head injuries thirty-two times.

But he cannot stay sorrowful and long-faced for very long. The basic nature of the man known as Jaws is one of unflagging optimism and relentless enthusiasm. This is a man drunk on life. He much prefers laughter to mourning.

177

So he says: "Thirty-two concussions goes a long way to explaining why I'm the way I am, doesn't it?"

And he giggles.

He played for the Rams, the Eagles, the Dolphins, the Chiefs. LA. Philly. Miami. Kay-Cee. He wasn't that physically imposing. Nothing about him, on the outside at least, indicated indestructibility. Six-feet-two, a buck-ninety. But he was tougher than cheap steak. He stood in the pocket as though rooted there. He was a willow lashed by a hurricane, bending, not resisting, going with the force, letting the storm blow itself out, just wanting to survive, to be around for the next storm, the next play.

He was sacked more than four hundred times in his professional career. Four hundred! That's four hundred car wrecks, four hundred helmet-clattering collisions, and it doesn't even begin to count all the hundreds of other times that creatures large and mean and pitiless fell on him after he had already released the ball.

The one hit that lives on in vivid video in the memory bank of every witness occurred in an Eagles game in Philadelphia, against the Chicago Bears. A defensive end named Mike Hartenstine, under a full head of steam, had an unimpeded path to Jaworski, who had his back turned and was looking the other way. Hartenstine homed in, a helmet-tipped missile. The area between Jaworski's shoulder blades was locked in his crosshairs. At impact, Jaworski resembled a crash test dummy. His head ricocheted violently. If ever there was a textbook illustration of a concussion, that shattering hit was it.

"When I got to the hospital," Jaworski recalls, "the neurosurgeon told me he had been watching the game on TV, and when he saw that hit he told everyone on duty to get ready, that they'd be bringing me in."

And yet Ron Jaworski played the very next Sunday.

It never occurred to him not to.

He prided himself not so much on his bravery as his durability. No matter what they did to him, he would be hunkered down under center the next game. And the game after that. And the one after that. He started 116 consecutive games, which is believed, even now, to be a record for quarterbacks. Certainly there were times when he played that he shouldn't have, but awareness of the danger of concussions was not nearly as prevalent then as it is now.

"Of those thirty-two concussions, there were only two when I was really out," he says. "And I remember telling my wife just before the game, the one after that Hartenstine hit, that I hoped that I'd get hit early, just so I'd know I was OK."

During what would be his final season, the damage that he was courting—that dance with death he insisted on, the grim consequences of what could happen to him—finally began to seep in. He became aware that something wasn't right, that he was squarely in harm's way, when he was barely hit yet still sustained all the buzzing effects of a concussion.

"A cornerback came on a blitz," he remembers, "and I ducked away so that he only got me a glancing blow, really just kind of brushed my helmet, but even then the stadium started to . . . well, what I like to call twinkle. And I remember I thought to myself then: 'You know, maybe you shouldn't be doing this.' "

When Larry Holmes, once the heavyweight champion of the world, was knocked out by Mike Tyson, he was asked what it felt like. Holmes smiled ruefully and replied: "Man, they was taking my picture!"

Jaworski laughs. "Yes, that's exactly what it feels like. You really do see all those lights exploding in your eyes."

This is how the American Medical Association Home Medical Encyclopedia explains a concussion and the temporary blackout that usually accompanies one: "The loss of consciousness is due to disturbance of electrical activity in the brain."

In other words, your cerebral wiring is short-circuited. Your fuse box temporarily goes tilt!

"I knew how to roll with the hit, how to soften the impact, how to absorb the real force of it," Jaws says. "The funny thing was, it wasn't a concussion that ended my consecutive game streak. It was a broken leg. It happened in St. Louis. I was on the bottom of the pile, and my left leg snapped. Like snapping a matchstick."

He still has a steel plate and some screws in his left leg. But other than that?

"Nothing. No problems. No after-effects. No headaches. No disorientation. No dizziness."

Nothing at all that would indicate having suffered thirty-two concussions?

"Nothing. Nothing at all."

A grin. Then:

"Which is too bad, because that means I don't have an excuse."

Now comes the terrifying and intriguing part: If anyone would give him the chance, he'd be back out there this very minute, concussions be damned. Wouldn't he?

"Absolutely. It wasn't my idea to quit. But in the fifth game of the 1989 season I blew out my knee. We were playing the Raiders in the Los Angeles Coliseum. I was down, and Howie Long rolled over me. The doctors said I had two choices. The first was a cast for eight weeks and then retirement. The second was total reconstruction of the knee, followed by all that rehabilitation, all that therapy, about a year's worth. And even then, there was no guarantee.

"I was in my seventeenth season and inside me I knew it was over. I knew something was telling me to move on."

So he officially retired. And a month went by, then two. His leg began to knit. Three months passed, four. Soon, it would be time for camp. Five months passed.

"And I'm feeling better. I'm ready to play. I recognize that itch. Fortunately, no one had any use for a thirty-nine-year-old with bad legs."

So he stayed retired.

"It was kind of like staying dead. I mean, the game was such a passion for me. The appeal was the competition. It's what I miss even now. That first year away I was miserable. Absolutely miserable. Something terribly important had been taken away from me."

Like all of them, he had become an addict. He was hooked on the rush that comes from the game, a rush so powerful that he could ignore thirty-two concussions and think, quite seriously, about going out and risking thirty-two more. Potent drug, football.

"Yes, you come to need that adrenaline. I guess about as bad as a user needs his fixes."

He found a way to stay close to the source. He did radio work, and then began a television career on ESPN that has flourished and has made him more famous and more recognized nationally than he ever was as a player.

"That work that kept me around the game, that made it easier for me to stay retired. But notice I said easier, not easy. It's still a poor substitute. You're around the game, close to the players, but it's like everything is coming through a filter. It's not the same. The emotions aren't there on Sunday like they are when you're playing, all those unbelievable ups and downs."

He lives in South Jersey, close to the headquarters of NFL Films, and during the season he studies film of eight to ten games each week, which means he is dissecting anywhere from twelve hundred to fifteen hundred plays, the better to prepare himself for his analyst's role.

"I actually watch more film now than I did when I was playing. Those film sessions, they're the next best thing to playing. But only the next best thing."

Even now, almost a decade after his last hit, he finds his body betraying him, trying to seduce him, trying to lure him back to the sweet rush of adrenaline.

"I'll be on the sidelines, broadcasting a game, and if they'd hook me up to a monitor, I bet I'd be off the charts. It's like my body is acting on its own, all that jerking and twitching. I swear my body is telling me: 'Yo, it's time. Let's suit up!'"

He has to fight to resist.

Jaws recommends the Bergey Burger for lunch.

181

He orders one for himself. The sandwich is named in honor of Bill Bergey, the mule kicker of a middle linebacker who was Ron Jaworski's teammate in Philadelphia in the 1970s. Like Jaworski, Bergey has enough enthusiasm, enough unbridled zest for life, that if converted to wattage would be sufficient to light up most of the East Coast.

Lunch is being served in the Jaws Restaurant, which is located just off the lobby of the Holiday Inn (Proprietor: Ron Jaworski) in South Philadelphia. The hotel is situated about one hefty Jaws spiral away from Veterans Stadium, the very arena where Ron Jaworski absorbed so many of those sacks, so many of those concussions, and to where he kept coming back for more.

He is trim and fit, sartorially turned out in suit and tie, mustache clipped and tidy. He exudes the quiet swagger of the quarterback. He has the look of the wealthy, successful, and shrewdly diversified businessman that he is. Despite all of the physical damage he sustained, there is not the slightest hint of any slurring of words. If you didn't know him, if you hadn't seen him play, you would never suspect that he is anything but a tycoon, safe behind a desk, or that he had ever sustained any sort of injury more serious that a paper cut from opening another fat check.

Most of all, he gives off an aura of positively radiant health. This is not some punch-drunk old warrior shuffling along, a puppet with his strings snipped. Indeed, if this is what thirty-two concussions do to you, maybe we all ought to consider lowering our heads and ramming into a wall or two.

"My father died at fifty-one, from a heart attack," he says. "So I get a really thorough physical exam every year. Stress tests, the works."

At the mention of his father, his face softens. Ron Jaworski owes all that he has to football, and he owes football to his father.

When he was in high school, in the gritty steel town of Lackawana, New York, Jaworski played baseball as well as football. He had an arm right out of Smith & Wesson. He was drafted by the St. Louis Cardinals. He wanted to go with them immediately. But his father pushed for college first.

"My dad worked in a lumber yard and he wanted something better for me. But you know how teenagers are. All I could see was a major league career. When you're seventeen years old, your idea of preparing for the future is looking at next week."

So his father arranged for an introduction to reality.

"The summer before my senior year in high school, he had me go to work in a steel mill. The Ryerson Mill. My job was straightening rods. Pull out a crooked rod, put it in the straightening machine. Pull out another crooked rod, put it in. After a week, I wanted out. He made me stay two more weeks, just to make sure I got the point. I thought the sky turned orange at six in the evening everywhere, just like it did there, when they blew out the blast furnaces."

A mill towns is often referred to as "Hell with the lid off." Jaworski nods his head in somber agreement.

"I have so much respect for people who work at those jobs," Jaworski says. "Those weeks in the mill will stay with me forever.

"And my father was my biggest booster. My freshman year in college, all I did was hold for placekicks, but he'd drive three and a half hours each way just to see that. My biggest disappointment in life is that he never got to see me play in the pros."

His father died in 1971, when Ron Jaworski was about to begin his sophomore year at Youngstown State. It was a small school but he got to throw and throw and throw. The Rams, impressed with his arm, drafted him in the second round. Desperate to fit in, he took on a lifestyle that wasn't really him. He cringes at the memory of what, for a time, he became.

"I'm a shot-and-beer guy at heart, from a mill town, and there I was trying to be Marina del Ray martini-cool. Of course I was scared and insecure, so I tried to cover that up by being cocky. I figured the only way I could call attention to myself was with my mouth. So I was saying things like, 'There's a place reserved for me in the Hall of Fame. All I need is playing time.' What a jerk."

He shudders.

But he outgrew that soon enough. When he did get to play, his arm set them all to buzzing. The papers dubbed him "The Polish Rifle." (He has mounted on a plaque in his home an official Polish rifle—the barrel is bent backward so that whoever fires it gets his head blown off.)

He pushed to be a starter. He pushed too hard and alienated management. The Rams balked and traded him to the Eagles. It turned out to be fortuitous for Jaworski. Coach Dick Vermeil became a father figure to him. Each year Jaworski got better and so did the Eagles, finally reaching the Super Bowl in 1980.

Along the way, he became known as Jaws. The name was hung on him by his next-door neighbor at the time, Doug Collins, who was then a star guard for the Philadelphia 76ers, and would later be a coach in the NBA and an analyst on television.

"He didn't come up with Jaws because of that shark movie, though," Jaws says. "Dougie said it was because my mouth was always open, talking."

He rolls his eyes.

"Talk about the pot calling the kettle black."

Collins was even more outgoing, more hyper, more naturally gregarious than his neighbor. The two of them carpooled frequently. The conversation must have sounded like the car radio set on permanent scan.

Jaws led by exuberance as much as by example. Philadelphia took to him, but only grudgingly, slowly, because that is the nature of the city. Philadelphia's athletic heroes tend to be embraced only in the twilight of their careers. Jaworski actually became more popular after he was traded away, because the fans came to miss the zing in his arm that they had taken for granted, and because he had made their beloved Iggles winners, and mostly because of his incredible toughness.

At the time, no one, including Jaworski, knew about all the concussions he had sustained. Even if it had been made public knowledge, the reaction of the people in Philly wouldn't have been one of concern or alarm. It would only have endeared Jaworski more to the Eagles zealots, who want their players to be as hardy as sidewalk weeds.

"I was never worried about myself," he says. "But I was worried about what might happen up in the stands. My brother Bill, I was afraid he might turn around and pop some guy who was on my case. And my kids were there, you know, so you're imagining them going: 'What'd that guy call Daddy?' "

And of course there was someone else to worry about.

Liz.

"Only girlfriend I ever had," he says. "I was sixteen, she was fifteen. I was the quarterback, she was the cheerleader. Just like in all the old movies."

They married in 1975. They have two daughters and a son. During one game, ESPN spent the entire weekend following Liz around. It happened to be the game in which Ron Jaworski and Mike Quick teamed up on a fairly incredible touchdown pass of ninety-nine yards.

"I never knew, until I saw that film they made of her, but she never sat during a game. She couldn't. She was up and pacing all the time."

His voice thickens with affection. And admiration.

He snorts.

"Football wasn't hard. What she did was the hard part. Taking care of the house. Taking care of the kids. Taking care of me."

That last part was the most demanding chore.

"Oh, yeah. Liz used to say there were two Ron's—Ron A and Ron B. Ron A was the guy from January to July. The father and the husband. The guy without football. Ron B was the guy from July to January. The bastard. I'd get that competitive mindset. When you're in that mood, you don't want to be around anyone. You want to isolate yourself.

"On Saturdays during the season, we'd have practice in the morning and then at night check in at a hotel. I'd just go right from practice to the hotel. I didn't want to go home because I knew what a real joy I would be to be around.

"Liz can tell you stories, how she'd have to throw me out of the house. But without her . . ."

His voice trails off. He cannot put the sentiment into words—but then he doesn't really need to. Liz Jaworski is every bit as outgoing and extroverted as her husband.

"The pressure to win was so enormous on him," she says. "During the season, from Tuesday to Friday, he was Ron the Angel, and from Friday to Tuesday he was Ron the—you'll have to excuse me—Bastard. He'd be there with you, but not really. His body would be there, but the rest of him would be a million miles away. And you knew what he was doing—he was watching football films in his mind.

"The injuries were actually the last thing on my mind—until they happened. I hated it, just hated it, when he would play after a concussion, but there was no one who could talk him out of it. It was the booing, the fan reaction . . . that's why I'd pace. I'd go down a ramp and then when I heard the play start, I'd come up, look, then go back down. I just couldn't sit and listen to the boos."

She and the children packed up and followed him from Philadelphia to Miami and then to Kansas City.

"And we enjoyed most of it," she says. "But after three years, our one daughter was ready for the eighth grade, and I told Ron: 'I don't know if you're ready to stop or not, but we are.'"

Ron Jaworski did extraordinarily well away from football. At one time he owned six golf courses in Pennsylvania, New Jersey, and Delaware. Plus two gyms, two sporting goods stores, a resort lodge in the Pocono Mountains, and a telecommunications company. The memory of those few days in the mills has driven him.

"We're very lucky," says Mrs. Jaws. "Ron got to play for seventeen years, and there are hundreds of players who have to leave after just a few years, before they want to. Then you look at the divorces, the retired players who aren't doing well physically or are struggling financially . . . we're very thankful."

So they plan on keeping their partnership going another thirty-four years?

Mrs. Jaws doesn't hesitate with her answer: "At least."

He battled and fought and then fought some more
But then he stumbled and faltered. Listen, no roar

He crumbled in silence, alone and in tears
This day comes for all, just silence, no cheers

The game drifts away but your life still goes on
You hear the same music but it's not the same song

Gerry Feehery, C-OG 1983-87 Philadelphia; 1988 Kansas City
Excerpt from his poem, "A Boy . . . A Dream . . . A Man . . . A Reality"

"When you're done, it's done. You'll never ride a roller coaster that good again."
Gerry Feehery, C-OG 1983-87 Philadelphia; 1988 Kansas City

"It took several years for me to realize my career was over. Before making an NFL roster players hear a thousand times that they are not good enough. Every NFL player has the mentality to shut out doubts about their ability, to play hurt, to push on and perform when it is not believed they should be able to. Therefore, when you are watching a game on TV two, three, four years after your retirement, deep inside you believe that if I really wanted to, if I really applied myself, I could play again. Reality is, those days are truly gone."
Paul McFadden, 1984-87 Philadelphia; 1988 New York Giants; 1989 Atlanta

"My transition wasn't traumatic. Why, I kept my same friends before and after and during my career. I never got out of touch with my roots. My family was my life, not football. I never forgot that I was just plain me and not the 'star' in a football uniform on Sunday afternoon. My goal while a player was to make enough money to send all of my four kids to college without relying on an athletic scholarship. I achieved that goal. I feel better about that than the championship ring I have, but never wear."

Anonymous player

Cynthia Zordich

GREAT EXPECTATIONS
The Bill Fralic Story

Even when he was little, he was big.

When he was nine years old, he was 5-feet-10 and weighed 175 pounds.

When he was twelve, he was 6 feet tall and 210 pounds.

When he was thirteen, he was 6-feet-3 and 235 pounds.

His fate was sealed, of course. Call it biological destiny. He would be a football player. Everyone said so. It wasn't as though he had a choice, or a say in the matter. Because if he had . . .

"I played Little League baseball and I always wondered if I made a mistake," he says, a bit wistfully. "Baseball was fun. Football was never fun. It never is when you're a lineman. I remember being at camp one time and watching the band and thinking how much that looked like it would be fun."

He may have had a musician's soul, but he had a football player's body.

He grew up in Western Pennsylvania, where football is religion, and in Pittsburgh, at a time when the grit of the steel mills and the fire from the blast furnaces defined the city, a city that doted, then and now, on its football. When H. L. Mencken described Pittsburgh as "Hell with the lid off," the city accepted it as a tribute. It is proud even now of its shot-and-a-beer, show-up-for-work-no-matter-what toughness.

Bill Fralic had two older brothers, Joe and Mike. His father, William, was a former Marine who worked in the mills. His mother, Dorothy, was a waitress. Their home was a place of nurturing and nourishment. The children were large and healthy. Boys being boys, they turned a lot of the furniture into kindling.

"My whole identity was wrapped up in being a football player then," he remembers.

He can be reflective, analytical, dispassionate about it now because he was able to forge a new identity once football was taken away from him.

At age eleven, he was trying out for the Morningside Bulldogs, a sandlot team that boasts—and without an argument—that it is the winningest team in the world. There was no weight limit. Most of the boys were five years his senior. He was so raw that his brothers had to show him how to dress, what pad went where.

Almost immediately, he sustained a fracture. His left forearm snapped in two. The bone was held in place by a sleeve and a pad, and when they were removed, his arm flopped over like a dead tree branch.

"I remember I didn't cry," he says, pridefully.

This high threshold of pain would stand him in good stead over the next twenty years.

Because he was so big for his age, he didn't play football with his peers in those early years. He was always in against older kids.

"It was better for me," he says, "going against older, bigger people. It was get better or get killed."

In the summers, he and his brothers caddied. But there was one summer when his brothers worked in the mill. Their father thought it might be instructive and motivational. It was.

"They came out of the mill and told me: 'You don't ever want to do that.' The way they said it was very convincing," he says, smiling tightly.

So football would be a way out. Instead of steel, Bill Fralic turned to iron. He felt an instant affinity for weights almost from the first moment he tried lifting them. He liked the feel of the pump, the way oxygenated blood swells the muscles, the psychological purging that comes when the sweat runs off you in rivers.

He became a fanatic pilgrim to the weight room and remains dedicated even now. At thirty-five, he is 6-feet-5 and 240 pounds, which is 50 pounds under his playing weight, and he is sculpted.

The waitress who places the club sandwich in front of him asks: "The guys at the next table wanted me to ask you, are you a professional football player?"

He smiles and answers: "I used to be."

He pauses for effect.

"In another lifetime."

"I thought so," she says, stroking his arm.

He rolls his eyes, but he cannot help but be flattered.

When he turned to the weights, he found one that he couldn't lift. It goes by the name of potential and it is impossibly heavy. There is no load more crushing to carry around than other people's expectations.

When he was nearing the end of his collegiate career at the University of Pittsburgh, there was speculation, printed, that he might even become the first lineman ever to win the Heisman Trophy.

He wasn't, but he was an All-American on every such team that was compiled. He did get Heisman votes, in both his junior and senior years. And he was the second player chosen in the NFL draft, which is quite a coup for a grunt.

In high school, he was the pubescent version of Hercules. The girls swooned, the guys churned with envy.

"I was always physically advanced for my age," he says. He pulls a tan baseball cap off his head, reattaches it firmly, looks you square in the eye, and adds: "And I emphasize the word physically."

And emotionally?

"I'd like to think I have finally caught up in that area," he replies.

To be told at every turn, from a very young age, that you are marked, that you are expected to perform the extraordinary, well, surely that can become exasperating.

And suffocating.

"My expectations of myself were every bit as high, maybe higher, than other people," he says.

At Pitt, in his very first game, he was graded out by the offensive line coaches at one-hundred. It is a mark hardly ever attained. And yet he couldn't allow himself to enjoy it.

"I thought the grade was overly generous. I looked at the film and I thought I saw several mistakes that I had made," he says. "I'm an optimist at heart, but I'm also a realist. I've always been able to put myself outside myself. I don't get upset over things I can't control. My glass is always half-full, and if it looks like it's getting empty, I always feel like tomorrow we'll find some water to fill that glass up."

It was when he became a professional player that the burden he had carried around for so long suddenly came into focus. Jeff Van Note, one of his fellow grunts on the offensive line of the Atlanta Falcons, told him: "You know what potential is? That's French for, 'You ain't done squat yet.' "

Bill Fralic laughs as he recounts this, clearly pleased even now, after all those seasons. It dawned on him that just living up to his own expectations was full-time work, and the rest of it, the worrying about other people's expectations, the living up to other people's standards, was energy unwisely spent, passion squandered on a hopeless cause.

When he first began to commune with the iron, his already-large frame began to firm up and grow even larger. Of course once he was big, being simply big wasn't enough. He had to be massive. It was inevitable that he would experiment with anything that promised to make him bigger, stronger.

He had two separate flings with steroids while he was in college. They were brief, a month each time, but intense. The effects were impressive. Of course, long-term use has a frightening price. Eventually the bill comes due and it can be staggeringly ruinous—high blood pressure, damaged liver, rippled kidneys, impotence, and wild mood swings, the infamous roid rages.

"You can take all the juice you want but by itself it won't do anything. It helps you recuperate faster and more efficiently, but you still have to lift and work out," he says.

He did, demoniacally. And then his father confronted him.

"He told me, 'You don't need that stuff. It's wrong. It'll kill you.' I would have just agreed with him and promised to stop, and then just kept on taking it," he says. "I was willing to try anything that would give me an edge. We were all experimenting. It's natural to do that at that age. But it occurred to me that if I did keep on using it, then I'd never really know if I could have made it without using the stuff.

"So I quit. And so whatever I did in my career, at least I know I did on my own. No help beyond a cup of coffee. And I feel better being able to sit here and talk about it, knowing that I didn't cheat."

195

In fact, he went full-circle, from casual experimentation to crusading against steroids. While he was still playing pro ball he testified before Congress in support of legislation to combat steroids.

"We need to protect some guys from themselves," he says. "I figured just by playing the game we were doing enough stuff to ourselves without putting another bullet in the chamber."

Where he played, down in the pit with the other dancing bears, the "stuff" they did—and do—to themselves and to each other is frequently unspeakable.

He offers his hands for inspection. The fingers are astonishingly long. A classical pianist would ache for such a span.

"There was a time," he says, wryly, "when they were a lot longer."

All of them, every one of them, has been broken at least once. The knuckles look like small mountain ranges. He is fortunate, though, that they do not haunt him with dull throbs or piercing stabs.

"They're a mess aesthetically, but at least they don't hurt. You get them caught in a face mask or in a jersey or up under pads, the stuff happens so fast . . . this one, the right pinkie, it got shattered. They X-rayed it at halftime and found it was in about twenty pieces. They gave me a glove to wear for protection. It made a pretty good weapon—you could just come straight up with it and smack a guy right in the chops."

For much of his career he was a one-armed player. His left elbow was a mess that would have to be surgically cleaned out from time to time. This would provide temporary relief but inevitably pieces of bone and ligament and cartilage would break off and collect like pebbles in a streambed.

Most offensive linemen either already have elbow problems or they develop them soon enough. To pass-protect, blockers use their fists. They jab like jackhammers. The quickest, surest way to at least slow, if not stun, some three-hundred-pound raging bull of a pass rusher is to punch him in the sternum. This process is repeated a million times, and eventually pieces of the blocker begin to wear away and chip off.

But Bill Fralic's most persistent pain comes from the pinched nerves in his neck, another occupational hazard for an offensive lineman. When you're not punching to pass-block, you're using your helmet as a battering ram to run-block. Mash your head against a wall often enough, and the supporting cables begin to give way.

"I'd go to the chiropractor two, three times a week to get the vertebrae back in line," he recalls, and instinctively reaches with his left hand for the back of his neck, just above his right shoulder, and winces. Some things you take to your grave.

Sometimes he would twist and stretch the parts of him that hurt, and it would sound like milk being poured on a bowl of Rice Krispies.

Then there were the knees.

"Drain them and play, drain them and play, drain them and play," he says softly, as though reciting a mantra. "And one time after one of the surgeries they told me, 'Oh, and by the way you don't have a posterior cruciate ligament anymore.' Of course I kept on playing anyway."

He shakes his head.

"The things we did for the game. I look back at some of it now and say, 'You dumb-ass.' "

On a bank of TV screens on the wall behind the bar, football is being played. The Colts against the Patriots. The new gun, Peyton Manning, is getting his baptism from an old gun, Drew Bledsoe. Bill Fralic never looks. Even when the crowd reacts to an especially violent hit, or greets a touchdown with a guttural roar, he pays no mind.

The Falcons, the team that employed him for eight of the nine years he played pro ball, had played a home game that afternoon. He had a ticket. But he didn't go.

"I stayed home and sat in the sun," he says.

There is no guilt in his voice, only contentment. The break from football, it would seem, has been clean and total.

"Pretty much," he says. "I'll watch a game on TV from time to time, and go to a Falcons home game on occasion. That's about it."

But then comes a sigh and a confession: "At times, I still miss it. When you're down there, it's not especially glamorous. You're hammering on a guy and he's hammering on you. You take turns being the nail and the hammer. But there's something about being in the arena . . .

"I miss the highs and the lows. I miss the extremes. See, the game itself is so simple, so direct. You have a chance to prove yourself and there are all these mood swings in a three-hour period and then it's over and you move on with your life. It's all so clearly defined. You win or you lose. There's a bottom line.

"The reason I think we all miss it so much is because you never find anything in life to duplicate the feelings you get from football. There's no outlet for your aggression. Well, I mean, not unless you're going to break the law. And in the business world there are some emotional surges from time to time. You close a big deal and there's some exhilaration, but it's just not the same. Not quite the same."

Is it because in football everything is so sharply defined, the borders and the boundaries understood by everyone in the arena?

"Yes. I loved that part. I was on bad teams almost my whole career, so I experienced a lot more losing than winning. But even after you'd gotten your ass kicked, you still felt good about having been in that arena. You'd had a chance to test yourself against people who felt the same way you did, for the most part, who understood they were testing themselves against you."

After the eight seasons in Atlanta, he was traded to Detroit. His last game was in early January of 1994. It was a playoff game. The Lions lost to the Green Bay Packers.

He sat there on a stool in front of his dressing cubicle for a long time afterwards, in no hurry to strip off the uniform he knew he'd never put on again. He'd made his decision about retiring.

And he knew it was the right decision because while he sat there, waiting for that post-game euphoria, that familiar, soothing rush of satisfaction . . . it never came.

198

Nothing came. Not relief. Not fulfillment. Not anger. Not nostalgia. Nothing at all.

"All I had was this hollow feeling," he remembers. "There wasn't bitterness or sorrow. There wasn't anything but that hollowness. I took that as a kind of confirmation. It really was time to leave."

His body had a sizable vote in that, of course. "By that time there wasn't a part of me that didn't hurt. I couldn't remember having one day that didn't have pain in it."

But his pride was the loudest voice of all. The same pride and ego that drove him to reach, or surpass, all those expectations that had accompanied him since he was nine years old detected that his play had begun to slip.

"And my ego couldn't accept just being an average player. The reality was clear to me—you aren't what you were."

He could have stayed and gotten by, for at least another season, maybe two. It's done all the time. But he felt he owed it to himself, and equally, to the game.

"The game had been so good to me, I had too much respect for it to just settle for collecting a paycheck from it."

Withdrawal wasn't as easy as he thought it would be.

"For the whole first year after I had quit playing I had dreams of going to games. They were incredibly real. I mean I'd wake up and look around and think I was actually in a stadium, or a locker room."

For three seasons, from 1995 through 1997, he was on the radio, doing color and analysis of the Falcons games. But, increasingly, he found it an unfulfilling substitute.

"Frankly, it was kind of boring sitting and talking about it after you had played it."

He felt mostly relief when his radio contract ran out and was not renewed.

He lives outside Atlanta and has an insurance agency that employs a couple dozen people and specializes in servicing trucking companies.

"I am very," he says with a wry smile, "what I presume to be happy, and that includes being without football. Because, in a way, it's still with me. I have nothing but good memories. And the best part is, I don't yearn for the past."

There is a bridge that must be crossed by all who leave the game or have the game taken from them. When you get to the other side, you meet the other you. Not all players get across that bridge. Bill Fralic appears to be one who did.

"It's not as meaningful to me, football," he says. "I don't need it any longer for my identity. And I know that, physically, I feel a lot better at thirty-five than I did at twenty-five."

Not that there isn't some lingering restlessness. Not that he doesn't cast about with some uncertainty in his life.

He lives with a woman named Susan Hunter and has for at least five years. They first began dating in 1983. She also works at his insurance firm.

"I think," he says, "that she misses football more than I do. The social part can be pretty appealing. But the thing that matters most is, she has been very loyal and very supportive.

"She tells me: 'I'm the best teammate you've ever had.' She's right. Oh, is she right. I have put her through hell."

He pulls on a beer.

"And I still do."

He struggles to assess what the game has meant to him.

"Its impact on my life is immeasurable. I can't imagine my life without having had football in it. I really don't know how to put into words how lucky I am.

"It's the great leveler, the game. It lets you find out so much about yourself. Oh, you have to give up your body, but in the grand scheme that's probably a fair trade-off because, really, it's only a vehicle anyway.

"The greatest thing you take away from the game is that no matter how bad everything seems, you don't quit. You don't ever, ever quit. Even if you're down in the dirt and getting stomped, don't quit."

And if he one day has a son?

There is no hesitation in his response.

"I wouldn't push him. If he didn't want to play, fine."

He pauses.

"But, I'd sure encourage him to . . . "

He looks across the room, beyond the bar and the TV, beyond the hotel lobby. He seems like a man who is looking back over a bridge, a bridge that he himself crossed once upon a time . . . and not so very long ago.

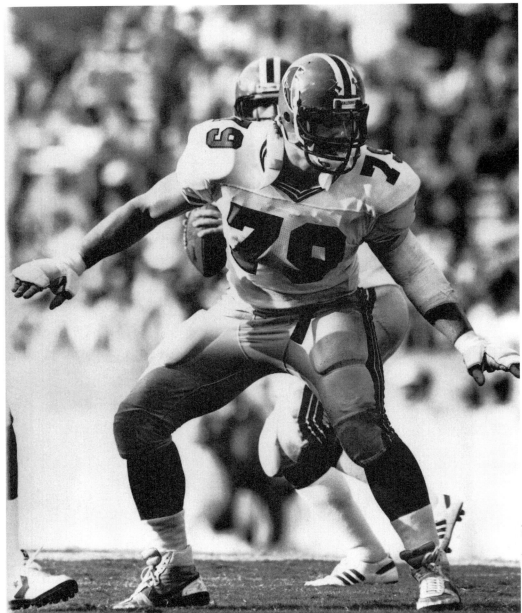

Cynthia Zordich

TALL AIN'T ALL
The Stump Mitchell Story

They would be playing a game of pickup football. He was only four years old, shorter and younger than the rest of them, but they would fall all over themselves trying to catch him. It was like trying to grab hold of your shadow.

They would run up behind him and reach out to grab him, and, suddenly, he wasn't there.

He was over there instead.

But when they would sneak up on him over there, he was—poof—somewhere else. It was as though he could see them without moving his head, as though he could see what was on his left, what was on his right, and—this was the scary part—even what was behind him.

So that's what they told him, in that blunt, unthinkingly insensitive way little kids do: "You got eyes in the back of your head, Stump! There's something wrong with you, Stump."

At first, what they said scared him. He laughed off their taunts, but secretly he couldn't help wondering: Am I some kind of freak? Then he would make someone else miss him, and he would run away, laughing, and after a while he decided this ability, this thing that enabled him to see where others couldn't, was a gift. And he would come to believe that this extraordinary peripheral vision was a compensation of sorts.

It was to make up for the height he would never have.

Stump Mitchell would never be taller than five feet, eight inches. And for all of his football life his height would be held against him.

"If you're smaller than everyone else, you always have to prove yourself," he says. "Especially in football, people have it in their minds that bigger is always better, and if you're not big then you'd better be really, really fast."

And he wasn't that, either. Not until much later in his career. But he had that remarkable vision. And he had a burning in his belly, a secret yearning that almost every person who has ever been vertically challenged can identify with: "I'm gonna show 'em. I'll show 'em."

He put a name on it, his longing. And whenever he was denigrated for his size, he would whisper to himself: "Tall ain't all."

At this particular moment, early in March of 1999, only days away from a milestone birthday, Stump Mitchell contemplates being forty, and celebrates having proven that, indeed, tall ain't all. It is six in the morning and it is raining in Seattle. Stump Mitchell is already at his desk in his new job, which involves showing those running backs in the employ of the Seattle Seahawks how to make tacklers miss and then afterwards mutter in frustration: "I still don't know how he got away. Guy must have eyes in the back of his head."

A distinguished ten-year playing career in the National Football League is behind him. It was a triumph against considerable odds. It was also a triumph accurately foretold by a man named Alvin Glover, who has been, and still is, a coach and a mentor of several generations of men who have grown up in the hamlet of Kingsland, Georgia. Kingsland is located about thirty miles north of Jacksonville, Florida, and it was here that Alvin Glover watched Stump Mitchell running away from bigger, faster kids, and told him: "You have talent. You could be special."

Stump Mitchell couldn't have been more than seven years old.

"That man made me feel twelve feet tall when he said that," he says.

Stump was christened Lyvonia Albert Mitchell.

To this day, he has no idea why. But he is eternally grateful to his older brother, Trezzavant, for nicknaming him Stump.

Initially, it was because he resembled a stump, short to the ground, squatty. But later, when he had proven his toughness, people said that he seemed as hard and unyielding and durable as a stump. It became a nickname of which to be proud.

He was raised by his mother and grandmother and "by anyone else who saw me doing wrong. It was a small town and the community pretty much raised everyone. We all watched out for each other. There were no drugs in those days. We were always playing sports and that pretty much kept us from getting into trouble."

In the ninth and tenth grades he lived in Florida, with his aunt. He went out for the football team. Up to then, he had thought he was fast.

"There, I was just fast enough to play the offensive line and be a linebacker," he recalls.

He tried to make up for lack of size and speed with recklessness on the field. His reward was a fractured collarbone. He was in a cast for six months and his aunt, terrified of further injury, forbade him to play football ever again. So he really had only one choice.

He moved back to Georgia.

There, he became a running back, and during his senior year in high school he rushed for sixteen hundred yards. But it was Stump Mitchell's other two numbers—5-8 and 150— that discouraged the college recruiters. One school finally expressed slight interest.

The Citadel.

But they only called because Johnny Newton, a friend of Stump Mitchell's who was also from Kingsland, had played football at The Citadel and raved about Stump to the head coach at the time, Bobby Ross.

"Coach Ross told me, 'You'll have to wait your turn.' But every year somebody would get hurt and they'd end up having to play me."

By his senior year, they no longer had to be convinced. Stump Mitchell ultimately rushed for more than four thousand yards in his collegiate career. As a senior he was second in the nation, less than two hundred yards behind George Rogers of South Carolina, who would win the Heisman Trophy.

Tall really ain't all.

"I really liked school," Stump Mitchell says. "I was OK with the military part of it. No, I was better than OK with it. It's a great place for a young man who desires to be successful. You learned self-discipline, you learned to take responsibility for your actions, you learned self-reliance. I picked up good habits there, habits that helped me later. When I was a rookie in the NFL, I'd go back to my room and study the playbook and get my rest instead of going out on the town. I was always fresh for practice. It was one more thing to make up for that bias against short guys that I always seemed to be having to fight."

He got his degree. And by the end of his senior season he knew something else for certain. He could play.

Alvin Glover had been right all those years ago when he watched the little boy with the eyes in the back of his head eluding tacklers. Stump Mitchell was going to be something special.

His promise and potential, however, seemed to have escaped the NFL. The 1981 draft began and the first round passed without anyone taking Stump Mitchell. The second round passed. Then the third, fourth, and fifth. The entire first day of the draft went by and his name had still not been called. On the second day, he was taken. In the ninth round.

"A round that no longer exists," he notes, with some relish.

The St. Louis Cardinals notified him by phone that they were proud to welcome him to the fold. If they were expecting a display of gratitude for their risk, they were sorely disappointed.

"Larry Wilson called me to tell me they'd taken me, and I was a real jerk. I was telling him stuff like, 'I was the second leading rusher in the whole country and you can't take me until the ninth round, what's wrong with you people?' And I kept on raving. I told him, 'I'm making your damn team, I'm telling you that right now. That's a flat promise.' I let my frustrations get to me. I apologized to him later. And I've always been grateful to the Cardinals. They were willing to give me a chance, and you can't ask for more than that."

The Cardinals soothed his frustrations with a signing bonus of $7,000. His salary would be $25,000. Per season.

That was front-page news in Stump Mitchell's hometown.

"They made it seem like I'd won the lottery," he says, laughing. "The funny part is, I probably could have made more if I'd just come back to Kingsland and went to work for the paper company there."

He was the softest sort of touch, anxious to share his new wealth. In almost no time, the bankroll that had seemed so fat was gone. All of it.

"I'm a nice guy," he says, matter-of-factly, "and I was naive then, and kind-hearted, probably to a fault. You come back to where you were raised and they treat you like the conquering hero . . . I wanted everyone to share in my good fortune and I got carried away, and to tell you the truth I got in debt before I ever got to training camp."

In camp, he knew he would have to prove himself all over again, demonstrate anew that tall ain't all, and just when he thought he had them convinced, he came down with turf toe. It doesn't sound like much, one damaged toe, but it is an incredibly painful injury and can be terribly debilitating.

"It was the only time I've ever been afraid," he admits. "I was afraid I'd never get my chance."

But he did. They put him in to return a punt, in a preseason game in Seattle, and the first time Stump Mitchell touched the ball as a pro he took a low, line drive kick that had been mis-hit and darted past tackler after tackler. He made them look foolish. He looked like he had been doing it for years. It also struck some of the Cardinals that the rook, the short guy, seemed to have eyes in the back of his head, the way he got away from people.

"And the Cardinals," he remembers, "they were like, 'Well, OK, at least we've found something he can do.' And then the next week, against Kansas City, I had a couple more good returns and they used me in some third down situations and I caught a pass. I was starting to feel comfortable."

If he didn't have the team convinced by then he certainly did the next week, against the Bears. He cradled the ball on a kickoff one yard deep in his own end zone and didn't stop running until he was in the other end zone.

Then the season began. Stump Mitchell didn't miss a beat. In the opener, against Washington, the rookie went sixty yards with a punt. He could have gone seventy. Or eighty. But sixty was all he needed. Sixty got him into the end zone. First NFL game, touchdown.

His dazzling debut didn't go unnoticed.

"We were in warm-ups for a game against the Cowboys," he says, "and I'm at mid-field catching some punts and Drew Pearson and Tony Dorsett come up to me and start in: 'Go easy on us now, Stump. You be careful out there, don't go showing us up.' And I'm all bug-eyed. I mean, Drew Pearson! Tony Dorsett! I'd been watching those guys on television and now here they were, in the flesh, and talking to me. I don't think my feet touched the ground the rest of that day."

Besides his special vision on the field, Stump Mitchell burned with the small man's desire to continually showcase what he could do instead of what he couldn't, and so he became a daredevil standing under punts. He insisted on returning every one of them. Every one.

"I was bound and determined that I wasn't going to signal for a fair catch," he says. "It became a point of pride with me. I went more than a hundred in a row without one."

The Cardinals used Otis Anderson as their featured running back but they found more and more uses for Stump Mitchell, especially as a receiver of screen passes and swing passes, routes that would widen his field of vision even more. He had played a lot of baseball and volleyball as a kid, and as a result his hands were soft and sure. And he loved playing fox and hound with a linebacker.

"They were always running over people in close, giving you big hits, but when you could get them out in the open and they'd have to cover you, well, I don't mind confessing to you that I wanted to totally embarrass them."

And did. Frequently.

Then he ran into something that he never saw coming, even with those eyes in the back of his head: The law of averages.

When the 1989 NFL season began, it was Stump Mitchell's ninth. That's a lot more than the actuarial charts give you, especially when you're out there trying to make big people miss and not always succeeding.

In the third game of the season, against the Giants, he was tackled from behind by their linebacker, Carl Banks.

"I thought that somebody had fired a cannon," Stump Mitchell remembers. "It sounded just like a cannon."

It was his knee, the left one, exploding.

He didn't go down. But he was hung up, limp, helpless, totally vulnerable to anyone who wanted to deliver the kill shot.

"The safety had a clear run at me," he remembers, "and he could have really unloaded on me. But he pulled up and all he said was: 'Go down.' He must have known it was bad."

They knew it was bad on the Giants bench.

"As soon as I got hit," Stump Mitchell says, "I heard Bill Parcells yelling for the trainer to get out there. A doctor came out and I still remember how his voice sounded. He said:

211

'We've got a problem here.' "

Inside his left knee, there wasn't much that wasn't torn, ripped loose, or grotesquely stretched. But even now, a decade later, what stays with him is the kindness and the concern that was shown to him by the opponent's fans.

"I got so many calls and cards from people in New York. I know that city takes a lot of grief, but the respect they showed for me, it really took my breath away."

Things were not so kind on his own team. The medical verdict: Your career is over. Subtly at first, and then with increasing transparency, a badly injured player finds himself being ostracized. After a few weeks, or months, he becomes a leper. Even as he showed up each day for the drudgery and the psychological discomfort and the physical pain of rehabilitation, Stump Mitchell could feel he was now an entry on the debit side of the ledger, no longer productive, no longer regarded as an asset.

A player unable to perform is the same as a broken machine in a factory. It is a liability.

And an injured player is an uncomfortable reminder to the rest of the team of what could be waiting for them. Slowly, imperceptibly, you find yourself being squeezed out.

"What hurts," says Stump Mitchell, "is you miss the give-and-take with the guys in the locker room, all the camaraderie. It hurts when people no longer want anything to do with you. It's like they're saying, you're not in the fraternity anymore. You lose all sense of belonging. It's a very lonely feeling."

By the 1990 season, he was ready to return. He had rehabilitated his knee and had actually gotten faster. He had hooked up with a trainer, Bruce Frankie, who had worked with him on biomechanics, stride, and arm motion, and to his delight Stump Mitchell discovered that while speed is usually something you're born with, it is also something you can acquire.

"I was all geared up and ready for my first contact," he recalls. "It was a scrimmage against San Diego. But they wanted to put me in with the third string, against the Chargers' first string defense. I thought that was a sure invitation to get injured. I thought I deserved more respect than that. I'd given them nine good seasons, I'd given them my body, and I didn't think it was asking all that much to be respected in return, at least respected to the point you weren't being thrown in there as fodder for someone to beat up on."

He dressed and went back to his dorm room. The next day he met with the coaches and was assured he would be starting, with the first string, in the next game.

Instead, he was released.

"The doctors and trainers wanted to restrict me to practicing once a day in camp, and the coaches didn't like it. Maybe they thought I was dogging it, but they should have known me better than that. I really think I should have been put on the physically-unable-to-perform list. I wasn't some naive innocent, I know this is a business, and I know exactly where you stand in the grand scheme of things. Still, I felt like they slighted me. I didn't think the relationship should have ended that way."

Now, however, from the distance of years, his anger has abated, and he says simply: "That's over. There are no hard feelings. I'm not bitter. Carrying a grudge, that's about the heaviest thing you can put on yourself. I've come to see that it would be a waste of energy."

He spent many hours in rehab being iced. Maybe all that ice cooled the fires of resentment.

"Maybe. I never could understand why we couldn't win. I wanted to, in the worst way. When they released me, I wanted to prove them wrong. I was offered tryouts by Washington and Philadelphia and San Francisco, and they all examined me and they all said the same thing, that I was probably three to four months away from being able to perform."

While he was trying to get ready for a comeback, a part of his life was turning to ashes. After five years, his marriage was breaking up. He and his wife Rita had a son, Lionel, and a daughter, Gail. Their parting, he says, was amicable. They still speak and he sees both his children.

He kept working out, aflame to prove that he could still play, and in March of 1991, the Kansas City Chiefs offered him a contract.

"I was doing OK in camp and in the preseason, and then in a game against Detroit I took a kickoff and everything was setting up just perfectly. I only needed to make one more cut and I'd have clear sailing. One more cut and I could see I'd go all the way."

He planted with his right foot and made one of those tire-squealing, rubber-burning accelerations, and he heard that familiar sound. Somebody had fired another cannon. His right knee turned to tapioca.

The trainers bent over him and he told them: "You guys aren't going to believe this, but I just tore up my other knee."

His diagnosis was absolutely correct. He wouldn't ever play in the NFL again. But that didn't mean he wouldn't try. And it didn't mean he wouldn't come back and play football anyway.

"I spent 1992 coaching in the World League, with San Antonio," he says. "But I kept right on rehabbing. I was stubborn. I was going to play football again, no matter what."

He would remind them all over again: Tall ain't all.

And he did, the very next year. He played in the Arena Football League, for the Arizona Rattlers. He played both ways, and on special teams. He was a throwback. He was a sixty-minute man.

"That was the most fun I've ever had, that one season," he says.

It was the validation he needed, the redemption. When the season was over, he felt the restlessness subside. No more burning for vengeance. He was at peace. The time was right.

It was a good time to let go.

"I could still run, but something in me said this was when I should call it quits. It wouldn't hurt so much."

He migrated naturally to coaching, spending two years at Casa Grande High School in Arizona, taking a team with a 3-7 record and turning them into playoff qualifiers in the next, sending kids on to Brown and Brigham Young and Hawaii. Then he moved to the collegiate level, to Morgan State, where he was an assistant for one year and head coach for three.

The pros inquired about his availability. He declined. But when the Seahawks called in February of 1999, he accepted the position of running backs coach. Again, it just felt right. It was time.

"I felt like if I turned down one more offer from an NFL team it would be the last one I would get. The word would get out that he's stuck there, he doesn't want to leave, and no one would be calling."

Football left him, as it leaves most who play it, with reminders. Limps. Aches. Twinges. Arthritis. Tendinitis. Stump Mitchell can put a check mark after each of them. Forty approaches, and some mornings it feels like seventy.

"When I was at Morgan State, I was benching four hundred and some," he says, wistfully. "But that last year in pro ball, I got back spasms and a bulging disc, and so I have my good days and my bad days.

"My last year as a player, I weighted 195. Now I'm like everyone else, 215 and fighting gravity, behind a desk and talking about things instead of doing them."

He laughs, and there is no echo of bitterness. He has made his peace with this situation, too.

"I try to walk on the treadmill about every day, but there are some days I have to walk sideways, though I try not to show it. I do notice I spend a lot more time in the hot tub."

They all love football. Fiercely. Sometimes, football loves them back, and sometimes it doesn't, and what's that old saying? You always hurt the one you love . . .

"Aw, football is a part of me," says Stump Mitchell. "I wouldn't trade that part of my life for anything.

"See, the best part I got out of it was knowing that there wasn't anything I couldn't overcome. A man could go his whole life and never find that out, couldn't he?"

Why, yes. Yes, he surely could.

"Recently I was tossing a football around with a buddy who thought I was being a bit too frisky. He said, 'Come on, you're a has-been.' I thought about it and then retorted, 'Yeah, but that's better than a never-was.' I had a wonderful ride, I had a turn."

Todd Christensen, TE-FB 1979 New York Giants-Oakland; 1980-81 Oakland; 1982-88 LA Raiders

"The adjustment to deciding what to do each day, rather than having coaches make those decisions for me, was tough. I missed the adrenaline. I missed the guys, although when rookies started calling me 'Mr. Mecklenburg' I should have known my time had passed. It's been three years and twenty pounds since I last put on a helmet. I'm closer than ever to my wife and children. I can get right out of bed in the morning without a limp. I work when I want to, but usually I'm at home with my family. I loved football, and I know that I was fortunate to make a living doing something I loved. Now when I visit training camp, or stop by the Broncos training room, I can't believe that I put myself through that. It's a young man's game, and #77 has grown up."

Karl Mecklenburg, LB-DE 1983-94 Denver

"No one can discount the transitional dilemma that most players have faced upon retirement. The biggest gift we could ever give the active player of today would be the discipline to pursue their second career during the off-season, so that their self-esteem would not be so challenged upon retirement from the game. They would wake up the next morning, with a feeling of hope, direction, and most importantly, a feeling of belonging to something. 'A warrior heart—with no battle to fight'—we will always have the heart of a warrior, but we need to know who the enemy is going to be, before it's too late."

Chuck Detwiler, DB 1970-72 San Diego; 1973 St. Louis

"It was my last lick and I knew it. When I say I sold the ship, I mean it was a collision. I felt that tingling sensation. The next year I ended up getting into coaching and I had serious withdrawal. I'd go to the locker room really early in the morning on a game day, put a helmet on and just beat my head against the locker. I needed that hit. (Niners linebacker) 'Hacksaw' (Reynolds) would tell me I had one more left in me, one more shot to give. I told him, 'I'm going to save it.' I wish I could give it up Sunday for my players."

Ray Rhodes, DB-WR 1974-79 New York Giants; 1980 San Francisco
Prior to his final game as head coach of the Philadelphia Eagles
From an article by Phil Sheridan in the December, 1998 Philadelphia Inquirer

218

Cynthia Zordich

CLOTHESLINES AND YORKIES
The Tommy McDonald Story

The mailman stops to insert the day's delivery into the metal box on West Valley Forge Road in King of Prussia, Pennsylvania, just outside Philadelphia.

"I'm going up there," the visitor says, nodding toward the house at the top of a slight incline. "Be glad to take that."

"Sure, thanks," the mailman says. "Here."

"By the way," the visitor asks, "just to be safe, this is the McDonald residence, isn't it?"

And the mailman sits up just a little straighter and volunteers, in a voice rising with prideful emotion: "Sure is. Home of Tommy McDonald, Hall of Famer."

He pauses for effect.

"And my idol."

Halfway up the driveway, the visitor hears the mailman's parting line: "Nobody had hands like him, you know?"

The man who answers the door, the sixty-three-year-old one-time wide receiver with the peerless hands, has in those peerless hands a wriggling, inquisitive fur ball.

Tommy McDonald and Jingles, a six-year-old Yorkie with a cold nose and a warm heart, are a team, constant and inseparable.

The similarities are inescapable. Yorkies are yappers, wee and wiry, full of bark, jumping about this way and that, quivering with nervous energy, full of themselves, demanding to be noticed.

Tommy McDonald played football like a Yorkie.

"All my life," he agrees, "all I ever heard was, 'You're too small. You'll only get hurt.' Well, sir, I made that my fuel. That was what fed my engine. I'd show them."

And so he did. And with a mighty vengeance.

In the summer of 1998, Tommy McDonald became the smallest player ever inducted into the Professional Football Hall of Fame.

"There are some in there who are five-ten," he says.

He is five feet, nine inches.

The five pro teams he played for listed him at 175 pounds. They lied. Every one of them. By anywhere from eight to ten pounds. He might have been 166, tops.

He was a Yorkie among Saint Bernards. And the Saint Bernards made room for him.

He was fearless. He would run routes over the middle, smack into turf that belonged to the carnivores, the linebackers with their clothesline forearms, and the safeties who hit you like they had blackjacks. He would flit into that no-man's-land, bounding along up on the balls of his feet, and snag a spiral when some fang-tooth would bust him, and he'd drop like a man shot.

And he would always bounce right back up, like a yapping Yorkie, and trot back to the huddle.

"Ohhhh, but that'd make 'em mad," he says, smiling at the memory. "I made that my signature, that bouncing up, just to let 'em know they hadn't hurt me, that they weren't going to intimidate me."

He leans forward and makes a whispered confession: "But I'd get back to the huddle and I wouldn't be able to breathe. I'd always tell the quarterback: 'Take your time calling the next play, 'cause I'm dyin' here.' "

He played without a face mask. He was the last pro to do so.

"In those days, it was just a single bar, not that much protection, really, and it distracted me. I never did get my nose broken. But I did get four helmets broken. I was always blessed with good reflexes. I could see the hit coming and I'd turn my head. They'd get the helmet, but not me."

"(Dick) Butkus hit me in the neck one time, and I thought he'd killed me. And (Ray) Nitschke . . . some of the hits he gave me. He really put one on me this one game and right after the hit he said: 'Now let's see you bounce up from that one, you bleeping little runt.' "

"I always thought Ray's number was 99. But it was 66. I guess it was because every time I saw it, I was on the ground looking up at him."

He rummages among some framed photographs in the den. His voice grows soft, oddly, openly affectionate, as he talks about the middle linebacker of the Green Bay Packers who delivered such ferocious licks.

"Ray . . . I had really looked forward to seeing him when I went into the Hall of Fame. But he . . . he up and died on me . . . "

Ray Nitschke passed away just as winter was giving way to spring in 1998.

Tommy McDonald's eyes fill.

221

"Oh, gee, I didn't mean to do this. Get all emotional, I . . . It's just . . . "

He cannot finish. He weeps.

It is a poignant moment, a sixty-three-year-old man who was celebrated for his soft, sure hands, standing in the den of his home on an afternoon in April and mourning a fallen warrior, a cherished opponent, a man who had tried again and again to decapitate him.

Such is the power of the bonds that link the men who play the game, that link them to the game and to each other. Football consumes them and then it ties them to each other, and those ties are as certain and strong as umbilical cords.

Tommy McDonald dries his eyes and returns to his sofa, and Jingles leaps in a light, single bound, circles once, twice, nestles in beside him. He strokes her, clears his throat.

"So, the title of this book is going to be *When The Clock Runs Out?*"

That's the plan.

"You know what you ought to add at the end of that title?"

What's that?

"You ought to add 'tick . . . tick . . . tick . . .' "

Why?

"Because that clock," says the man with the peerless hands, "doesn't ever really run out. You think it will, but it doesn't."

You mean even now, thirty-two years removed from your last game, at the age of sixty-three, you still want to play football?

"You'd better believe it, brother. I'd love to be playing today . . . "

He smiles hugely.

222

"Especially the way they throw the ball today. They got guys catching eighty to ninety balls in a season. Imagine that."

But, Tommy, you haven't played since 1966. You're a grandfather. Surely the fire has turned to cold ashes by now.

His smile is one of patience and pity.

"Let me tell you something: The two worst days of my life were when they made us play after JFK was assassinated and when I had to leave the game. I never felt such an emptiness.

"I had this appetite for the game, for the competition, and one day somebody says to you: 'Thank you very much, but we have no further use for you.' I asked, 'Where did my twelve years go? How did it go so fast?' When you realize the curtain is coming down, you're scared. You get a fear you've never felt before. The thing that matters so much to you is being taken away, and there isn't a single blessed thing you can do about it."

"Sure, part of you is afraid of what's to come. I mean, now you have to get a real job. But what you're afraid of is how much you're going to miss it."

"This isn't like any other goodbye you'll ever say. People who never played can't understand it. This isn't something you can just turn off. It's not like closing a door."

Tommy McDonald rubs one of his peerless hands through his hair. Next to him, Jingles, on her back, snores softly. He rubs her belly.

He played his first seven seasons with the Eagles, then had one year with Dallas, two in Los Angeles, one in Atlanta, and the last one in Cleveland. When Tommy McDonald played, athletes, unlike other professionals in other lines of work, had no control over their jobs. Lawyers don't get traded. Bankers don't get traded. Doctors don't get traded. Football players do.

And at the whim of somebody else.

"First time I was traded, I was in shock. What did it mean, exactly, traded? To where? For what? I mean, who? No-trade clause? We didn't know what that was. And if you asked, you were a troublemaker. And the part that hurt the most was the first I heard about it was in my own car, on the radio.

"It never gets any easier each time you're traded," he says, frowning. "Who likes to be rejected? And then the day nobody wants you. The Falcons put me on waivers and nobody took me. I think that's when the reality of the situation hit me. When you're available to anyone who wants you, only no one wants you . . . "

Then the years roll back and you're the littlest kid all over again, the scrawniest one, the last one picked when the bigger, older ones choose sides. The unwanted one.

"When I cleared waivers, I thought that was the end. But then Gary Collins got hurt in Cleveland and the Browns needed a receiver. I was grateful for the chance, but I knew it was only one of those . . . what do you call it when the governor calls at midnight?"

Stay of execution?

He snaps his fingers.

"That's it. I knew that was going to be the last year and I'd better get on with my life."

And yet, even after he had made that concession and that confession, when training camp rolled around the next year, he found himself looking at the telephone.

"Vince Lombardi had left Green Bay and was coaching in Washington," he says. "I had been in awe of him and my dream was to play for him. I had heard that he had said, 'You give me eleven Tommy McDonalds and I'd win the championship every year.' So there I am, my first year of retirement from football, and I'm wanting to pick up the phone and call Vince Lombardi.

"I had it all rehearsed. I would ask for a tryout as a walk-on. I would tell him I wanted to try playing defensive back. I had always been a good tackler. I'd tell him all I wanted was a chance to show what I had, what I could do.

"I never made the call, though. I could never work up the nerve to pick up that phone."

He sighs. But it is not a plaintive sigh, not a regret of what might have been. It is a sigh of gratitude.

"Maybe a part of me was trying to save me from myself."

———————————

Roy.

It's a town, not a person. Tucked in the northeast corner of New Mexico, there were barely three hundred souls living in Roy in the summer of 1934, when Tommy McDonald was born.

"It was a little bitty farming town. We raised some wheat, some corn, fattened some cattle. My dad read books and from them learned how to be an electrician. He opened a small shop but there wasn't enough business to support us. So we moved to Albuquerque, just before my junior year in high school."

Tommy McDonald's voice, all these years later, still has echoes of Roy in it, a faint, dusty drawl that suggests sagebrush and adobe, wide open spaces and a sky without end.

"It seems like the Big Guy in the Sky is always looking out for me," he says. "Always putting me in the right place at the right time. If we hadn't moved to Albuquerque, nobody from any college would ever have seen me play football."

He scored twenty-six touchdowns his senior season, as a little bitty single wing running back who was quicker than a jackrabbit. In the state track meet, he won the 100. And the 220. And the 180-yard low hurdles. And he got two more gold medals as a member of the 440-meter and 880-meter relay teams.

His track accomplishments made Bud Wilkinson perk up his ears. Wilkinson doted on speed. He was the head football coach at Oklahoma University who put together a juggernaut that still has not seen its equal.

In his four years at Oklahoma, Tommy McDonald never knew what it was like to play in a losing game. The Sooners won forty-seven in a row! Yet the prospect of unequaled success in football is not what persuaded McDonald to go to Oklahoma.

"Bud Wilkinson told me: 'Don't come here for the football. Come here for the education. You're gonna spend more of your life without a football than you are running with one.' That sold me."

In his senior year, in 1956, McDonald received the most first place votes in the Heisman Trophy balloting, but finished third overall behind the winner, Paul Hornung of Notre Dame, and the runner-up, Johnny Majors of Tennessee. (When the Pro Football Hall of Fame asked its members for nominees from among those players who had been previously passed over, the most ringing endorsement of McDonald was given by Hornung.)

The Eagles drafted Tommy McDonald, in the third round. He asked for $12,000 and held his breath. He also asked for a signing bonus of $1,000. He was astonished to receive both. He used the bonus to make a down payment on a car.

A station wagon.

Why not a babe car?

"Because I was married."

And so he was, to Miss Oklahoma of 1955.

He and the former Ann Campbell had met in college. They wed in January of 1957. She got a job as a secretary while her husband played football.

Their marriage lasted two years. There were no children.

"We decided it just wasn't working out for either one of us," he says. "We parted on friendly terms."

His first time in Philadelphia he came to collect the Maxwell Trophy, and he went to a travel agency in the center of the city to arrange for a flight back home. As soon as he walked in the door, a woman stood and pointed at him and screamed:

"It's HIM! It's the Kissing Bandit!"

He thought maybe it was a practical joke. But the police were there in an instant, snapping the cuffs on the little jackrabbit from Oklahoma.

"There had been a series of robberies of ticket agencies in town," he says, grinning at the memory, "and every time the robber was about to make his getaway he'd give one of the women a kiss. The papers were full of Kissing Bandit stories. Personally, I never thought I resembled him all that much, but that woman sure thought I did.

"The cops are telling me to spread-eagle and I'm nodding my head up and down and saying: 'Yeah, the Eagles, I'm gonna play for the Eagles.' And they're looking at me, you know, all five-nine of me, and one says: 'Yeah, and I'm gonna fly.'

"The Eagles' offices were only about a block away and I'm pleading with them to call Vince McNally, who was the general manager. They finally do and he hustles down and verifies who I am, and then he really chews them out. Later, I got a letter of apology from the mayor."

His first five weeks as a professional, Tommy McDonald mostly sat. And stewed. The Eagles were well-stocked at running back. But in the sixth game of the 1957 season, on November 24, playing against the Washington Redskins, the Eagles ran out of receivers. Tommy McDonald ran into the huddle. The quarterback was Sonny Jurgensen, a raspy-voiced gunslinger with a short temper and a knack for winning football games. He looked at the new guy, the little Yorkie receiver, and told him: "Take off and I'll hit you."

So much for complex strategy.

Of course Tommy McDonald remembers every stride: "The ball was underthrown but I came back for it and got position and jumped up for it and I ran 'til I got to the end zone."

Sixty-one yards in all. Touchdown.

Later in that game, he scored another one.

"Charley Gauer, he was our offensive coordinator, he said: 'You know, kid, I think maybe we found a position for you.' "

They loved him in Philly. They loved his yapping Yorkie courage and bravery, the way he cut off his sleeves and ran around in swirling snow bare-armed. All over town, kids took scissors to their jerseys to imitate him. They practiced jumping up after getting hit.

"What nobody knew," he says, "was that I cut sleeves so I could get a little more reach. Long sleeves bind you. I needed all the help I could get. Cut the sleeves, you got maybe an extra inch of reach."

In the 1958 season, he played six games with a broken jaw. The first game after he broke it, with everything wired shut, he scored four touchdowns.

"They told me they were gonna break it every year."

In the 1959 season, he dove for a ball and separated his shoulder. He came back to the huddle wincing and rubbing his arm.

"I've done something bad to my shoulder," he said in the huddle.

Van Brocklin looked at him and snarled: "Shut the bleep up and catch the bleeping ball!"

He did.

He played the final four games of the season with a separated shoulder.

"They'd shoot me up . . . you know, Novocain."

He looks alarmed.

"Maybe we shouldn't say that . . . "

Relax, Tommy. Surely the statute of limitations has run out on that by now.

He caught almost five hundred balls in all, for nearly nine thousand yards. He scored eighty-four touchdowns, which is remarkable for anyone, but even more extraordinary for a Yorkie mixing it up with all those Saint Bernards.

The statistic he is proudest of, though, is this: Out of a possible 155 games in his twelve-year professional career, he missed only three—two with a torn hamstring, one with a kneecap swollen beyond belief.

Too small? Hah!

Along the way he met an Irish lass named Patricia Ann Gallagher.

"Blind date. Guy tells me: 'This girl is so beautiful, your teeth will hurt.' He was right."

Yes, he was. Pictures on one wall of their den are a testimony to that. She is a willowy blonde with a bouffant hair-do, he a Yorkie with a buzz cut. Beauty and the jackrabbit. They are in a convertible. Their smiles could light up the night sky for a grand opening. They look incredibly happy.

They ran off and got married on September 15, 1962. It was a Saturday. The very next day, Tommy McDonald and the Eagles played the St. Louis Cardinals in Philadelphia.

Tommy and Patty have four children, two sons and two daughters, and five grandchildren. None of them live farther apart from their parents than twenty-one miles. Tommy and Patty live in the first house they bought, in April of 1963.

"To this day," she says, "there are people who are introduced to me, and the first thing they say is: 'Oh, you were Miss Oklahoma.' And I have to explain to them that, no, I'm not. And then they say: 'Oh, well are those Miss Oklahoma's children?' And I always say: 'Well, they sure felt like mine when I was having them.' "

She laughs easily and frequently. If there is any bitterness, she learned how to bury it long ago. The newest grandchild has arrived just three days ago. She has just returned from holding her, and she is aglow.

"We never talked football," Tommy says. "She never mentioned the games. Patty's a private person. She always let me dig a hole for myself and she would always say that when the dirt started to fall in on me she'd be there to dig me out. Even after all these years, I'm still finding out new things about her."

She smiles at that, pleased. "You support each other, but you have to have your own identity, too," she says.

On one of their den walls is the cover of a *Sports Illustrated* magazine dated October 8, 1962. The headline is: "Football's Best Hands." Tommy McDonald is reaching for the ball, both arms outstretched in the classic pose. But it is not the standard sports photograph. Rather, it is an artist's watercolor, done in swirls and curlicues of green.

"The man who painted that is eighty-three and still working," he says. "I called him when I saw the cover and asked if there was any way I could get the painting. He sent it to me."

It hangs on the wall at the other end of the den. It is a symbol of Tommy McDonald's passage.

That painting so stirred him that he began a portrait business while he was still playing football. He employs six artists. Their work includes every Heisman winner and thousands of athletes, celebrities, and judges.

"It helped keep me around football, and I needed something that would. I had to be weaned off the game. I couldn't just quit cold turkey. I still play racquetball, mostly because I need something that will burn off the fire. I still want to compete so bad . . . "

He appears to have survived all those hits and all those bounce-ups with astonishingly good health.

"Only time my body tells me I ever played the game is when I first get up in the morning. When I'm out of the bed, I have to take baby steps most of the way across the room."

He rises from the sofa and does a shuffling little gait, almost a soft-shoe right out of vaudeville. Jingles lifts her head and observes this with the canine version of a big smile.

He returns to the sofa, still quick and nimble.

"Gee, every time I read an article about a player retiring, I think to myself, 'Boy am I glad I don't have to go through that again.' "

But aren't you still going through it?

Tommy McDonald scratches Jingles behind the ear and thinks about that.

"You know, that's true. It never really does end. You think it goes away, but it doesn't. You get traded, you retire, it's adios, we don't need you any more. But the thing is, it may not need you, but you need it. So you deal with that the best you can."

The man with the peerless hands seems to be doing exactly that.

Cynthia Zordich

*"My high school coach once said,
'Stick your foot in a bucket of water,
then take it out. The hole that's left
is how much you'll be missed.' "*

Todd Christensen

BRAIN SURGEONS AND LONG SNAPPERS
The Todd Christensen Story

Is there a more thankless job in all of sports than that of the snapper?

The position itself fairly reeks of submission. Legs splayed, head down, the snapper is helpless to defend himself, as vulnerable as a turtle flipped onto its back.

He looks at the world upside down and backward. He is a human croquet wicket. He is expected to rifle an accurate spiral back to the punter or the holder while blocking out the indignities that are about to be visited upon his body.

And, of course, he is accorded no mercy at all.

"Everyone wants to tee off on you," says Todd Christensen. He laughs. It is the laugh of a survivor.

He laughs because he is an ex-snapper now, because he snapped and lived to tell about it, because he started out playing that specialized, sadistic position at a height of six-feet-three and three-fourths inches and left the game at the same height. No small feat, considering how the opponents like to stomp the grape-breaking, wine-making tango on your vertebrae.

"If they can't block the punt or the kick, they figure they can at least beat up on you, and maybe make you flinch just enough the next time to put one over the kicker's head," Christensen says.

In his eleven years in the National Football League, a career that was almost four times as long as the average, the fiercest lick he ever took was on a punt.

Todd Christensen and the Raiders were playing the Houston Oilers, and Ray Guy, the Raiders' Cannon Leg, hit a rare bad one, a sideways shank. Todd Christensen shot up out of his snapper's stance and angled toward the ball. He knew he was likely to be needed on the tackle, and so was concentrating on getting to the ball, to the exclusion of all else.

Which meant he was set up for a blindside.

"Adger Armstrong," he says, identifying the culprit, slowly drawing out the name of the perpetrator the way a man will do when he is recreating a wreck and wants to get the details just right.

Adger Armstrong might as well have been equipped with crosshairs on his helmet. Christensen never saw him coming.

"I'm taking my time here because I don't want to exaggerate," he says, "but I know for certain that I went at least four yards up in the air. It was one of those hits that they show in the film room the next day and they keep running it back and guys are whooping and yelling: 'Show it again . . . show it again.'

"They kept showing it and showing it . . . they must have showed that hit at least a dozen times. I know when I came down, I tried to get up and my legs wouldn't work. I was only about eight, maybe ten yards away from our bench, so I crawled to it on my hands and knees, like a dog that had been hit by a truck.

"Guys on the sidelines are screaming at me, 'Get up. Don't let 'em know they hurt you. Get up . . . get up!' And I'm mad and yelling back at them: 'I'm trying to . . . I'm trying to . . . but my legs won't work.'

"This was very early in my career and I remember thinking at the time, I can't afford to get hurt, I haven't proved myself, I haven't proved to anybody that they need me."

Remarkably, nothing was broken.

"Sometimes," he says, appreciative of the irony, "you break something and never know it 'til a long time later. I remember running a pattern over the middle and Randy Gradishar was the linebacker in the area and he saw it coming and I'm thinking: 'Please don't throw it high.' And of course it was high and I went up to get it and he helmeted my ribs and they took me to the locker room and I said I was sure some ribs were broken.

"So they took the X-rays and they said: 'No, nothing broken here. But those other two breaks have healed nicely.' And I'm like, what other breaks? I didn't know I'd broken anything . . . you know, you'd just wrap it tight and keep playing. I never figured I could afford the luxury of any time off. I might not have a job when I came back."

When you do come back, there is always the possibility of another titanic hit. And there is the possibility of something hurting that never hurt before.

"We played Cleveland later in my career and I ran a tight-end seam pattern and Ray Bolton of the Browns really clocked me. Of all the strange sensations, of all the things to hurt, my rear end went numb. Completely dead. I mean, I had no feeling at all back there, and I've never experienced anything like that before or since, and I was panicking.

"The trainer hustles out and I'm screaming: 'I can't feel my ass! Do something!' So he gets some analgesic balm and a couple of guys form a circle around me so no one can see what's going on and he's shoving handfuls of this balm down my pants. It kicked in then, like an army of fire ants, and I jumped up and said: 'OK, thank you very much, let's go play some football now.' "

Like the rest of them, he tells his war stories with obvious relish. It is what bonds them, one generation to another, like veterans of combat. The game may change slightly over the years, technology may improve, but the essence of football is eternal. The collisions, viewed from a distance, are recalled with a certain reverence, and almost always retold with humor.

At the moment, Todd Christensen is reviewing his collisions amidst some breathtaking scenery. Winter mist shrouds the Wassach Mountains. February in Utah can stir primal feelings in you. Each inhale is pure and sharp. He lives with his wife, Kathy, and their four sons in Alpine, thirty-five miles southeast of Salt Lake City and several light years removed from the smog and clutter and gridlock of alleged civilization.

A thoughtful man, given to curiosity and intellectual exploration, he sprinkles the words of Emerson and Thoreau and Shakespeare in his conversation. It is not lost on him that the mountain home with the warming fire and the spectacular view is all made possible by a game. Rather than shrink from that thought, he embraces it.

"Everything good that has come my way did so because for eleven years I caught passes, and I was privileged to do so in a very select fraternity. Football has my undying gratitude. I'm not one of those guys who says that football didn't define him. The heck it didn't!

"Thoreau speaks of man seeking always not for something to do but something to be. We all want to find something that defines us. Well, I did, and it involved a football. And I think that's why those of us who play it for a living have such a difficult and painful time separating ourselves from it.

"Look, at last count there were 3,580 accredited brain surgeons in this country. There are, what, 1,600 in the NFL. What boy grows up wanting to be a brain surgeon?"

The question hangs in the air, like an icicle.

He laughs now, to soften what he is about to say.

"If it hadn't been for the streak of antisocial behavior I inherited from my father and the super-competitiveness I inherited from my mother, I wouldn't have been much of a football player. If I had been a brain surgeon instead, I might have done society some good."

But Dick Butkus, who remains to many of us the quintessential middle linebacker, has always said that each of us is born for a purpose. And for a few, that purpose is to play football.

"I don't shy from that philosophy at all," Todd Christensen says.

And then he cuts to the heart of why football's hold can be as abiding as the tug of the umbilical cord.

"Where else do you spend six days preparing and then for three hours you pour yourself out? And then you resurrect yourself. There is absolutely no way to replace that."

"See, it's not the money, it's not the crowds, it's not the fame. In fact, as you spend more and more time in the game, it's not even the winning and the losing. At the end, the losing didn't bother me nearly as much as it did earlier. I was still playing and that's all that mattered."

"The game is all."

Eventually, of course, it will be taken away from you.

"Yes, we know that," he says, measuring the words, "and what haunts you is the knowledge that no matter what you do, you're never going to be as good as you were in any other endeavor."

He falls silent.

So silent you swear you can hear the snow falling on the mountains.

The trainer for the Penn State wrestling team delivered him into the world.

This occurred in the summer of 1956. Ned and June Christensen were living in Belfont, Pennsylvania, at the time. It was a small town—a village, really—near State College.

"There wasn't a hospital close by, so the trainer did the honors," he says, "and right from the beginning it was like I was destined for the locker room. My father is five-nine and my mother five-five. I tell them I was their mutant child. But I am eternally grateful for whatever DNA it was that put me past six-three."

When he was four, he was introduced to the game that would eventually consume him. His brother Merrill, who was three years older, handed him a well-worn football in the front yard and gave him his very first instruction: Tackle the guy with the ball.

Dutifully, Todd Christensen bent, snapped the ball back to his brother out of the shotgun formation, and turned around and promptly tackled him.

"I could only get better, after a start like that."

He did, of course. And quickly. His family moved to West Virginia and then to Eugene, Oregon, where track and field is a passion, and in an all-comers meet, at the age of six, Todd Christensen ran sixty meters in 9.2 seconds, and took home a trophy.

"We're all desperate for validation," he says, "and that experience awakened something within me. I can still remember being in Miss Woodson's second grade class. I was eight and she asked us to write what we'd like to grow up to be, and I put down SPORTS! in huge letters. Miss Woodson suggested, diplomatically, that perhaps I might want to consider aiming just a bit higher.

"But I was hooked. I'd go down to Country Lane Park and put a football under my arm and I was Jim Brown. I'd punt and kick field goals. We'd play and for some reason—perhaps lack of brains—I wasn't afraid to lower my head and ram straight ahead, even against bigger, older kids. I don't know where it came from but I was pretty fearless, to the point that the rest of them would say, 'OK, Todd can play but he can't run with the ball.' "

By the time he was fourteen, his trophy was gone, having been swallowed by flames. Unattended candles had set curtains on fire, and on Christmas Eve half of the Christensen's house burned to the ground. No one was hurt, and the family, having little use for material possessions, never regarded it as that much of a tragedy. Besides, the TV set was still intact. It was an old black and white, and while his mother forbade him to watch it on Sunday, he would sneak peeks in autumn afternoons. It was then that he first saw black helmets with NY inscribed on them. He was mesmerized by Y. A. Tittle and Alex Webster and the other Giants.

Impatient for genetics to kick in, he yearned for a way to flesh out his seventy-pound body and persuaded his parents to invest in a set of weights, crude but serviceable barbells and dumbbells, made of water and sand and covered with hard plastic. His body responded and it set a pattern, a regimen, that is still unbroken. Thirty years later, he works out every day, and it shows.

He and the neighborhood kids held backyard decathlons, a sawdust pit behind one house, a pole vault pit behind another. By high school, he was good but not great. He was All-District but not All-State as a running back. He was a bulked-up point guard on the basketball team. He hit home runs but struck out far too often. He never stopped training, though he did so in a time before lifting and running were fashionable. He was, literally, a self-made athlete. Had he not spent all that time training, he says, there is not the slightest doubt in his mind that he never would have played in the NFL.

He found out just how unexceptional he was perceived to be when his father received a phone call from Provo, Utah. Lavell Edwards, the new head football coach at Brigham Young University, said: "Bishop Christensen, I understand you have a football player in your house." When Todd Christensen arrived at the BYU campus, Lavell Edwards told him: "We've looked at films of you, and frankly we're not all that impressed."

Christensen, seventeen and full of himself, was offended and determined not to go to BYU. He visited other campuses. Nothing felt right. BYU called with an offer. The Cougars were allotted thirty scholarships and they were offering Todd Christensen the thirtieth one. His mother told the family: "Let us drop to our knees and offer a prayer of thanks and gratitude."

"And me, I was like, what do you mean, grateful?" he says, laughing. "They made it sound like charity. But of course I accepted it."

He went to BYU as the seventh-string fullback. But then, in a burst of stunning good fortune for him and calamity for the six ahead of him, the other fullbacks were visited by injury, and on opening day Todd Christensen found himself starting, against Hawaii. He even scored a touchdown.

During his stay at BYU, from 1974 to 1978, the school's fabled passing attack was born. Todd Christensen didn't get to run all that often, but there was compensation—he became an accomplished pass receiver. He played in two postseason all-star games after his senior year and caught ten balls and was named MVP in the Blue-Gray game. He scored the winning touchdown with an up-and-over drive in the Senior Bowl and so impressed his running backs coach, Joe Gibbs, that Gibbs was moved to tell him: "I think your future is on special teams."

It occurred to him that he was underwhelming talent scouts at every turn.

At that time, most teams did their own individual scouting or used combines. The mass meat market of today, the come-one-come-all tryouts, hadn't yet come into fashion. Todd Christensen shrewdly knew he would need any edge he could create for himself to offset his lack of the natural blessings, such as foot speed.

He bought a pair of souped-up track shoes, and when the first team (the Green Bay Packers) came to scout him, he ran on an indoor track, changed to those shoes on the sly, and asked to start standing up rather than in the conventional stance. (His explanation: "Your first movement starts the stopwatch and if the first movement is your hand flying up, then you're on the clock before you've ever taken a single step. Starting from standing up, I was already ahead.")

His feet should have worked as swiftly as his brain.

He ran the forty, to the astonishment of the Packers, in 4.51 seconds. Then he shaved three-tenths off that. The Dallas Cowboys, who at that time put heavy stock in certain tests, rated him the best athlete in the draft. Not the best football player, but the best athlete. They were the defending Super Bowl champions. They drafted him with the last selection of the second round.

His rookie season ended before it began. In the last preseason game, against the Pittsburgh Steelers, he was playing fullback and was tackled by Jack Lambert. His right foot caught in the turf. The turf gave. His foot didn't. The fracture left him on crutches, and he passed away the boredom of the entire regular season by becoming a weight room fanatic. He vented his frustration by pumping. Thomas (Hollywood) Henderson took to calling him "Todd-Zilla."

Tom Landry, the coach, was not as impressed as Henderson. Todd Christensen returned for the 1979 season, played in the Hall of Fame game and then didn't play again in the preseason, and was cut. He was picked up by the Giants almost immediately, however, and the owner, Wellington Mara, came up to him in the locker room and told him exuberantly: "You're going to help us."

Mara apparently was in the minority, because shortly afterward, when Todd Christensen returned to his hotel room near the Meadowlands, the message light was flashing in his room. Ray Perkins, then the Giants coach, had called to cut him.

"By this point," he says, "my self-confidence was nonexistent. I was getting rejected at every turn."

The rejections were only beginning. Some of them he brought on himself.

The New England Patriots called. "I asked them were they going to bring me in because they were interested or just because one of their players got hurt."

He snorts.

"It made no sense, my attitude. I should have been elated that teams were calling."

The Chicago Bears were next. He turned them off, too. The Philadelphia Eagles flew him in. He tried to compensate for his earlier brashness with extra confidence ("I can do anything athletic!"), but it was misinterpreted as cockiness. He flew back to Dallas.

The Packers were next. He went to Green Bay but Bart Starr, the coach at the time and a fiercely loyal man, couldn't bring himself to cut any of his players to make room.

Back to Dallas. Back to his wife and growing family. He and Kathleen had met at BYU, when they were introduced by her brother. Almost immediately after they met, she went to Jerusalem for six months. A long separation is almost always the end of it. But not for them. They wrote. On the Fourth of July, 1976, they had their first kiss. There were, he says, fireworks in every sense. They married two days after he played his last college game.

By now, it seemed that only his wife wanted him. He told her that maybe he'd better go back to college, to grad school, and then the following year make the rounds to the remaining teams that hadn't rejected him. But there would be one more call, and from a most unlikely source.

The Oakland Raiders.

He sat on the grass with Al Davis and they talked for half an hour.

"They actually cut a guy to make room for me," he remembers. "Talk about bolstering your ego. After all that rejection, someone finally wanted me."

On the surface, at least, it looked like an odd coupling. The Raiders were well-known then as a haven for cast-offs and rejects and retreads, the hole-in-the-wall gang of the NFL. How would a Mormon fit in with this assemblage of renegades and outlaws?

Quite nicely, as it would turn out. Before his football career was over, he would win two Super Bowls, lead the league in receptions, make All-Pro, and pave the way for a post-football career in broadcasting. He agreed to a staring salary of $42,000 a year, which was the same starting salary called for in his contract with the Cowboys, and he took up temporary residence in a hotel room, at $275 a month.

"All the Raiders cared about was what you did on the field," he says. "They didn't want robots. That was fine with me because I had never been a conformist. They encouraged individualism. The only question they ever asked about a guy was: 'Can he play?'"

When his career ended, Todd Christensen first joined NBC-TV as the color analyst, from 1990 through 1994, and then went to ESPN.

"My departure from the game was ignominious," he says, a sharp edge of lingering regret in his voice. "I'd had gall bladder surgery and lost a lot of weight. I was the second-to-last cut before the eighty-nine season."

Leaving the game wasn't his idea, but he jumped with a golden parachute billowing behind him—money in the bank, all limbs reasonably intact, TV beckoning. There was no emotional trauma that first year away from the game.

"I thought, hey, what's the big deal with this retirement stuff?"

And then another season rolled around and he was seized by an urge that sent him rushing to the phone.

"I remember when Marcus Allen kept coming back season after season and they'd ask him why and he'd say because I only want to leave when the tank is empty. Well, I felt I still had something in my tank. I thought, I should have called Bill Walsh or Joe Gibbs. So then, every year after I'd retired I was calling teams. Now, how pathetic is that?"

He has another confession:

"Just a little over three years ago, I was running pass patterns trying to impress the Anaheim Piranhas of the Arena Football League. I'm thirty-nine years old, catching passes in a driving rainstorm, from the coach, who is Babe Parilli and who is sixty-five."

He relates this somewhat sheepishly, but there are also traces of pride. He is a little embarrassed by his addiction, but a little proud, too.

"I'll tell you an even funnier one," he says. "Just yesterday I got out my track shoes and had my son time me. I did a four-six-three."

The snow falls on the mountains, and Todd Christensen still runs pass routes.

"And even now," he admits, "when I go out and catch the ball, it's so pleasurable, so aesthetically pleasing, the feel of the ball. I catch a pass and go: 'Ohhhhhh . . .' "

Cynthia Zordich

"During the ten years of my career it was interesting and painful to see how many of my teammates stayed too long. It was either a case of getting benched, traded, cut or injured. There is, even now, much bitterness among these guys because of what happened. It was apparent watching these situations being played out, that my teammates couldn't walk away gracefully. In my situation , it fortunately had a happy ending. I remember clearly the next year [after I quit] when training camp opened, being at Dewey Beach, with my family, with the temperature being in the high nineties and feeling like a genius for having made the decision to leave. We continued living in Maryland for another five years after retirement and never went to a Colts game. There was closure and no reason to get back into that world. I feel extremely fortunate to have had that opportunity. We were one of the finest teams of that era. There are seasons in a person's life. It is apparently hard for most to leave the arenas where they found fame and adulation. There is, however, the voice of reason that says it is time to go to the next season."

Bob Vogel, OT 1963-72 Baltimore

"We're blessed with the opportunity to live our dreams and not many people get to do that. Problem is in the NFL you don't do much to prepare for when you wake up from that dream. For as we play, my feeling is that we have to prepare not to play."

Mike Quick, WR 1982-90 Philadelphia

"I don't want to be in this book."

Michael Zordich, SS 1987 New York Jets; 1987-88 New York Jets; 1989-93 Phoenix; 1994-98 Philadelphia

248

Cynthia Zordich

HANDS OF THE HAWK
The Larry Wilson Story

First, Larry Wilson busted up his right hand.

He clawed at a ball carrier to bring him down and got his hand stuck in the man's head gear. Larry Wilson yanked and pulled, but he was caught as sure as a wild critter locked in a trap. The other man twisted and heaved around, and pretty soon there was this sound, like someone cracking walnuts.

Only they were the bones in Larry Wilson's right hand.

Somehow, he didn't scream.

"But I do believe I may have shouted out a couple of bad words," he says.

Then, Larry Wilson busted up his left hand. He was on the ground, at the bottom of one of those grunting, snarling piles after the play had ended but the biting and pinching and cursing had not. Someone—he couldn't tell who exactly, what with half of a building on top of him—-saw his hand just lying there, so inviting, and they stepped on it, deliberately it seemed, and then ground their cleats in for good measure, like you'd step on a cigarette to grind it out.

This time, Larry Wilson's bones sounded like someone chopping kindling.

"I believe I did make a noise I'd never heard before," he says.

That was in a game in 1965 against the New York Giants. The next Sunday, Larry Wilson and the St. Louis Cardinals were to play the Pittsburgh Steelers. He played.

With casts on both hands.

And he intercepted a pass.

He earned himself a place in football lore forevermore. Larry Wilson: The man who played an entire game with broken hands and got a pick! Can you believe it? He already had the reputation as one of the true tough guys of the National Football League and now there was a story that would last long after he was gone. Even now, when the talk turns to daring deeds and great physical feats, Larry Wilson and his two broken hands are the objects of extravagant, boisterous toasting.

The man himself draws on a smoke and exhales a small blue plume and a chuckle. He has watched, bemused, as over the years the story has been embellished with each elaborate retelling. As is frequently the case with war stories, it is difficult now to determine exactly where the legend ends and the man himself begins.

"Every year it would grow a little bit more," he says, laughing. "Pretty soon they had me playing with two broken arms. One day, they're liable to have me in a full body cast."

Still, the truth doesn't diminish the deed.

"What actually happened was, I broke the middle fingers of both hands, and everyone thought that was pretty hilarious," he recalls. "Then I'd messed up some of the other fingers pretty good, bent them and stretched them, so they used wires and pins and connectors and I don't know what-all, and they got everything pretty well tied down. And I went

250

out and played, and Bill Nelsen, who was the Steelers quarterback then, was kind enough to throw me a pass, for which I have been eternally grateful."

He got the pick with his left hand and had to make a nifty little move to get to the ball. Then he began to run with it.

"I should have scored a touchdown," he says. "I should have run it back all the way."

But there was a cluster of Steelers waiting to intercept him. And Larry Wilson, being one of those players who would prefer to run through you than around you, squared his shoulders, lowered his head to battering-ram level, wrapped both those busted mitts around the ball, and leaned forward, bracing for the collision.

Only there wasn't one.

Somehow, he shot right through the knot of would-be tacklers, untouched.

And then he promptly fell down.

"I was leaning too far forward and I was all set to get hit, and when I didn't I just kind of fell over," he says.

Face-first?

"Pretty much."

He lights another smoke and pokes fun at himself.

"Not a very heroic ending, it is?"

Nor was there sympathy to be found on his own sidelines.

"Oh, they really got on me, my teammates. They said it looked like I'd tripped over the chalk stripe. Asked me to teach them some of that fancy footwork."

It was the defining play of a sturdy career lasting a dozen years, all of them with the same team. He was one of the best safeties ever, one of those players who performs way beyond

251

his natural gifts. He seemed to be equipped with a radar in his helmet, tracking the ball in flight, sensing where it would be coming down.

Ball-hawking, they called it.

Larry Wilson just seemed to know what pattern you were going to run and where the ball was going even before it was snapped. It had nothing to do with foot speed or reflexes or even instinct. It had everything to do with studying, watching film, watching flickering images on a grainy screen until your eyes blur and tear and you stumble out of the room into the sunlight blinking like an owl at high noon.

He would study the film over and over, looking for patterns of predictability and situational tendencies. He loved the preparation. But then there wasn't anything about football that he didn't love, even the boring and the routine, the stuff that other players detested.

"For me, it's the perfect game," he says. "Football was fun. I enjoyed practice, I enjoyed the running and the hitting, I guess because it was a way of proving yourself. I liked to get after people, mix it up.

"And it was a chess match back there, trying to see how they would snooker you, what kind of traps they'd be setting for you. I needed every little edge I could get. I wasn't bigger than hardly anyone else, and the ones that weren't as large sure were a helluva lot faster."

He claimed to be six feet tall.

"Maybe just a whisker over," he says.

Uh-huh.

And 185 pounds.

Yeah, right. With an anvil in each pocket, maybe.

But he hit like he was big. He would stick his helmet into a gizzard and explode like a hand grenade. In an open field, he would hang on and get bounced along like a rodeo cowboy trying to wrestle the steer to the ground. When he got a hand on you, he didn't let go. He stuck like a cocklebur sticks to dog fur.

And he could jump. He could jump halfway to the moon. No one could figure out the source of all that s-p-r-o-i-n-g-g-g-g, but it became obvious you couldn't get the ball over his head. Maybe that jump came from all that squatting he did as a kid working in the potato fields.

Larry Wilson was born on March 3, 1938, in Rigby, Idaho, near Pocatello and Idaho Falls. Population about three thousand. Not the roof of the world, but up there in the eaves, all right. Big Sky country. A man can turn around and not bump into anything.

His mother died of spinal meningitis when he was only ten. His father was a drayman.

"That means he drove a wagon and delivered stuff," says Larry Wilson. "Later, he drove a truck for Utah Power and Light."

There is a note of pride in his voice. His father did hard, honest labor and was proud of it. He passed the same values along to Larry and his younger son, John. A man was judged by the strength of his back, the strength of his word, and the strength of his convictions.

School would be interrupted, and so would the high school football season, for a few weeks in the autumn for the potato harvest. More hard, honest labor. Everyone took part.

"You'd start out the day bending over," Larry Wilson remembers, "but pretty soon you'd be squatting, and by the end of the day you were pretty much down on your hands and knees."

You'd plunge your hands into the ground and pull out the potatoes and drop them in a basket, and when the basket was full you would empty it into a gunny, or burlap, sack. A sack would hold anywhere from sixty to eighty pounds.

"You'd get three cents a sack," he says. "Sometimes four.

"Everyone paired up, and it was important to get yourself hooked up with a good partner. You wanted to be with someone who'd dig like a dog going after a bone he'd buried."

Given his work ethic, it seems safe to assume that Larry Wilson was a good potato-picking partner.

"Damn right I was!" he responds. "We whipped right through them spuds. What you learned was that the harder you worked the more money you could make. That was a darn good lesson. Still is, for that matter."

He had three friends and they all lived within a block of each other. Next door to the house in which Larry Wilson lived was a vacant lot. They were always there, the four of them. A "Field of Dreams," in Rigby, Idaho.

"The fire department would sound a siren at nine o'clock every night, and you knew you had to be home. Either that, or get a good whipping. Nobody had a car. It was pretty hard to get into any trouble."

There was a backboard in that vacant lot, and for a long time Larry Wilson thought his sporting future lay in basketball. He also played football and softball and ran track. He was especially adept at the hurdles and the high jump—it turned out that those potato-picker legs could produce some serious hang time.

Because he was good enough at just about every sport, colleges came calling. He accepted a football scholarship from the University of Utah. The decision was not his.

"My father liked what the coaches told him—they said they guaranteed I'd be going to class and that I'd get a degree. That was important to him. He wanted me to have it better than he had."

He wanted a future for his son that would stretch beyond the potato fields.

Larry Wilson played both ways, running back and defensive back, and he was good, but there was no inkling of just how good he was going to be. The professional scouts liked his durability and the way the ball always seemed to be near him, and vice-versa. In the 1960 draft, he was chosen by two teams—the Cardinals and the Buffalo Bills, who were of the rival American Football Conference.

254

Larry Wilson settled on the Cardinals for one reason: money.

"They gave me $500, which was $500 more than the Bills offered. But it turned out that it wasn't any sort of signing bonus. It was an advance on my salary."

His salary for the 1960 season was $7,500.

When you're not that many years removed from the three cents a bag of spud-picking, $7,500 looks big.

"More money than I could visualize at the time," he agrees.

He reported to training camp, intending to be a running back for the Cardinals. But the team was locked in a contract dispute with the legendary defensive back Dick (Night Train) Lane, whom they would finally end up trading to Detroit.

"I got switched to defense and started at cornerback," Larry Wilson remembers, "and the very first preseason game we played the Baltimore Colts and I look up and staring back at me is the great Raymond Berry. Well sir, the first pass of the game went to him and it was for a touchdown. The second pass to him, I finally pulled him down at the two-yard line. And then they stopped passing for a while, so I got run over by Alan Ameche. The Cardinals had seen enough by then. They moved Jimmy Hill from safety to corner and put me at safety.

"Then we have our last preseason game and it's at San Francisco. I packed my bags and brought them with me. I mean, I packed everything I owned because I figured after that showing against the Colts I'd be cut, and this way at least I wouldn't have to fly all the way back to St. Louis to get my stuff.

"The 49ers had R. C. Owens. He made the 'Ally Oop' pass famous. They'd lob the ball up in the end zone and he was a great jumper, he'd just go up and get it. But I could get up pretty good, too. All that high jumping, or the spud-picking, or maybe both. Anyway, I knocked down a couple of those Ally Oop passes, and the next thing I knew, I wasn't being sent home after all."

No, he wasn't being sent anywhere.

Well, except later, when he would be sent to Canton, Ohio. In 1978, Larry Wilson was inducted into the Pro Football Hall of Fame.

They named him Jed.

"Boy, he was one tough little bugger, the toughest person I ever knew," says Larry Wilson, who is not exactly a slouch in the tough department himself.

Jed was the middle child, one of four children born to Larry and Dee Ann Wilson. Jed was born with spina bifida, a congenital defect in which part of one or more vertebrae fail to develop completely, leaving a portion of the spinal cord exposed. It occurs in about one of every thousand babies.

It sounds like good odds, until you're the one confronting them.

The defect left Jed Wilson paralyzed from the waist down, and locked in a wheelchair his entire life.

"He lived twenty-five years," Larry Wilson says, "and I never heard him complain."

They went fishing together a lot. "Jed liked that, just the two of us. You could talk if you wanted, or not. There's something about water that's gentle, you know?"

And Jed was like the water?

"Yeah, he was. He took what was given him and he never asked why. Just did the best he could with what he had. He was an inspiration to me, and I think to everyone who was ever around him."

Larry Wilson fires up another smoke. There has been some compensation for the loss of a son. His two surviving children have made him a grandfather. Seven times.

He and Dee Ann began going together when both were in high school. They married when he was a sophomore in college. After twenty-eight years, they divorced. He recites their history without any evident anger or bitterness.

He married Nancy nineteen years ago. They live in the Arizona desert, on a golf course on the Phoenix-Scottsdale border. He can stand out on his patio and smoke and look at the purple mountains.

"Yeah, it gets hot in the summer, but the winters and springs are great, and I don't miss the damn snow even a little bit," he says.

He is employed by the Cardinals still, as vice president, and their association is in its thirty-ninth consecutive year.

"Never been with any other team, and, really, never wanted to be," he says.

His playing career ended after the last game of the 1972 season. His body, as durable and indestructible as a cactus, had finally begun to yield.

"I still had my enthusiasm for the game," he says, "but I got beat up pretty good that year. I had a punctured lung, and I pretty well figured that was it for me. I'd been lucky, really. I got my toes broken one game—and listen, that'll get your attention—but they shot 'em up and I played. The only time I had to stay in the hospital was one year at training camp I got stung on the thigh by a bee, of all things, and I had a bad reaction.

"Anyway, after twelve years I was starting to show the wear and tear. I was older and slower, and they wanted me to go to strong safety and I wasn't interested. I had always played on the right side—we didn't call them strong safety or free safety then—you just played one side or the other."

He knew the game, inside and out, and he thought maybe he'd like to be a coach so he could still keep playing those chess matches, although from a safer distance. Coaches didn't get their hands or toes broken.

"But the Cardinals' owner, Bill Bidwill, he felt like they needed a pro scout, and so I agreed to take that job," he says. "When I was playing, in the off-season I'd worked for the Cardinals and for a brewery and for a savings and loan. You had to supplement your income in those days. Football wasn't enough to live on, although by my last season I believe I finally got up into the sixties (thousands).

"Believe me, I'm not complaining. Working in the winter gave me a chance to meet a lot of people, and football opened a lot of doors."

The moment that so many of them dread—the arrival of their first training camp out of football—did not turn out to be especially painful for Larry Wilson.

"I've been lucky that I never got very far away from football," he says. "That first summer after I had retired, in '73, I went to camp and I did what I'd always fantasized about doing when I was a player. I got me a soda and I sat in the bleachers and I watched them running and sweating down there in all that heat and humidity, and I leaned back and poured that cold drink down my throat."

Not that he didn't suffer from separation anxiety.

"Those first few years," he admits, "are hard. I went to all the games, of course, and you know you watch them and you can't help yourself. You start out and you promise yourself you'll be calm, you'll just be a spectator. But it doesn't take long until you're knee-deep in it. You get involved. There'll be a play and you'll hear someone shouting: 'How can they do that?' And then you look around and you realize that that voice, the one that's doing the shouting, it belongs to you."

Did he ever feel the urge to play again?

"I've had a bunch of urges," he says, laughing. "I still try to stay involved. I still sit in on the pregame meal. I'll even confess to you that I still spend time making sure I know our opponent."

Twenty-seven years removed from his last game as a player, Larry Wilson still studies film, still charts tendencies. The game is in him as deep as a cactus needle.

As a player, he was one of those who couldn't wait around for the team bus on game day. He'd take a cab to the stadium, drink coffee with the equipment people, let the adrenaline simmer, leisurely allow the anticipation to build. He savored it.

"I hated to be rushed," he says. "I had my routine and I wanted to be able to follow it. I wanted everything to be right, to be just-so."

He was, of course, a slave to superstition. He had to put on the armor the same way, the exact same way.

"I had the same set of thigh pads my whole career," he confesses. "They were pretty well shot by the end, all taped up and the insides gone, but I wasn't about to let go of them."

Now he is into his sixties and Larry Wilson still has that distinctive profile, the creased face and the hawk nose and that jutting prow of a chin that suggests an uncommon toughness. And inside, he still boils on game day.

"I still get all fired up," he confirms.

And on those Sundays when the Cardinals are up against it and he can't stand to sit any longer, he rises from his chair and goes outside, up on the roof of the stadium, and fires up another cigarette and begins to pace, back and forth, blue plumes swirling around his head.

At home games, they say it sounds like Captain Ahab pacing the deck of the Pequod, looking for Moby Dick.

But no, it's just Larry Wilson, a tough man trying to will victory.

Cynthia Zordich

*"Give your hearts, but not into
each others keeping.*

*For only the hand of Life can
contain your hearts.*

*And stand together yet not too
near together;*

*For the pillars of the temple
stand apart,*

*And the Oak tree and the cypress
grow not in each other's shadow."*

Excerpt from The Prophet, *Kahlil
Gibran on marriage*

THE OAK AND THE CYPRESS
The Kimberly Lewis Story

He was huge. The first time he stood in front of her, she wondered to herself: Where did the sun go?

Her first instinct was maternal. She wanted to take care of him. As though someone six-feet-six and three hundred pounds needed anybody to look after him.

But Kimberly Lewis, nee Kimberly Katharine Broer, had always had a soft spot in her heart for strays. She was attracted to them. She always wanted to help. Raised in love, she wanted to pass it along.

Besides, he was not only enormous, he was handsome and a football player at a school where football was everything. He was the center of campus attention, turning heads wherever he strode. Plus—and this was the clincher—they made a strikingly attractive couple.

263

She grew up in Lincoln, Nebraska, home base for the University of Nebraska and its mighty, corn-fed football machine. On autumn Saturdays, when the Cornhuskers play at home, the stadium becomes the third largest city in the state. Everyone wears red. The arena looks like some monstrous hemorrhage.

She was raised in a loving, attentive household, by parents who encouraged their children to become independent and self-reliant, to think for themselves, to be curious and inquisitive, to always have a sense of wonder, to not only answer questions but to question answers.

This was what they were taught: If a thing has already been done, then all that should mean is that you know you can do it, too. And if a thing has not been done, then all that should mean is that you can be the first one to do it.

Her mother had been an orphan. She survived being shipped from foster home to foster home without becoming embittered, but she did develop a strong survival instinct. To her two daughters and her two sons she would pass along this advice: Don't depend on anyone else. It is right to give your heart to someone, but don't give away your legs, because you never know when you are apt to have need of them—you should always be able to stand on your own.

Kimberly Lewis's mother has been true to her own advice—she is an interior designer and owns clothing boutiques and antique shops. Kimberly Lewis's father owns a construction company. It was his firm that built the south-end addition to the university's football stadium. He was a generation ahead of his time—he did not feel the least bit threatened because his wife looked beyond the traditional role of homemaker and wanted something more.

"He's like my mother, he believes that everyone should have their own identity," says Kimberly Lewis, her voice husky with pride.

"We were, we still are, a very close family. We'd sit down to meals together. Everyone was encouraged to contribute to the conversation. We were urged to debate, to look at an issue from more than one side. My brothers and sister, we were each other's best friends. We played out in the pasture. There wasn't any trouble to get into."

For almost as long as she can remember, Kimberly Lewis felt a stirring within her. There was a dancer inside trying to get out. She yearned to be a ballerina, but she was going to grow to be tall and lithe and willowy, five-feet-ten, with long, supple legs that were ill-suited for ballet. That didn't mean they were ill-suited for other forms of dance, though.

Her mother took her to a Broadway musical, and the little girl was smitten.

"My parents were always encouraging us, telling us to go for our dreams, that there's nothing we can't do if we put our mind to it."

Her parents indulged her dream. They sent her to New York, Los Angeles, Chicago, to Europe, wherever there were dance conventions. She seemed a natural, and coupled with her aptitude for dancing and choreography was a killer work ethic. She danced all through high school, then enrolled at the University of Nebraska. She majored in business, mindful of her mother's advice—always have something to fall back on, always have a way to take care of yourself, just in case . . . just in case it ever comes down to you against the world.

One of her brothers, Kurt, played defensive end for Nebraska. When Kimberly Lewis was in her junior year, Kurt introduced her to the Huskers' starting center, Bill Lewis. Two years after that, they would marry.

Their dating was a heady time. The football team never seemed to lose and Bill Lewis was the pivot on those mammoth offensive lines for which Nebraska had become known. Autumn Saturdays were a swirl of lopsided victories celebrated in an endless round of parties. If it seemed like a fairy tale world, well, it was.

He was going to be a high draft pick, everyone agreed. A promising, lucrative career loomed. They made a tall, graceful, smashing couple who were easy to envy. Life seemed cast in gold. What was there not to like?

Her parents were against their relationship almost from the start. They sensed a mismatch.

"In retrospect," she concedes, "they were right. We were exact opposites. I don't know why I didn't listen to them."

265

Maybe because they had raised her to believe in herself, to make up her own mind, to stand up for her convictions.

And maybe because she had an urge to rebel this one time. Maybe a secret part of her wanted to take a walk on the wild side. Maybe, for once, she wanted to be defiant.

And maybe, most of all, because she had convinced herself that she was needed.

"I was going to show him love, show him what real love was," she remembers. "We had had foster children in and out of our home all the time I was growing up. Bill hadn't had the kind of family life I'd had. His family just wasn't very supportive, for whatever reasons. There seemed to be a distance between them. He went two years one time without ever speaking to his own mother. Me, I couldn't go two days without speaking to mine, and still can't."

Her nurturing impulse kicked in. She says what struck her about him was his anger. It seemed to her that he lost his temper easily. When a very large, very strong man gets mad, the rage can produce—well, she took it as a challenge. She would be the one to soothe him, the one to still whatever torment it was that drove him to such unreasoning anger.

"I am from a very nurturing family. I'm used to getting emotional sustenance, and now I wanted to give it. I had all these noble feelings . . . well, at least I thought they were noble. I thought I could help him. We all, every one of us, have a need to be needed . . . "

They were married in November of 1986. Bill Lewis wasn't the high pick in the draft that he had expected to be. Several rounds went by. Finally, the Raiders, then located in the Los Angeles area, took him.

They lived in El Segundo. By the next summer, she was pregnant. Bill, she says, became even angrier playing professional football. He was even more aggressive. He got in fights with teammates. He was subject to sudden, wild mood swings. She was unable to gentle him.

The day after Christmas, she says, he left her. Opened the door and walked out as casually as you'd go to the post office. The baby forming inside her was six months old.

She went back home, to Lincoln. She felt abandoned, but the sting of shame hurt even worse. She felt disgraced.

"We'd never had this kind of heartache in our home," she says. "I felt like a terrible failure. I cried myself to sleep most nights."

In March of 1988, she gave birth to a daughter and named her Taylor. The day after she got out of the hospital, she was served with papers. Bill had filed for divorce.

She cast about for something to cling to. She remembered that old stirring within.

Dancing.

It had always sustained her emotionally, had always given her a sense of fulfillment. She was good at it, and at this point she was in desperate need of something reassuring, something that could restore her sense of self-esteem and self-worth.

She moved to New York and lived with a cousin. She immersed herself in dancing. She taught classes. Taylor would sit in the corner, watching, absorbing. It is hardly a surprise that she loves dancing, perhaps with a passion even greater than her mother's.

The Raiders came to New York for a game. Kimberly Lewis's phone rang. It was her estranged husband. He wondered if he might see his daughter.

He might.

He came and they talked. He called. He called again. Soon, the phone calls increased. He said he was reforming. He said he was cleaning up his life.

He asked Kimberly and Taylor to move across the country and join him in Palm Springs. He said he wanted—no, he needed—a second chance.

"He came to my brother's wedding and he apologized to my parents. It was like he was on his hands and knees. He promised that he would be a loving husband and father."

She was torn and vulnerable. She was accustomed only to success and happiness. Defeat was a stranger. This was a chance to expunge the blot from her record.

"No one in our family had ever gotten divorced," she says. "I had never failed at anything before. I wanted to prove that I could make it work."

From a distance, she says she now realizes it was foolish pride and vanity on her part, and that neither make a very good basis for starting a marriage or trying to resume one.

There had been no alimony, no child support. She had been on her own, she had become resolute and independent. She had become her mother's daughter. Now she was going to be giving it all up. She hesitated. And then she committed.

"And I had to fall in love with Bill all over again," she says.

He was traded to the Cardinals. The three of them moved to the Valley of the Sun. Sitting in a hotel room in Arizona one day, she was channel-surfing and happened across an NBA game between the Phoenix Suns and the Los Angeles Lakers. The game itself held no appeal for her, but something in the background did.

"I noticed that the Lakers had the Lakers Girls but Phoenix didn't have any cheerleaders or dancers. Just on an impulse, I pulled the telephone directory out of the drawer and looked up the Suns' number in the yellow pages and gave them a call. They referred me to the marketing department. I called them. They said, well, we already have the gorilla mascot, you know, and he's very popular. Thanks for the offer, but no thanks."

She kept calling anyway.

"I'll sew the costumes myself, I'll take care of everything, just give me the chance," she told them.

Finally, someone relented. They told her she could do the season opener, in November of 1990. It would be a one-game audition. Her mother flew out and helped her with the sewing. Almost one hundred girls showed up for the tryouts.

"I wanted a dance team that was skilled, with professionally-trained dancers who had had years of tap, ballet, and jazz," she says. "I wanted dancers that kids could watch and try to emulate."

The day after the season opener and that one-game audition, the Suns called her. With an offer, a one-year trial.

They passed the trial, and since then, the troupe she founded has performed on MTV, in Europe, in Mexico. The gorilla was worked into the dance routines. She had found an outlet for her creative energies, and a way to feel good about herself. Life seemed to be cast in gold again.

She got pregnant a second time. A son, Alexander, was born in April of 1992. But it wasn't just her family that was growing. Her reputation as a choreographer spread. More and more aspiring dancers wanted to take lessons from her.

But another part of her life was in trouble. Her marriage was crumbling again. The Cardinals released Bill Lewis. The New England Patriots picked him up. It meant uprooting again and moving back across the country. It meant giving up all that she had established on her own. She was certain that it wasn't worth it this time. She told him she was staying.

"In my heart, I knew my marriage wasn't any good anyway," she says. "I couldn't pretend any more. I was forced to confront that. He'd be gone four, five days at a time. And then when he went to New England, two weeks would go by and he wouldn't call."

She does not absolve herself from blame or responsibility. She agrees that a marriage is a partnership and does not succeed, or fail, on the actions of just one of the involved parties. It is a shared endeavor.

"It never was me that he loved, not really. It was football," she admits.

It took her a while to realize this, she says. It took a passage of time and a healing of emotional wounds. And it required her to set aside any hard feelings she had for him and try to objectively assess herself.

"I know that he thought that I was high maintenance. I'm not what he wanted. We really were opposites. I'd have dinner parties and he'd be off playing golf. He wanted to be with his buddies more than with me. I think that Bill's friends became his surrogate family.

"The football parties, the high lifestyle, all the travel, the see and be seen, that's not reality, that's not a world you can live your whole life in. It's one thing when you're in college. But you grow up. Or at least you're supposed to. Your values change. If they don't . . . "

The bonding that football players do, she says, became his emotional sustenance.

"I think," she says, "that almost everyone who played on the Cardinals' offensive line with him, they are divorced now. Their ex-wives and their kids still live in the Phoenix area and the kids come to my studio. The players sometimes will come to see them dance at recitals and other performances. You look at their faces and you know how much they love their children. Really, it tears at your heart."

On her own again, now with two children, she thought of what her mother had told her while she was growing up: "Think a lot of yourself." She meant that if you believe in yourself, if you believe in your abilities and your determination, that you will have a strong start to surviving, to living.

Kimberly Lewis took out a small business loan. She started up her own dance studio. She outgrew that one and doubled its size, and outgrew that one and expanded again. She has more than a thousand students. She owns a clothing store that is next door to the dance studio. And in June of 1999, in partnership with her brother Kurt, she will open a new athletic club.

As independent as she was, she was shaking when she went in to apply for that first loan. "I'm lucky. I realize that I have a lot of opportunities that my mother never had. It wasn't that long ago that a woman would have been turned down for no other reason than she was a woman. I picked a good time to be born."

Kimberly Lewis has a habit of getting directly to the point. She is purposeful and deliberate and she projects a no-nonsense air. Her stride is brisk, and those long dancer's legs inhale the ground in big gulps. She is justifiably proud of what she has done, most of it largely on her own. But she does not gloat or allow herself any twinges of vengeance. And of her twice-failed marriage and her ex-husband, she says: "I don't want to put him down. I don't want there to be hard feelings. I don't want to say that there weren't times when he wasn't wonderful. That wouldn't be fair and it wouldn't be true, either. We did have two children together, after all. We still talk, maybe once a month, and it's cordial. I think he's happy. I hope that he is. He sees Alex every other weekend.

"I do not talk hard or mean about him and I don't put him down around the children. I don't want their minds poisoned and I don't want them exposed to pettiness. It's important that Alex have a father, one he knows, not a stranger. And I don't want Taylor to grow up automatically hating all men. That's not fair and that's not right. I was raised in a family in which you respected your father. And I think that should apply whether there's a divorce or not."

As for herself, it is obvious she has built an extraordinary career in business. But she also says, somewhat wistfully it seems, that she is not the brusque, impatient, get-outta-my-way businesswoman she sometimes might appear to be.

"I am strong emotionally," she says, "mostly because I've had to learn to be. But actually I'm emotionally softer on the inside than I let on."

For self-protection?

"Probably. I think maybe you put up defenses out of some instinct. But I do like to laugh. I'm not a man-hater. And I hope someday to fall in love again. I'd like someone to share a life with."

There was bitterness and hard feelings for a time, of course. But the emotional scar tissue has accumulated, and the wounds are only scars now.

"I think the older you get you realize it's not worth it to carry a grudge," she says. "We all have emotional baggage that we carry around with us. Sometimes you don't realize how heavy that baggage really is until after you've put it down. I firmly believe that I am stronger now for having gone through what I did.

"You can go back and get an education. You can go to work. You can do whatever you want. You can balance your life. You can be a wife and a mother and have a career, too."

And she wants other women—and men, too—to know that the sooner they realize that professional football is seductive because it is more make-believe than real, the better.

"You think that the big money and the fame and that lifestyle is going to be there forever, but it's not. As a woman, you become known as The Wife. The Shadow. But you have your own identity and you should be aware of it. It's OK to watch out for you, to think of yourself.

"Football players are told always to believe in themselves. Women should, too."

"The Second Death"

They say that football players die two deaths. The first death comes when their career finally ends. My career has ended. No more cleats, no more banging helmets, no more cheers, no more headaches. Instead of the stress and worry of an impending football season, the notion of autumn is nothing more than brilliantly colored orange trees, just like in the postcards. I hear stories in the news about my former teammates losing weight in the heat, having last-minute battles over their contracts, getting injured.

Me? I'm at my home on a cool clear lake in upstate New York. I get up early and go swimming with my kids. I feel great. In the afternoon we take boat rides. I'll usually pull a couple of cold bottles of beer from the ice chest to knock off any remnant of heat that the breeze and the water haven't already dismissed, gaze at the rolling farmland that bounds the water, and wonder at this dying two deaths business.

Of course, it's easy to feel this way now. Training camp is the misery of the NFL experience. But what happens in a few weeks, when this training camp thing is over and the Sunday games begin? I keep telling myself and all my friends that even these games, the gems of the NFL experience, I don't miss. After all, I'm in the broadcast booth for FOX, and still a part of the show.

But who am I really kidding? As great as it is to stay close to this game, to talk about it, to be there watching, to get excited about doing television broadcasts, it really isn't quite the same, is it? I mean, why is it that so many people will sit down to watch those games on TV, to go the stadiums, yell and scream, laugh and cry? It's the game . . . There is nothing like it. It's the most grueling, challenging sport there is. Brute strength, cunning speed, gut-wrenching endurance are all wrapped up into one fast-paced, hard-hitting uproar.

So, the other day I was having lunch at this little coffee shop in town and a young boy came up to me holding out a football trading card.

"Are you Tim Green?" he asked. "The football player?"

I wiped my mouth, then smiled as I took the small child's card and pen. On its face was me, dressed in heavy pads and a black helmet. My arms, where they showed, were glazed with sweat. My face was contorted and my muscles rippling in a frozen moment of exertion. I looked big and strong and even ferocious. I felt that pocket around my heart filling with adrenaline.

"I used to play football," I heard myself say to the boy as I scratched out my name. As I handed the card back to that boy I took one more fleeting look at the image of myself, the ferocious one, and realized that I would never be that again, never be that football player. And in that moment, with those words, I think I died my first death.

Tim Green, LB-DE 1986-93 Atlanta
The Darker Side Of The Game
Published by Time Warner Books

Cynthia Zordich

THE ZIPPER CLUB
The Dan Reeves Story

Just before the anesthesia enfolded him in that deep, sweet sleep, he thought about what might happen when the surgeon took one of those gleaming scalpels and began to open him up, from stem to stern.

When the rib spreader had pried open his chest cavity, and his beating heart had been exposed, what would they find besides clogged arteries that were screaming to be Roto-Rootered?

The cardiologist would rummage around in there and then plunge his hand down deep into the very core of Dan Reeves and say: "Wait, what's this?" And he would draw out this thing that was attached to Dan Reeves, like some alien invader, and he would hold it up to the light.

And it would be a football.

He laughs at this suggested image, but he admits that it isn't all that far-fetched.

"Well, the game does have a way of getting inside you," he allows, in that distinctive drawl. "It gets in your blood and I don't think they've invented a transfusion yet that will get it out."

In December of 1998, at the age of fifty-four, the bill was presented to Dan Reeves, the bill for a life devoted to and immersed in football, for first playing it, then coaching it, and always, always, being a slave to it. The cost: four arteries so thick with plaque that they looked like gutters packed with leaves. No matter how his heart thumped with the effort, the blood movement was not much more than the drip-drip of a leaky faucet.

He underwent a quadruple bypass. The arterial plumbers cut him open to perform their special embroidery, and twenty-five days later—twenty-five days!—Dan Reeves was back on the sidelines, tethered to his headset once again, imploring his players and, despite his promises to the doctors, gesturing his disgust at the officials over a call he was sure they had blown, the veins in his neck engorged and throbbing.

On that day, the Atlanta Falcons, coached by Dan Reeves, outlasted the San Francisco 49ers, 20-18, in an NFL playoff game that was not decided until an incomplete pass fluttered to artificial grass on the last play of the game. It was not exactly the sort of test recommended by the American Medical Association, but Reeves had put the doctors' work under the severest sort of pressure.

"If I could get out of that one alive, I figured I might be good for another twenty-five years," he says.

Throughout the game, he looked like Moses parting the Red Sea. There seemed to be a force field around him that kept everyone—players, photographers, assistant coaches— five feet away from him. No one wanted to be the one who accidentally bumped into Dan Reeves and disrupted the delicate chemical balance of the blood thinners and caused him to . . . well, no one wanted to think about the dire possibilities. For his part, he made himself walk slowly and deliberately, like a man trying to negotiate a strange room in the dark.

But when a penalty flag was thrown against his team, he reverted to instinct and reflex and flapped his arms at the zebras in righteous protest.

276

"I wanted to yell at them, but my chest was so tight and still hurt and I was afraid I might tear something loose," he recalls.

When the game was over, his giddy players wanted to carry him off the field, or give him the ritual sneak-attack sideline shower from a barrel. But of course they didn't dare. So they settled for grinning at him. And pointing at him. And waving their fists.

Universal jock-speak. Sign language for: "This one's for you, coach." And for themselves, too.

The Falcons had been fowl most foul for almost all of their existence. As recently as two seasons before, they had won only three games and dropped thirteen. They changed coaches. They brought a Georgia son home. Dan Reeves has a drawl as thick as the red clay, and even though he had been practicing football at Dallas and Denver and New York all those years, he was still, at heart, as Georgia as a peach.

Falcons fans eagerly awaited the deliverance they were sure was at hand.

Of their first seven games with Dan Reeves as coach, the Falcons won exactly once. He called the team together. He told them he understood that they were accustomed to finding ways to lose rather than ways to win, that they had come to expect, however subconsciously, that at crucial moments in a game something bad was inevitable, that fate always seemed to have it in for them. Then he told them something most of them had never heard: He believed in them.

"Look, if I didn't believe in you guys, you wouldn't be here. We're in this together," he said.

"You know, we did have talent," the wide receiver, Terance Mathis, remembers. "I couldn't believe how we matched up with other teams, but we couldn't seem to beat them. And then Coach Reeves came in and he had instant credibility. He got us on the right track. He got our heads cleared. He told us if we do all the little things right, the big things will take care of themselves." The Falcons won six of their last eight games after that meeting.

Then they rode that momentum into the very next season and won fourteen of sixteen. Along the way, their coach went into the hospital for open-heart surgery. He told them he would be back with them for the playoffs. It was their destiny, and they had come too far now not to realize it.

He became one of the most compelling inspirations of the year, and the Falcons became one of sports' feel-good stories. They won that playoff game against San Francisco, with Reeves back on the sidelines with them just as he had promised, and the very next week they upset the favored Vikings in Minnesota.

The Falcons were going to the Super Bowl.

Falcons and Super Bowl? Look out your window; surely pigs are flying.

Falcons and Super Bowl? Check hell; surely it has frozen over.

The Falcons became the third NFL team, along with the Broncos and the Giants, that Dan Reeves had coached into the playoffs. Only Chuck Knox and Bill Parcells had managed that feat previously. Dan Reeves had won in the West, in the East, and now in the South. What he had done recalled the ultimate coaching tribute, made by Bum Phillips about Don Shula: "He can take his'n and beat your'n. Or he can take your'n and beat his'n."

Before Reeves, the Falcons had played the run 'n shoot offense, an unorthodox philosophy that floods the field with receivers and forsakes such traditional staples as the tight end and power running backs. It is a hothouse offense, meaning that it flourishes in domed stadiums or in warm climates, but it is far less effective outdoors, when exposed to the harsh and frequently unforgiving elements in late autumn and early winter. It is difficult to pass and pass in the rain and sleet and cold. The run 'n shoot is regarded by traditionalists and purists as too gimmicky.

Reeves junked the run 'n shoot. He went back to the very basics of football: Run it and stop the other guy from running it. Reeves ordered the ball to be given to running back Jamal Anderson again and again and again. Four hundred and ten times during the regular season, Anderson ran with the ball. It was a wearying, and record-breaking, workload. No back in NFL history had carried so many times.

"The man had faith in me," Anderson says of Reeves. "When someone puts all that trust in you, you want to produce for him."

In addition, Reeves installed Chris Chandler, who was often injured and usually stuck on bad teams, at quarterback. He responded with a career year. The Falcons loved their new-old offense. And their defense began creating turnovers faster than any other team in the league.

There is an old coaching adage that you shouldn't expect a mule to be able to sing opera and you shouldn't expect a tenor to be able to pull a loaded wagon up a hill. Reeves has adhered to that philosophy. He has won at Denver, at New York, and at Atlanta because he didn't ask players to do what they were unequipped to do. Rather than moan about their deficiencies, he played to their strengths.

Reeves became a head coach, at Denver, in 1981. Through 18 seasons, his teams have won 172 times, including the playoffs. They have been in four Super Bowls. And in every one of them, he has been the losing coach.

In some segments of society, that makes him a failure. It conveniently omits all that is required to even reach the Super Bowl, the unbending will and the extraordinary resiliency to keep trying to get back even after you have lost. Human nature, after all, is to give up after you have experienced crushing disappointment. To lose in the Super Bowl and then to be able to return to the very next one is a monumental triumph of desire.

"We don't seem to make much accommodation for the effort, only for the result," he says. "We judge you strictly on the basis of whether you won, and if you didn't, then everything else you accomplished . . . it's as though it never happened. That doesn't strike me as very fair."

Three of his four Super Bowl defeats were with the Broncos and with John Elway at quarterback. Elway finally achieved his vindication. Twice. His second of back-to-back championship wins was accomplished against Reeves's Falcons. From a distance, Elway and Reeves had sniped verbally at each other prior to that game. Before kickoff, there was a mutual cease-fire.

"It's a waste of words and energy to say hurtful things about another person, to carry a grudge," Reeves says. "I was happy for John. He's given everything to the game. He deserved his Super Bowls . . . although I admit that I'd be less than honest if I didn't say that I wish he had gotten that second one at somebody else's expense. But you need to have perspective."

Undergoing bypass surgery will do wonders for perspective.

He parks the car and removes the golf clubs. It is four months after the quadruple bypass. There is no hint of exertion in his voice, only anticipation. Indeed, if it weren't for the incision scar, the now-famous "zipper" that winds down a heart patient's chest and abdomen, you'd never suspect that only a few weeks ago Dan Reeves was on the cutting table.

"I thought that maybe the surgery might help my golf game," he says. "I hoped it might hurt enough when I swung that it would slow my swing down some."

He is playing in a celebrity golf tournament on this glorious spring day to raise money for charity. There are a lot of fat checkbooks anxious to play with Dan Reeves.

"I think more people know me, recognize me now than knew me before the surgery," he says. "That's what really hits you when you have a situation like that, the outpouring of love and prayer from people you've never even met."

And, no, he says, he didn't fear dying. "The Lord has a way of getting your attention. I figured if He was calling me home, fine. I was in His hands. I had learned long ago to cherish every day, to live life and not dwell on death. It's going to happen, to every one of us. But if all you do is think about dying, then you forget to live."

Besides, it wasn't as though he didn't know what it felt like to be in a hospital. It seemed like he spent most of the first part of his life in them.

He was born in Rome, the Rome that is between Americus and Andersonville, Georgia. He was born on a farm, in the winter of 1944, and he was sickly from the beginning. He had an infection between his bladder and kidney. Fortunately, antibiotics had just been developed. Unfortunately, they were delivered by injection.

He was only four, and he would lie there on the hospital bed, making himself very still, trying to be brave, trying not to cry, while they shot him. Six needles a day.

The other children could run and play. He watched them from a window. He made a promise to himself. One day, he would be the one doing the running, the one who would burst into the house muddy and panting and completely happy.

He started school early, when he was only five. Might as well, his parents figured. He can't run, so he can have more time for books.

He would turn out to be the classic late-bloomer.

"We played football on the farm, my brothers and cousins," he says. "And then I went out for football my freshman year in high school. I was the slowest player on the team. I made it, but barely."

It set a pattern. He didn't impress many people, but what he did was impressive. He was a quarterback, and his team always seemed to end up winning. He was the quintessential plugger and plodder.

He had a way of doing more with less.

He barely got a scholarship to college, but when he was done at South Carolina, in 1964, he had set ten school records. Nobody wanted him in the pros, but when he was done at Dallas, he had played eight years, as a back-up running back, a third-down specialist, and a master of the halfback run-pass option. He had played in the Super Bowl. More than once.

Yet he can't remember the last football game he ever played. He struggles, but for the life of him he can't bring it back, not a single detail.

"Wow! This is strange," he says. "My last season was . . . what . . . seventy-two? Yep. Seventy-two. And my last three years I was a player-coach. But I just can't remember anything about my last game.

"I knew I was ready to retire as a player. I'd lost a couple of steps and I'd never had any to lose anyway. The first time I ever had knee surgery, that's when I knew my career was going to be over one day. You start out thinking that you can play forever. But I had seven knee surgeries, and after the first couple I realized I'd better start preparing myself for life after football."

He got a broker's license and a realtor's license in the off-seasons. He thought only briefly about remaining in football once he retired from playing. He felt he owed his family, his wife Pam (they have been married thirty-five years and have four granddaughters), and his two daughters and son.

"Coach (Tom) Landry asked me if I wanted to be an assistant coach," he recalls, "but I felt like I should spend more time with my family. There are a lot of guys who would like to be an assistant coach so that they wouldn't have to leave the game. But there may not be an opening, and you're making so much money playing that it's a big pay cut and a huge financial sacrifice. You get accustomed to a certain lifestyle."

Dan Reeves's life without football lasted for one year.

He said he learned something in that time: "I learned how much I missed the game."

He was lost at sea. He went to a football game and sat in the stands.

"It was the first time I'd ever seen a professional game from there," he says. "And it didn't take me any time at all to start second-guessing, just like everyone else. I really missed being a part of it."

He tried, gamely, to help a developer sell townhouses. He tried looking at a wooded area and visualizing a mall. He tried plotting in his mind the path of a new highway. It was more fun to plot the arc of a long touchdown pass.

"I just wasn't comfortable," he says. "People always wanted to talk football with me, and I loved doing that. On top of that, I picked a bad time to become a real estate broker. That year interest rates skyrocketed. If I had been successful, I never would have gone back to football."

And, quite likely, to his undying regret.

He called Tom Landry to inquire if there was room for a broken-down running back and an unhappy real-estate broker. No. Sorry. Nothing right now.

Dan Reeves sighed and fought the melancholy that wrapped around him in snake coils.

A week later, Tom Landry called him. There was an opening. The Cowboys needed a special teams coach. The salary would be twenty thousand, half what Dan Reeves had made his last year as a player. He couldn't accept fast enough.

"Having to do without football for a year . . . it's true what they say about absence making the heart grow fonder. But I know that I really dedicated myself after that, because I knew what it was like to be on the outside looking in.

"The excitement, the adrenaline, the competition . . . there's no substitute for it out in the real world. And I think you reach a certain comfort zone. This is something you know, and something you know that you can do."

He served his apprenticeship under Tom Landry and after seven seasons became a head coach. In many ways, he resembled Landry. He wore a coat and tie on game day. His jaw was always set in determination. There was an air of courtliness about him, the southern gentleman's respect for manners and tradition. But there was some bronc-buster in there, too, and close to the surface.

He has always been mindful of his own playing career. He has always had a soft spot for plodders and pluggers, and is reluctant to cut them.

"Not that I don't love superstars, too," he says, laughing.

When he underwent his bypass, it was the twentieth surgery of his life. Twenty times under the knife. The operating room had become as familiar as the stadium.

"You go in treating it just like a football game, expecting to win. You don't ever expect not to . . ."

"I guess that's the essence of football. Isn't it?"

Sure does seem to be.

Cynthia Zordich

Cynthia Zordich

Cynthia Zordich

BEARS AND GRABOWSKIS
The Mike Ditka Story

Mike Ditka is quoting Mozart.

Ponder that: Mike Ditka and Wolfgang Amadeus Mozart.

An intriguing pairing, isn't it? Iron Mike and Wolfie the Big M. A football player and a musical genius. A throwback and a prodigy.

"An admirer came up to Mozart one time and told him, 'You know, I'd give my life to play as well as you.'

"And Mozart looked at him and said: 'I did.' "

Mike Ditka pauses long enough for that to soak in and to shift his gum to the other side of his mouth. Then he resumes chewing and spitting out what is on his mind, and all you can think about are . . . jackhammers. Mike Ditka goes through his chewing gum like jackhammers rip apart concrete.

He goes through life pretty much the same way.

"See, Mozart wanted to be the very best, so he put his heart and soul into it. He didn't set out saying, 'I'd like to be mediocre.' If you're going to set goals for yourself, then set some good ones," he says. "Say you want to be the best and then don't settle for some half-assed effort. It's a way to motivate yourself. See, I've never understood the notion that you don't work as hard as you possibly can, every day. How are you ever going to get better with that kind of an attitude?"

He stops for a breath and is partly contrite. He understands that he is rabid and, in his passion, occasionally irrational. He also understands that he cannot ever be any other way.

"Now I know I put way too much pressure on myself when I was playing football. It's only a game and all that. But, you know, you get out of something exactly what you put into it. And, boy, losing better bother you. I don't mean you shouldn't be able to accept defeat, but you shouldn't get to where you're comfortable with it.

"You lose, you ought to be gracious about it. On the outside. On the inside, though, you'd better be boiling. If you're not, you're going out there the next time and you're going to get your head handed to you all over again. It's easy to get used to losing, see. And once you accept it, then you invent ways to lose."

The jackhammers fall silent for a moment.

***

Mike Ditka was born at least a generation too late.

He would have been right at home in a leather helmet. He would have been embraced as a soul mate by men named Bronco.

His earliest recollection of just how frighteningly intense his competitive spirit is came during a Little League baseball game. He was catching, which, when you think about it, is the perfect position for him. Catcher, with its endless squatting in the dirt, is the closest position to football that baseball has. His brother, Ashton, was doing the pitching, though not especially well.

Certainly not well enough to suit his catcher.

So Mike Ditka, frustrated, replaced his own brother on the mound, banished him back behind the plate. Later, when the shortstop kicked away a ground ball that the pitcher was certain should have been an easy out, an exasperated Mike Ditka replaced the shortstop. If he could have played all nine positions at once, he would have.

"I know the manager was sitting there wondering what the hell was going on, but for some reason he never said anything to me," Mike Ditka remembers. "Maybe he thought I was some kind of psycho kid."

Later, when he was a Bear, opponents would wonder the same thing. So would some of his own teammates.

In his very first game as a professional football player, his team was losing to the Minnesota Vikings. Badly. When the Chicago offense came to the sidelines after another failed possession, the raw rookie Ditka sized up one of the Bears' offensive guards, the veteran Ted Karras, and offered him an unsolicited critique on his performance:

"Get the lead out of your ass and play harder!"

Karras answered with an oath and a punch.

"Aw, I was a rookie and rookies were supposed to keep their mouths shut," Mike Ditka says, "but that didn't stop me. It still doesn't. I say what's on my mind. I cared too much, probably. Took it too seriously, probably. Still do. Can't change. Maybe if it was some other game, but we're talking about football!

"You know, in a football game you can trick people for a while, but you'd better bloody their noses once in a while, too."

A month after Ted Karras took a swing at him, Mike Ditka got ready for his fifth game as a pro. The Bears were playing the Baltimore Colts, and his assignment as a tight end was to block a linebacker named Bill Pellington, whose reputation was that of a fierce, merciless, and sometimes borderline-illegal hitter. All week, the rookie was warned.

The first time the Bears snapped the ball, Pellington punched Ditka square in the chops. There were no elaborate birdcage face masks then, only a single, thin bar. Mike Ditka was pretty sure he had swallowed his face bar after Bill Pellington coldcocked him.

"We went back to the huddle," he recalls, "and I didn't even hear the play that was called. I didn't know if it was supposed to be a run or a pass, I didn't have the slightest idea what my assignment was. I was only thinking about one thing.

"When the ball was snapped, I gave a little head fake, just to give him something to concentrate on, and then I cocked my right and busted him hard as I could, right in the mouth."

On the next play, Bill Pellington punched Mike Ditka, and on the play after that Mike Ditka punched Bill Pellington, and it is Ditka's recollection that they went on like that for a time. Then, though no words were spoken and no peace treaty signed, they agreed to a mutual cease-fire. Not that they didn't keep playing hard, but they quit the punching. There was respect on both sides.

"I lost my temper, sure. I retaliated, sure. I instigated, sure. But I did it all within the rules. I just wanted to win."

He wanted to win not only in football, but in everything. Once, when he and Dan Reeves were assistant coaches with the Dallas Cowboys, they were playing a card game, and when Reeves won an especially close hand, he remembers that Ditka stood up, picked up the chair in which he had been sitting, and hurled it across the room.

It hit the wall, and all four legs stuck there.

"I thought to myself, 'Now here's a person who really hates to lose,' " Reeves remembers.

During those years with the Cowboys, Mike Ditka was never able—not that he even tried—to alter his approach to football: that it was, and is, a game best played in a fine fury.

For Ditka, it is a sport for carnivores.

The Cowboys, under the studious Tom Landry, took a more cerebral approach. At game plan meetings, Landry would go around the room asking each coordinator and assistant coach for his input, his thoughts on strategy. Each time he would get to Ditka, the response was always the same:

"Coach, what I think we should do is take the ball and shove it right up their ass."

Usually, this would be met with quiet snickering by the others, and Landry would purse his lips and shake his head. But one time Landry allowed himself a small smile, looked at Ditka with what appeared to be a certain fondness, and said: "Mike, you're still a Bear at heart. You'll always be a Bear."

Mike Ditka blinked and jackhammered his gum and asked: "Is that bad?"

Tom Landry smiled indulgently and replied: "No. No, Mike, it isn't."

Aliquippa, Pennsylvania. Steel town. Mills and forges and furnaces. Tough town. How tough? Ditka pauses for effect.

"When guys stole hubcaps, they did it while the car was moving."

His grandfather settled there, having immigrated from the Ukraine. The family name was Dyzcko. Mike's father, Mike, changed it to Ditka. His father was a Marine, in every sense of the word.

"I wouldn't have had it any other way," his son says, proudly.

They lived in a single house in a row of six, all attached. Mike Ditka and the other neighborhood kids congregated on the concrete and played sports. They played basketball in the winter, outdoors, when the cold and the wet made their hands crack and bleed. They kept playing anyway.

Mike Ditka's father played semi-pro football. He played with gusto. He didn't stop for anything, including the car he ricocheted off and broke his ribs on. He ran into it, catching a pass that was thrown beyond the end zone, into the street. Such unwavering persistence was a trait he passed on to his son.

The men of Aliquippa wore shirts pocked with burn holes from the showers of sparks that lit up the mills.

"The mill is not for you," Mike Ditka's father told him. It sounded like a promise. Like deliverance.

"Sports," his father said. "The way out is sports. You can get a scholarship."

He was a fullback in high school. He learned how to run away from people, and over them. He seemed to have been born knowing how to run over people.

The University of Pittsburgh took him. He came cheap—$14.96 a month. He used it for laundry. He had a lot of laundry; he played football, basketball, and baseball at Pitt. He played them all like he played football. When Pitt played West Virginia in one basketball game, the great Jerry West found himself being guarded by a crazy man with a crew cut and eyes that gleamed like an owl's at midnight.

In only fifty-one seconds, Jerry West scored three baskets and had three highly personal fouls committed upon his butchered body by Mike Ditka.

West later told Ditka: "I thought you were going to kill me."

And Mike Ditka grinned and said: "I couldn't get close enough."

He wouldn't have had a pro basketball career but he probably could have scratched out a minor league living as a catcher. In his heart, though, he knew there was only one game for him.

"To me, when you step on a football field, everybody is equal. When you come off it, though, everybody's not equal any more. Because somebody has won and somebody has lost. Somebody has dominated and somebody has been dominated. I was told to try to make everyone's all-opponent team. First, you whipped the guy across from you. Then you got around to whipping the rest of them."

When he was in college he was an usher at Steelers' games, selling programs. It didn't pay much but it was more than laundry money. After his senior year at Pitt, he was offered a whole pile of laundry money. Both the Chicago Bears and the Houston Oilers drafted him first.

George Halas, the legendary coach and owner of the Bears, offered Mike Ditka $12,000. The old man let the figure sink in, and then, in a rasping voice that sounded vaguely like a growling bear, he told Ditka: "By the way, son, that's the most we've offered anyone since Red Grange."

It was quite a tribute. It was also, says Mike Ditka, a bald-faced lie. Of course he didn't know that at the time.

Mike Ditka said he'd sign. Then, while in New York for an All-American banquet, he was introduced to Bud Adams, the owner of the Oilers. Adams pressed three one-hundred-dollar bills into Mike Ditka's right paw and said: "Have a good time."

Mike Ditka folded the hundreds very carefully and put them in his pocket. When he got back home to Pittsburgh he took them out and handed them to his mother, and as he was doing it, it occurred to him that no hit delivered or received on the football field had made him feel quite as good as he felt at that very moment.

The Oilers offered him $50,000 for two seasons. He swallowed hard and declined. He had given his word to Papa Bear. Besides, in his heart of hearts, he knew.

"Aw, heck, I was a Bear," he agrees. "I belonged there."

And so he did. His very first season, he was not only rookie of the year, but also the All-Pro tight end. In 1963, the Bears won the professional football championship. In every game that year, Mike Ditka would catch a pass and begin to steam down the field, tacklers bouncing like pinballs off of him. Some he starched with a stiff-arm. Some he simply trampled.

One year, he dislocated his shoulder and was outfitted with a harness. He couldn't raise his arm, but somehow he caught seventy-five passes that season. The Bears didn't just beat teams, they mauled them. They took pride in their toughness. If you were a Bear, you never acknowledged injury.

"There were thirty-six players on a team and there were only twelve teams," he says. "So if you let pain keep you out of the game, there was a pretty good chance you'd lose your job."

So he played when he shouldn't have, took shot after shot, and ended up with a deformed foot. In trying to compensate for that injury, he ended up with an artificial hip. One year he tore knee ligaments but played in the Pro Bowl anyway because it meant an extra $800.

And, yes, he knows what you're thinking.

"Aw, nobody forced us to do what we did. Listen, football isn't a right, it's a privilege. I know people say I'm old-fashioned and that I ought to sue. That's one of the things wrong with society. Everybody wants to sue. That whole mentality bothers me, that do-a-little, gain-a-lot. That's just me. I'm not saying I'm wrong or right. I don't know if I am or not. I just know that football gave me a lot more than I ever gave it, and I'll spend my life trying to give back."

The jackhammers are silent again.

In 1967, his beloved Bears traded him to the Philadelphia Eagles. He did two years hard time in Philly. The team was bad and he sustained a crippling injury, tearing the tendon off one heel. He passed his days, and nights, drinking. Hard and steady.

"I always say I went to Philly to learn humility," he says.

Burnt-out, bloated, wasted, and feeling used up, he thought about retiring. But then Tom Landry called him from Dallas. He became a Cowboy. The timing couldn't have been more fortuitous. The Cowboys were just coming into their own, just becoming America's Team. They went to their first two Super Bowls and Mike Ditka went with them. He even caught a touchdown pass in one of them and was about to run in for another, on a reverse, when he, excited by the prospect, misjudged the goal line and ran into one of his own blockers.

"They didn't razz me too much about that one," he says, laughing.

"You wouldn't think a Bear could mix with Cowboys, but they weren't the goody-goody people I'd been told, and they found out that I wasn't quite the hell-raiser they had been led to believe. I had four wonderful years playing for Dallas."

He began to suspect his time had come. Every day when he got up his body creaked and something hurt. For a while he was in denial about his mortality. But his body wouldn't let him deceive himself.

"You think it's going to last forever. You say to yourself that you have been blessed with this body that will always work and never get hurt, and even if it does you'll keep on anyway, if you can get enough shots and keep up your enthusiasm. You get spoiled. You get used to living the good life and you don't want to give that up.

"You try to lie to yourself. But one day you finally face up to the fact that you just can't do what you could ten years ago. I had lost a lot of weight, my back was really hurting, and I couldn't hardly run at all. A bunch of us played poker the night before a playoff game in 1972, and when I went to get out of my chair and go to bed, I couldn't straighten up. I was all bent over and shuffling. I was embarrassed. I must have looked like I was a hundred years old.

"Plus, my mental outlook wasn't the best. I was going through a divorce at the time. That'll just suck the life right out of you."

They won that playoff game and then played the Washington Redskins. Mike Ditka went over the middle and caught a look-in pass. The linebacker, Chris Hanburger, nailed him, dropped him like a sack of laundry.

"That's when I knew I was done," he says. "Chris weighed less than me. Any other time, he would have bounced off me and I'd have still been running. That was my last game."

His time away from football didn't quite last a week.

He had invested in a bar-restaurant in Dallas. He thought it would support him financially. He wouldn't permit himself to think about what would take the place of football and support him emotionally.

"I was standing there one night, place was packed and loud, and I'm thinking I'll be staring at this bar the rest of my life, when Tom Landry called and wanted to know if I'd like to come back to the Cowboys as a coach. My salary would be cut in half. I couldn't say yes fast enough."

He started out as coach of the special teams. Could there be a more perfect fit? He jackhammered his gum and raced up and down the sidelines in support of his kamikazes. He ate headsets and threw clipboards. He stomped along on that bum hip, and large, helmeted men gave him a wide berth, sensing that he teetered on the edge of sanity. Some people play football. Mike Ditka immersed himself in football. He coached the same way.

He spent thirteen years with the Cowboys, as a player and coach. But the Bears' umbilical still tethered him to Chicago, and in 1982 Papa Bear, in the market for a new head coach, called Mike Ditka home. The job interview took place at the kitchen table in George Halas's house. Halas asked the usual obligatory questions. Ditka squirmed impatiently but gave the standard textbook answers.

At one point, Halas asked Ditka what his philosophy of football was.

"Dammit, Mister Halas, you've known me most of my life," he thundered, crashing a fist on the table. "My philosophy of football is the same as yours—win the game and shove the ball up their ass."

The old man hid his smile. He agreed to a salary of $100,000.

The next year, Papa Bear died, at the age of eighty-eight.

Ditka wanted to restore the Bears to their "Monsters of the Midway" legacy. This was his first bit of instruction to his players:

"Every game, first play, knock the headgear off your man. And then do it three more times after that. We don't want people anxious to play us."

They weren't. Da Bears began to win and their popularity spread. Soon, they were cult heroes. Everyman's team. Grabowskis.

"There are teams that are fair-haired and some that aren't fair-haired," he explained at the time. "There are teams named Smith and some named Grabowski. We're Grabowskis. It's about a work ethic, an attitude. Our idea of dressing up is putting on a clean bowling shirt. We're appreciated in Brooklyn, Pittsburgh, Scranton, Wilkes-Barre, Birmingham, areas where people know all about hard work. We wouldn't fit in real well in Beverly Hills."

Da Bears. The samurai linebacker, Mike Singletary. The relentless runner, Walter Payton. The appliance, Refrigerator Perry. The Easy Rider quarterback, Jim McMahon. They were iconoclasts. They were led by a coach who looked more combustible than a tanker full of liquid nitrogen.

He threw whatever was in reach, and for variety punched things. Blackboards were a favorite, because he could put a hole in them and they made a delightful noise. In one moment of turbulence, he punched an equipment trunk. Bad move. He broke his right hand.

So he jackhammered his gum and grinned and waved his casted hand and told his team: "Win this one for Lefty."

They won a Super Bowl in 1985.

In 1977, five years after his divorce, he married his second wife, Diana, who is his equal in passion for life—she, too, regards it with a cocked head and bemused smile.

Asked how her husband deals with defeat, she replies: "When you're losing, everybody in the whole city feels it. And, believe me, my husband feels it more than anyone else."

He had known his first wife since high school. They married while he was in college and they had four children while he played for the Bears. He is unstinting in accepting most of the blame for their divorce.

"I don't know that it's so much that people change as their situations change, and it's whether you're able to adapt and adjust to all those changes that determine whether you stay together," he says. "They talk about how not having enough of something can hurt a marriage, but success can put a real strain on it, too. You look at what happens to players after they've won a Super Bowl. Divorce rates go up. So do bankruptcies. Funny thing is, sometimes it's harder to deal with winning than losing."

When he and the Bears parted in January of 1993, he took the usual path, the one that leads to a TV studio. He stayed for four years. He jackhammered his gum and spit out his opinions. As he aged, with that bushy mustache and the way his hair was slicked back on his large head, you couldn't help but think: Why, he looks kind of like a bear.

297

He spoke and he traveled. He played golf. He played golf like he played football. ("I've calmed down a lot, though.")

He lied to himself that he didn't miss football all that much. Then, when he was offered the chance to return to coaching, to take over the New Orleans Saints for the 1998 season, he jumped higher than a man with a bad back and a racing heart and an artificial hip should be able to jump.

"The game gets its hooks in you and it lasts a lifetime," he says.

"Part of it has changed. When I played, we weren't the Hollywood stars like they are today. You didn't give love taps to the guy you were going against. And you didn't get fined for hitting too hard. I'm not saying my way was the smartest, it's just the way I was, and am."

He probably cares too much. The stress of coaching forces him to take medication to control the rhythm of his heart, which tends to speed out of control.

"But if I cared less, I wouldn't be me. God created me to be in football, I'm convinced of that. If I had my way, I'd live to be Papa Bear's age. And stay in football right up to the end. Funny, the older I get, the more I see of myself in him. I'll stay as long as the game wants me."

He jackhammers the last of his gum and says out loud what you already know to be true:

"I couldn't exist without football."

Cynthia Zordich

Lance Rentzel: "Do you ever think about playing?"

Jim Brown: "No, but I dream about it!"

Lance Rentzel, WR-HB 1965-66 Minnesota; 1967-70 Dallas; 1971-74 LA
Jim Brown, FB 1957-65 Cleveland

"One night my college roommate and I were sitting around playing backgammon and talking about what we wanted out of football. Being practical, I said I wanted five years in the NFL, and a nice house in the suburbs. My room-mate was more ambitious, he wanted to be the best quarterback ever to play in the NFL. Well, seventeen years later we both got what we asked for. However, had I known our wishes were going to be carried out so literally that night, I would have asked for a better pension too."

Tom Flynn, DB 1984-86 Green Bay; 1986-88 New York Giants

"We had run our course at that point and it was over. And it is a hard thing to live with. You want to rage against the darkness. But hey, when your C batteries finally die, the darkness comes."

Larry Csonka, RB 1968-74 Miami; 1976-78 New York Giants; 1979 Miami

302

PHOTO CREDITS

FOREWORD
1. Alex and Andy Harmon, photo: C. Zordich
2. Eagles crowd (Tina Toscani in #36), Veteran's Stadium, photo: C. Zordich
3. Michael Zordich, Veteran's Stadium, photo: C. Zordich
4. Cindy Zordich, Veteran's Stadium, photo: Ed Mahan
5. Michael Zordich with M. V., Alex, Aidan, photo: C. Zordich

ROCKY BLEIER
1. Rocky Bleier, Vietnam, photo: Rocky Bleier private collection, reprinted with permission from *Fighting Back* by Rocky Bleier
2. Bleier, Notre Dame halfback, photo: Notre Dame Athletic Department, reprinted with permission from *Fighting Back* by Rocky Bleier
3. Art Rooney Sr., Bleier, photo: Rocky Bleier private collection, reprinted with permission from *Fighting Back* by Rocky Bleier
4. Robert Urich, Maury Gable, Rocky Bleier, photo: Greg Dursch/Wide World Photos, reprinted with permission from *Fighting Back* by Rocky Bleier
5. Bleier with ball (Pittsburgh Steelers), photo: Chance Brockway

CHUCK BEDNARIK
1. Chuck Bednarik, field of snow, photo: Al Dean/*Philadelphia Inquirer*
2. Bednarik, Gifford, knockout hit, photo: ©John Zimmerman/NFL photos
3. Bednarik running, photo: Laughead/Bradley
4. Chuck, Emma Bednarik, photo: Bednarik private collection
5. Playing the accordian for Emma, photo: C. Zordich

PAT SUMMERALL
1. Pat Summerall's putting green, photo: C. Zordich
2. Summerall interview, Amazing Grace, photo: C. Zordich
3. John Madden, Cheri Summerall, Pat Summerall, photo: Summerall private collection
4. Pat and Cheri Summerall, grounds of Amazing Grace, photo: C. Zordich

TOM BROOKSHIER
1. Tom Brookshier tackle, photo: Brookshier private collection, courtesy Philadelphia Eagles
2. Brookshier, CBS Sports, Veteran's Stadium, photo: Brookshier private collection, courtesy Eagles
3. Brookshier, tackle, photo: Brookshier private collection, courtesy Eagles
4. Brookshier with ball, photo: Brookshier private collection, courtesy Eagles
5. Tom and Barbara Brookshier with Rose, photo: C. Zordich

THOMAS HENDERSON
1. Thomas Henderson in uniform, smiling, photo: Chance Brockway
2. Henderson on grounds of former high school, East Side Field, Yellow Jacket Stadium, Austin, TX (now home of area youth football program personally funded, renovated, and organized by Thomas Henderson), photo: C. Zordich
3. Henderson's signature goal post spike, photo: Henderson private collection
4. Henderson, uniform, photo: Chance Brockway
5. Henderson leaning on goal post, photo: C. Zordich

VAI SIKAHEMA
1. Vai Sikahema, photo: Sikahema private collection
2. Vai Sikahema, photo: Sikahema private collection
3. Sikahema #36 Cardinals, photo: Chance Brockway
4. Sikahema, Eagles profile, photo: Ed Mahan, courtesy Eagles
5. Vai Sikahema, photo: Sikahema private collection

6. Sikahema #22 Eagles, photo: Peter Byron, courtesy Philadelphia Eagles

RONNIE LOTT
1. Ronnie Lott, San Francisco, tackle, photo: Chance Brockway
2. Lott, sideline, photo: Al Pereira
3. Lott hands on hips, photo: Chance Brockway
4. Lott, Pro Bowl, photo: Lopaka Photography, Lott private collection
5. Lott, Stephen Luczo, Seagate Technology (across from Lott), and friends, pre-Masters breakfast, Augusta, 1999, photo: C. Zordich

RAY RHODES
1. Rhodes profile, photo: C. Zordich
2. Rhodes profile with cap, photo: C. Zordich
3. Carmen Rhodes, photo: C. Zordich
4. Ray Rhodes, Danny Smith, photo: C. Zordich
5. Rhodes, "player evaluation," Lehigh University, photo: C. Zordich

RON WOLFLEY
1. Wolfley "exhale," photo: C. Zordich
2. Wolfley, sideline, photo: Jessen Associated, Inc./Arizona Cardinals
3. Wolfley #26, photo: Dino Lucarelli/Cleveland Browns
4. Wolfley, Arizona mountainscape, photo: C. Zordich
5. Wolfley, Mitch Aoto, KMVP Morning Show, Phoenix, photo: C. Zordich

JOHN BRODIE
1. John Brodie, Mario Lemieux Celebrity Golf Tournament, photo: C. Zordich
2. Brodie, Stanford University, photo: Brodie private collection
3. Brodie portrait, photo: Brodie private collection
4. Brodie, Lemieux tournament, photo: C. Zordich
5. Brodie with youngest daughter, photo: Brodie private collection
6. Bryn Brodie Chandler, granddaughter, photo: C. Zordich
7. Brodie family, photo: Brodie private collection
8. Brodie signing autographs, photo: C. Zordich

JOHNNY SAMPLE
all photos by C. Zordich, taken at University of Pennsylvania, Lotty Courts

RON JAWORSKI
1. Ron Jaworski, Wilbert Montgomery, photo: Bob Hill, courtesy Philadelphia Eagles
2. Ron Jaworski with Don Tollefson (FOX-TV), Veteran's Stadium, photo: C. Zordich
3. Philadelphia Eagles candid team photo: Jaworski private collection
4. Jaworski shouting at ref, photo: Jaworski private collection, courtesy Eagles
5. Jaworski family, photo: Jaworski private collection

BILL FRALIC
1. Senior, PHHS, photo: Gateway Publications/ *The Progress* 1981
2. Bill Fralic, University of Pittsburgh, photo: Steven Woltmann, Athlon Sports
3. Bill Fralic, Atlanta Falcons, photo: Jimmy Cribb, courtesy Atlanta Falcons
4. Profile W. P. Fralic, photo: C. Zordich
5. B. Fralic Penn Hills High School, '98, in background, newly constructed Bill Fralic Athletic Center, designed and financed by the W. P. Fralic Foundation (412-828-2199), photo: C. Zordich

STUMP MITCHELL
1. Coach Stump Mitchell, Seattle Seahawks mini camp, photo: C. Zordich

2. Mitchell with St. Louis Cardinals, photo: ©Scott Cunningham/NFL photos
3. Mitchell, Seattle mini camp, photo, C. Zordich
4. Mitchell, coach's position, photo: C. Zordich

TOMMY MCDONALD
1. Tommy McDonald with Jingles, photo: C. Zordich
2. Tommy McDonald with ball, photo: ©Bob Albright, 1954, Oklahoma Publishing Co., from the *Daily and Sunday Oklahoman*
3. McDonald publicity appearance, photo: Bernie Moser, Dufor Photographic Studios
4. McDonald, Eagles mini camp, photo: Montone, courtesy Philadelphia Eagles
5. McDonald Hall of Fame induction, photo: McDonald private collection

TODD CHRISTENSEN
1. Over what hill? photo: Christensen private collection
2. Christensen, Smithfield House, BYU, photo: C. Zordich
3. Christensen, Smithfield House, photo: C. Zordich
4. Christensen, photo: Chance Brockway
5. Christensen walks with father-in-law, BYU, photo: C. Zordich

LARRY WILSON
all photos by C. Zordich, taken at Arizona Cardinals training facility, Tempe, AZ

KIMBERLY LEWIS
1. Star pupil, Kimberly Lewis School of Dance, photo: C. Zordich
2. Student/instructor, K. Lewis School of Dance, photo: C. Zordich
3. Kimberly Lewis and the Phoenix Suns Dance Team, photo: Lewis private collection
4. Lewis morning dance class, photo: C. Zordich

DAN REEVES
1. Sideline, photo: courtesy Atlanta Falcons, Jimmy Cribb
2. Super Bowl Press Conference, photo: courtesy Atlanta Falcons, Jimmy Cribb
3. Signing autographs at Eagle Ranch, a Christian home for boys, Chestnut Mountain, Ga. (for information, call Eddie Staub, 770-967-8500), photo: C. Zordich
4. More autographs at Eagle Ranch, photo: C. Zordich
5. Practice field, photo: C. Zordich

MIKE DITKA
1. Coach Ditka, New Orleans Saints mini camp, photo: C. Zordich
2. Ditka publicity shot, photo: Michael Hebert/New Orleans Saints
3. Ditka mini camp evaluation, photo: C. Zordich

QUOTES
1. Don Meredith, photo: Chance Brockway
2. Dan Fouts, photo: Chance Brockway
3. Deacon Jones, photo: Chance Brockway
4. Bubba Smith, photo: Chance Brockway
5. Ronnie Lott, photo: Al Pereira
6. Frank Gifford, photo: Chance Brockway
7. Brian Sipe, photo: Chance Brockway
8. Reggie Williams, photo: Chance Brockway
9. Mike Jarmoluk, photo: courtesy Philadelphia Eagles
10. Gerry Feehery, photo: Ron Ross, G. Feehery private collection
11. Paul McFadden, photo: Chance Brockway
12. Karl Mecklenburg, photo: Chance Brockway
13. Bob Vogel, photo: Chance Brockway
14. Mike Quick, photo: Chance Brockway
15. Larry Csonka, photo: Chance Brockway